Liberty
and
Community

Liberty and Community

Canadian Federalism and the Failure of the Constitution

Robert C. Vipond

State University of New York Press

Published by
State University of New York Press, Albany

©1991   State University of New York

For information, address State University of New York
Press, State University Plaza, Albany, N.Y., 12246

Library of Congress Cataloging-in-Publication Data

Vipond, Robert Charles.
    Liberty and community : Canadian federalism and the failure of
the constitution / Robert C. Vipond.
        p.   cm.
    ISBN 0-7914-0465-X (alk. paper). — ISBN 0-7914-0466-8 (pbk. :
alk. paper)
    1. Federal government—Canada—History.   2. Canada—Constitutional
history.   I. Title.
JL27.V56   1991   90-32115
321.02'0971—dc20   CIP

10 9 8 7 6 5 4 3 2 1

To My Parents

Contents

Acknowledgments
ix

Chapter 1
Introduction
1

Chapter 2
Confederation and the Federal Principle
15

Chapter 3
Provincial Autonomy and Self-Government
47

Chapter 4
Provincial Autonomy and Imperialism
83

Chapter 5
Provincial Autonomy and the Rule of Law
113

Chapter 6
Provincial Autonomy and the Division of Powers
151

Conclusion
191

Notes
199

Index
245

Acknowledgments

This book began as a dissertation in the Government Department at Harvard University, under the supervision of Judith Shklar and Samuel Beer. Both were exemplary teachers. Encouraging, attentive and demanding, they triggered my interest in the ideological bases of Canadian federalism in the first place and, the dissertation completed, urged me to pursue my thoughts further. In responding to their challenge, I was aided by generous friends and colleagues who volunteered to read and comment on parts of the manuscript. I want to take this opportunity to thank: Blaine Baker, David Bell, Joe Carens, Ramsay Cook, Steve Dupré, Donald Kommers, Ron Manzer, Jenny Nedelsky, Peter Oliver, Paul Romney, Peter Russell, Carolyn Tuohy, Jeffrey Tulis, Graham White, and Bob Young. Paul Perron provided moral support and sound judgment throughout the enterprise. Kathryn McPherson generously assisted in preparing the index. I owe a special debt to Dick Risk, my colleague at the University of Toronto, who listened to half-formed ideas cheerfully and patiently. Our ongoing conversation about the subjects covered in this book has made writing a real pleasure.

The research for this book led me to impose on the good graces of more research librarians than I can name here. However, I want especially to thank Edward Phelps and the staff at the Regional Collection, University of Western Ontario Library for the assistance they provided in sorting through the David Mills Papers. And I owe a great deal to Linda Oliver and the helpful and forgiving staff at the Pratt Library, Victoria College, University of Toronto.

The Olin Foundation awarded me a junior faculty leave fellowship, during which time much of this book was written. The University of Toronto Law School, through the Connaught Fund, provided crucial financial assistance. Guy Charlton, Soraya Farha, Jael Lazaridis, and Barry Weintraub served as dedicated and thoughtful research assistants.

Marion Smiley and Bernie Yack introduced me to the State University of New York Press; for this and their friendship I thank them. At SUNY Press, Peggy Gifford and Diane Ganeles guided the manuscript gently and expertly. I would also like to acknowledge the *Canadian Journal of Political Science* and the *University of New Brunswick Law Journal* for permission to reprint material that first appeared in their pages.

My greatest debt, though, is to my wife, Gina Feldberg, whose probing questions have made me more skeptical of the claims of liberal theory, but whose indomitable, critical spirit has reinforced my faith in liberal practice.

CHAPTER 1

Introduction

For the past twenty-five years the Canadian polity has lurched from one constitutional crisis to another. The rise of secular Quebec nationalism in the 1960s triggered a series of challenges to the stability of the political system and established the urgency of basic constitutional reform. The prime minister of the day, Pierre Trudeau, raised the stakes by pronouncing that the "the whole Constitution is up for grabs."[1] A number of provincial governments, especially from the West, pressed their own constitutional agendas with increasing vigor. And while all of this was going on, the Parti Québécois took office in Quebec, formed a government, and prepared to put the question of sovereignty-association to the electorate. The result was that as the obsession with constitutional reform grew through the 1970s, so positions hardened; and as the stalemate deepened, so the situation in Quebec made constitutional reform that much more urgent.

Yet even when the impasse was finally broken in 1982, the passage of the Constitution Act, 1982 (including a Charter of Rights and Freedoms) did not produce instant constitutional harmony so much as it superimposed a set of new controversies on a cluster of old ones.[2] On the one hand, the Quebec National Assembly followed Premier René Lévesque's lead, repudiated the 1982 settlement, and triggered a fresh round of negotiations to "bring Quebec into the constitutional family." The product of these discussions, the Meech Lake Accord,[3] quickly became as controversial as the Constitution Act itself. On the other hand, litigation under the Charter of Rights quite quickly forced (or allowed) judges and lawyers to address squarely a range of social issues with an authority they lacked before 1982. Through it, Canadians have begun to learn what Americans have long known; namely, that dealing with the constitutional implications of issues such as

1

freedom of expression and abortion can create deep political divisions.

Why has Canada's recent constitutional experience been so difficult and discordant? One reason is that constitutional debate has come increasingly to center on two "competing conceptions" or "alternative visions" of what the country is or ought to be; conceptions which, if not totally incompatible, have nevertheless helped to polarize political debate. Highly schematically, one is built on a liberalism that emphasizes individual liberty, views the state as a means to protecting liberty, and typically looks to the national government for leadership. The other stresses the value of community, is more likely to encourage collective choice, and tends to recognize the importance of provincial governments as the guardians of regional identities.

This tension between liberty and community, as I will call it, has manifested itself most clearly in Quebec, where collective identity has always been a crucial political issue; where the Charter of Rights was openly resisted on the grounds that it would thwart attempts to preserve the province's cultural distinctiveness; and where explicit constitutional recognition that Quebec is a "distinct society" within Canada remains the price of ratifying the 1982 settlement *ex post.* Yet the tension between liberty and community has not been confined to Quebec. Pierre Trudeau's pan-Canadian vision, in which language and other rights would be judicially protected and nationally enforced, was meant to serve as a counterpoise to the view, popularized by former Prime Minister Joe Clark, that Canada is "a community of communities." One of the stock objections to the Charter of Rights among English-Canadian critics was that judicial review would undermine "a sense of community"[4] and make it difficult to produce social policy in line with "community values."[5] And the notion that Canadian constitutional politics is best understood as a "dialectic" between "polar positions" remains very much alive. Indeed, it has become an almost standard reflex, especially among English-Canadian commentators, to portray recent constitutional developments, up to and including the Meech Lake Accord, as a "complex compromise among competing views"[6] of the Canadian polity.

This book, a study of the legal and political ideology of the provincial rights movement in Ontario between 1867 and 1900, has two principal objectives. The first is to understand the deeper historical structure of these "alternative visions" of liberty and community in Canada, especially and principally English Canada.[7] The premise of the study is that, for all of the important changes wrought by the Charter of Rights, constitutional discourse in Canada cannot fully escape the long shadows cast by the constitutional tradition. I have

chosen to concentrate on the legal and political thought of the provincial rights movement because it offers what is arguably the most
searching and accessible English-Canadian account of the questions
of liberty and community. What I try to explain is how a particular
claim of community—provincial autonomy—became a legitimate,
durable, indeed central constitutional value that continues to inform
constitutional debate in Canada—in a way, for instance, that the
doctrine of states' rights does not in the U.S.

Beyond its genealogical value, however, this historical recon-
stuction of provincialism in Canada is intended to challenge the
dominant mode of thinking about the core principles of federalism
and liberalism here and now. Indeed, it is meant to throw into question the analytical usefulness of the dichotomy between liberty and
community as it is usually understood. It has become all too easy to
reduce the central constitutional question facing Canadians these
days to a stark choice between provincial power and the protection of
individual rights—or perhaps some more or less acceptable compromise between the two. My goal is to show that, if the constitutional
tradition is taken as a point of reference, then this way of stating the
choice misreads the past, distorts the choices available to us in the
present and constricts our view of the future. The early theorists of
provincial rights did not assume that community and liberty were
"binary opposites"[8] secretly or openly at war with each other. On the
contrary, they argued consistently that their defense of community
was a means to protect liberty. They were not completely successful in
that endeavor, but their reluctance to view liberty and community as
competing and contradictory political goods may still serve as a useful
corrective to what has become the dominant view.

I argue, in short, that the real challenge facing Canadian constitutional politics is less to control the competition *between* liberty and
community than it is to find principled ways to mediate the tensions
within Canada's distinctive (and somewhat more communitarian)
form of liberalism. If it is too easy to reduce our constitutional choices
to some formula like 'provincial power versus individual rights', then
some better and more nuanced theory is needed to sort out the
internal dialectic within Canadian politics. While this book will not
provide such a theory in detail, it will at least provide a defense for the
construction of such a theory. In that sense, my goal is to create an
"alternative past" from which to view these "alternative futures"
afresh.

When John A. Macdonald, Canada's first prime minister, rose in
the Canadian assembly in 1865 to defend the blueprint for the federal
constitution, he candidly admitted that he had wanted to create a

simple union in which there would be one government legislating for the whole of what was then called British North America. A simple legislative union, he argued, would have been "the best, the cheapest, the most vigorous, and the strongest system of government."[9] Macdonald realized, however, that such a system was "impracticable"[10] in a diverse country like Canada because it simply would not be acceptable to those regionally based populations—especially French Canadians—who feared the "absorption" of their "individuality."[11] Ever pragmatic, Macdonald ultimately had to accept a system in which the central government would lead, but in which "separate provincial organizations would be in some degree preserved."[12] The Confederation settlement, he concluded, created a constitutional "happy medium,"[13] a scheme of government that combined "the strength of a legislative and administrative union" with the "sectional freedom of a federal union, with protection to local interests."[14]

Macdonald accepted the compromise proposal cheerfully because he was convinced that the concessions he had been forced to make in the direction of federalism would not undermine the almost imperial authority of the federal government to build the nation. For one thing, it is clear that, from Macdonald's perspective, these concessions to regional or provincial "individuality" were directed principally at Quebec. The principle of local independence of course applied to all the provinces, not just Quebec, but Macdonald apparently assumed that parochial loyalties would have little lasting appeal in English Canada. The Maritime provinces had distinctive laws, and Macdonald granted that these different legal traditions should be protected. But he also believed that these differences were relatively trivial, especially in comparison with French Canada, and he hoped that once they joined Confederation the Maritimers would assimilate their laws to the rest of the country.[15] As to the well-known demands for local control over local affairs made by the Ontario Reform party, Macdonald had almost nothing to say at the time of Confederation. Ontario, like the other provinces, would be given some measure of control over its own affairs, but he seems to have assumed that most Ontarians would be more interested in managing everybody's affairs from Ottawa than in controlling merely their own from Toronto.

Moreover, even if he was wrong about the disappearance of the spirit of localism, Macdonald believed that the central government would have little to fear from the provinces because Ottawa had been dealt the superior constitutional hand. The national government had been given "all the great subjects of legislation,"[16] including the apparently unqualified power to regulate trade and commerce, and a general, residual power to act for the "peace, order and good government" of the country. Beyond these positive powers, the constitution came equipped with a number of supervisory mechanisms—including the power to veto any provincial law—with which the federal government could defend itself against provincial attacks. As he put the matter to a political friend who was apprehensive that the provinces would grow too strong: "By a firm and patient course, I think the Dominion must win in the long run. The powers of the General Government are so much greater than those of the United States, that the central power must win in the long run. My own opinion is that the General Government or Parliament should pay no more regard to the status or position of the Local Governments than they would to the prospects of the ruling party in the corporation of Quebec or Montreal."[17]

In the end, Macdonald underestimated both the depth of localist sentiment and the ability of a political opposition, the provincial rights movement, to construct a powerful counter-vision from the core principle of provincial autonomy. As it was expounded in its mature form in the 1880s and 1890s, the constitutional doctrine of provincial autonomy consisted of three separate, but related, claims, all of which were arguably derived from the "federal principle" and supported by the British North America (BNA) Act.[18] First, the provincialists argued that the federal principle means, at a minimum, that the federal government has no right to interfere in those subjects placed within the control of the provincial legislatures, just as, conversely, the provincial governments have no right to infringe upon federal jurisdiction. Federalism means that each level of government is supreme or sovereign within its sphere, which is why the BNA Act conferred upon each "exclusive"[19] authority to legislate on a given set of subjects. Second, the provincialists argued that real federalism requires a balanced division of power in which neither level over-whelms the other. In this sense, federalism implies political parity, and the autonomists argued that the division of powers outlined in sections 91 and 92 of the BNA Act established a rough balance between national and provincial powers respectively. Third, the provincialists argued that federalism means contractualism. Confed-eration, they said, was created as a compact among the provinces which, according to the act's preamble, had "expressed their desire to be federally united into one Dominion."[20] If amendments were to be made to the compact, it followed that provincial consent alone was required. So defined, the doctrine of provincial autonomy became the standard against which Prime Minister Macdonald's actions were relentlessly judged, and the ideal in light of which the impurities of the constitution were identified.

It is a measure of the success of the provincial rights movement that by the turn of the century the federal veto powers over provincial legislation had been largely discredited; the courts had placed Macdonald's centralist reading of the BNA Act in grave doubt; and the most eloquent defenders of provincial autonomy had infiltrated enemy lines and were sitting in the national cabinet. Only the "compact theory" and its implications for constitutional amendment failed to take hold in the generation after Confederation—and even here the more recent success of a modified version of the compact theory suggests that the autonomists did not suffer total defeat. By 1900 the interchangeable terms "provincial rights" and "provincial autonomy" had become "clichés of Canadian constitutional discussion."[21] And they remain central to Canadian constitutional politics to this day— witness the West's efforts to have provincial control over natural resources constitutionally bullet-proofed,[22] the Supreme Court's dictum that basic constitutional amendment requires substantial provincial support,[23] Quebec's initiatives to place limitations on the federal spending power,[24] and the steady stream of cases in which the Supreme Court of Canada has acted as the "umpire" that will define and protect the spheres of federal and provincial jurisdiction.[25]

What was the original appeal of the constitutional doctrine of provincial autonomy? What is the legacy of the provincial rights movement for contemporary Canadian politics? This study attempts to answer these questions.

II

The provincial rights movement was the first constitutional protest movement in post-Confederation Canada, and its importance has not been lost on those who have attempted to understand the evolution of the Canadian constitution. There exists, indeed, a large and burgeoning literature which attempts to account for the autonomists' success. As the methods of studying political phenomena have proliferated in the last generation in Canada, so have the explanations for the rise of the provincial rights movement. At the risk of oversimplification, one can discern four different approaches to the study of the provincial rights movement: political, institutional, sociological and economic. These approaches are obviously not mutually exclusive, and most accounts expressly avoid unicausal explanations. Nevertheless, it will be helpful for the purposes of clarity to disentangle the major threads.

The politics of late-nineteenth-century Canada was dominated by strong partisan competition, and many observers have quite sensibly wanted to place the provincial rights movement squarely in the political context of party development. They note that in the years after 1867 the rivalry between the provincial governments and Ottawa became virtually synonymous with the competition between the Liberal and Conservative parties. They suggest that partisan considerations motivated both sides, and they argue that the success of the provincial rights movement must be considered in the context of the rise of the Liberal party in Canada. From this perspective it is thus not coincidental that provincial rights came of age when Laurier became prime minister and Liberals controlled most of the provincial legislatures.[26]

Others take a more specifically institutional approach. They note that the creation of party discipline within Parliament created a form of cabinet government in which political authority came to be concentrated in the first minister. When cabinet government is combined with federalism, the potential exists, therefore, for what Richard Simeon calls "federal-provincial diplomacy,"[27] in which heads of government are able to negotiate on behalf of their constituencies in a way that roughly resembles interstate negotiations and diplomacy. And the fact of the matter is that in the early years provincial premiers (most notably Oliver Mowat of Ontario) were simply shrewder, cannier, more skillful diplomats than their federal counterparts.[28]

Still others prefer a sociological explanation of the rise of provincial autonomy. They argue that the so-called Fathers of Confederation attempted to establish a political framework that simply contradicted the stubborn sociological reality that Canada is a country of strong regional and ethno-cultural loyalties. As Alan Cairns has put it, the BNA Act was just "too centralist for the diversity it had to contain."[29] For him, the provincial rights movement was, therefore, the agent of a natural and almost inevitable self-correction.

Finally, a wide variety of economic explanations have been advanced, the common thrust of which is to show that the provincial governments were able in one way or another to attract the support of influential private interests while the federal government was losing the support of its economic constituency. According to Garth Stevenson, for example, "the fact that Toronto capitalists gained less than they had expected from the annexation of the West" and so abandoned Macdonald's Tories, was a "contributing factor" to the rise of provincial rights.[30]

Now, this brief summary obviously does not do justice to the subtlety or complexity of the historical scholarship produced in the last generation. Yet even in this highly schematic portrait a paradox appears. The paradox is that in attempting to account for one of the pivotal constitutional episodes in Canadian political history, most historians and political scientists have resorted to some extra-constitutional standard of explanation—to partisan political competition, to institutional design, to sociological realities, to economic factors and so forth. It must be emphasized that the provincial rights movement was at base a constitutional movement. Its advocates realized that the thing they wanted—whether prestige, power, protection for certain cultural values, or economic independence—depended on expressly constitutional reforms. The explanations summarized above generally recognize the constitutional character of the provincial rights movement, but they tend to discount the importance of the constitutional debates and controversies themselves. However different these explanations may be in detail, they seem to agree that the constitutional issues and arguments are ultimately less important in explaining the success of the provincial rights movement than are broader political, institutional, sociological and economic variables.

Actually, this paradox is simply resolved. The explanations summarized above represent a common attempt to overcome what has been perceived as the too narrowly legalistic account of Canadian constitutional development that prevailed in the 1930s, 1940s and 1950s. Most studies of constitutional development written in those decades tended to concentrate on the interpretations of the BNA Act rendered by the Judicial Committee of the Privy Council (JCPC), the court of final resort for Canadian constitutional cases until 1949. This concentration on the legal aspects of Canadian constitutional development grew out of the political controversies of the 1930s. Many of the most prominent constitutional scholars of the era—F. R. Scott, W. P. M. Kennedy, V. C. MacDonald, Bora Laskin and others[31]—were extremely critical of the way in which the Judicial Committee had eviscerated the Canadian version of the New Deal. Their study of earlier judicial cases simply underscored their conclusions by demonstrating that the JCPC's provincialist tilt was longstanding. Through a consistently restrictive interpretation of the powers available to the federal government, the JCPC had derailed the political development of Canada by undermining Ottawa's capacity to build the nation.

The difficulty is that this legal account of the provincialization of the constitution distorted and oversimplified a more complex historical phenomenon. As Alan Cairns has put it: "It is impossible to believe that a few elderly men in London deciding two or three constitutional cases a year precipitated, sustained and caused the development of Canada in a federalist direction that the country would otherwise not have taken."[32] Precisely because the legalistic interpretation of the provincial rights movement oversold itself so badly, recent scholarly studies have gone out of their way to find alternative explanations.

Taken as a whole, there is no doubt that recent scholarship has done much to produce a rich and textured explanation of *how* the constitutional reformers of the late nineteenth century succeeded in thwarting Macdonald's grand design. It has been rather less successful, however, at understanding just *what* it was that the provincial rights movement set out to reform. Stated baldly, most students of the provincial rights movement assume that the meaning and function of the legal reforms to which the provincial autonomists addressed themselves are self-evident and unproblematic. They assume, more specifically, that Macdonald and the provincial autonomists were competing to control the definition of the newly-formed federal constitution in a way that would suit their interests; that the dispute between them can be understood in terms of winners and losers; and that, therefore, the interesting part of the story is the dynamic of the dispute itself and its resolution. That, indeed, is why almost every study begins, implicitly or explicitly, from the assumption that the most important and interesting question is why the provincial autonomists were as successful as they were.

To be sure, an explanation of the success of the provincial rights movement is one part of the constitutional story in late-nineteenth-century Canada, but it is by no means the whole story. For beyond acting in concrete and clearly defined cases to secure provincial autonomy, the provincial rights movement used the law as a way of giving order to their political life and of connecting the new and sometimes perplexing forms of federalism to older, deeply cherished cultural symbols and values. In this sense, the constitutional quarrels in which the autonomists became engaged were not simply attempts to advance certain political, social and economic interests; they were also episodes in an ongoing process of cultural self-definition. The anthropologist Clifford Geertz has led the way in suggesting that, at a deeper level, law exists as one of the ways in which people make sense of the world around them and make it coherent. As Geertz puts it, "law" provides a way by which we sort out and give meaning to social "facts."[33] Far from being a mere instrument of political interest, Geertz tells us, law serves both to reflect and embody distinctive "visions of community." Law "contributes to a definition of a style of social existence."[34]

Geertz's approach, which has been applied by scholars to other constitutional questions,[35] would seem to be particularly helpful here because it would connect the struggle for provincial rights to the larger process of defining a distinctive Canadian political culture. From this perspective, the story of the provincial rights movement is important because it reveals a generation of politicians, not otherwise given to articulating their deepest beliefs, wrestling consciously with what was a novel political and legal form—a federal constitution. Interpreted in this way, the provincial autonomists were not simply interested in thwarting Macdonald, advancing their political interest, or what have you. They were also concerned to show how a federal constitution could be fit squarely and comfortably into a larger, pre-existing, and deeply rooted cultural system. The provincial autonomists believed the Macdonald constitution was unacceptable because it was incoherent in Geertz's sense of the term: that is, it could not be reconciled with the constitutive symbols that anchored their self-identity. Provincial autonomy, understood as part of this larger cultural system, simply fit better with the deepest ideals of late-nineteenth-century liberalism: with the desideratum of self-government or political liberty, with what the autonomists considered to be the lessons of successful imperialism, with their deep faith in the rule of law, and with their abiding devotion to the protection of individual freedom. In coming to terms with federalism, the provincial autonomists were also coming to terms with themselves.

Actually, one of the virtues of this Geertzian approach is that it does, indeed, help to explain the success of the provincial rights movement in its struggles against Macdonald. All else aside, the provincial autonomists were extraordinarily skillful in deploying such powerful cultural symbols as self-government, home rule and the rule of law, and they used arguments derived from their common cultural experience to great advantage. Beyond this, the Geertzian approach helps to explain the dynamics of the political struggles of the late nineteenth century. It helps to explain why political parties, acting as cultural lightning rods, played such a central role in the provincial rights saga. Still more importantly, this method makes it easier to understand why such apparently mundane "facts" as widening streams, enforcing insurance contracts and conferring honorary titles became controversial "law." Seen through Geertz's lens, these "facts" assumed extraordinary importance because they provided opportunities for "imagining the real."[36]

I must emphasize again, however, that my principal interest here is not to provide yet another account of why the provincial autonomists succeeded as well as they did. Rather, my reason for viewing the claims of provincial autonomy as a form of cultural expression is to uncover the deeper structure of the autonomists' worldview. What I attempt to do in this study is to recapture a piece of what Geertz would call "local knowledge" by showing how the autonomists in their own quite distinctive way made sense of the constitution in light of prevailing cultural norms; how their understanding of provincial autonomy in turn shaped their larger "vision of community"; and how this whole process led them to incorporate and project the tensions and contradictions of the larger cultural system they inhabited into their constitutional doctrine. In this sense, provincial autonomy was a legal and political ideology; it provided a way to express a set of basic and comprehensive political preferences.

I am attracted to Geertz's method as well, speaking now as a political scientist and a student of comparative federalism, because it provides a way to understand the continuities and discontinuities between the world of the provincial rights movement and our own; to understand a longstanding constitutional dispute across "historical phases."[37] Neither cultural ideals nor the facts through which these ideals are endowed with meaning are static. Both "law" and "fact" are constantly being revised in light of each other. Alan Cairns, among others, has pointed out that the current constitutional debate in Canada is, in its own way, a struggle for the control and definition of key cultural symbols which involves "the potential restructuring of the psyche of Canadians."[38] One premise that informs this work is that it will be easier to understand this cultural and symbolic dimension of the current debate when it is placed in the larger historical context from which it is derived. Another is that the study of comparative constitutional federalism can be enriched by an analysis of federalism that is less obsessed with legal cases and more sensitive to the cultural context of constitutionalism.[39]

III

This study does not pretend to provide a comprehensive account of the activities of the provincial rights movement in Canada. At the same time, I have attempted to select the story's time, setting and cast of characters with a view to producing a representative account. A word about what is covered and what is not covered in this book is, therefore, in order.

First, I have chosen to concentrate my attention on the period between the promulgation of the BNA Act in 1867 and 1900 because the provincial rights movement was particularly active and particularly effective in the formative period of Canadian federal development. John A. Macdonald once likened the constitution to a mold that takes time to set. The metaphor is instructive because it conveys a sense both of the contingency of constitution-making and the deep conservatism of constitutional practice in a mature legal system.

Macdonald's opponents exploited both the contingency and the conservatism brilliantly. For while the meaning of the constitution was still in flux, the provincial autonomists developed a constitutional vision that directly challenged, and in many ways ultimately supplanted, Macdonald's centralist orthodoxy. Yet once settled, the idea of provincial rights became a fundamental and almost unchallengeable constitutional principle to which later generations could turn for legitimacy. The provincial rights movement thus had a formative, and apparently permanent, influence on the meaning of Canada's federal constitution. It is through them and during the period covered by this study that the idea of provincial rights, now ritually declaimed, was injected into the Canadian political tradition.

In those early years the call for provincial rights was heard throughout the country. Quebec politicians were responsible for some of the earliest and clearest statements of the meaning of constituttional federalism, and Quebec's Premier Honoré Mercier helped to organize the first coordinated provincial attack on Macdonald's interpretation of the constitution. A powerful movement to secede from Confederation took hold in Nova Scotia in 1867-68, and a second repeal movement asserted itself there in the 1880s. Yet as Christopher Armstrong has noted, the "heart and soul"[40] of the provincial rights movement in those years was in Ontario. It was in Ontario that the decisive constitutional challenges to Macdonald were launched, and it was there that the larger argument for provincial autonomy was spelled out with the greatest clarity. Ontario has long since ceded its leadership as the defender of provincial rights to other provinces— notably Quebec and the western provinces. In the early years, however, Ontario led the movement for autonomy. It will, accordingly, be the focus of this study.

As a number of scholars have pointed out, the controversy over provincial autonomy quickly became a partisan issue in Canada, led by elites but beamed toward a broader audience. Within Ontario, the provincialist position was associated most closely with the Reform (or Liberal) party, whose leaders used every medium at their disposal— parliamentary speeches, the Reform press, political picnics and election campaigns among them—to cement the connection between Reformism and provincial autonomy. Precisely because the doctrine of provincial autonomy was transformed in this process into a party slogan in which the leadership gave the cues, there was relatively little serious division of opinion within Reform ranks about the meaning and implications of the term. For that reason, I have not attempted to provide a complete roster of provincial rights opinion. Moreover, I have not assumed that those who were responsible for leading the provincial rights movement from one constitutional skirmish to another were necessarily the best exponents of the autonomist position. Thus, some of the characters who will appear in what follows —for instance Oliver Mowat (premier of Ontario from 1872 to 1896) and Edward Blake (who served briefly as premier before becoming Liberal MP and national leader of the party)—will be familiar to many readers; others, especially David Mills (longtime MP, editorialist and lecturer) will be less so. Whether more or less familiar, I have chosen them because they developed the ideology of provincial autonomy most clearly, most comprehensively and most thoughtfully; they are the pillars on which the study rests.

Finally, I have made no attempt to reconstruct every dispute or rehearse every case that bore on the question of provincial autonomy. Given the way in which almost every political question was perceived to be colored by federalism, comprehensiveness would have required nothing short of a complete history of Ontario, if not Canada. Rather, I have concentrated on a number of pivotal episodes, taking my cue as to the actual selection of topics from the words and actions of the provincial autonomists themselves. Thus chapter 2 discusses the meaning of the Confederation settlement by focusing on the ambiguity of the term sovereignty as it was understood in pre-Confederation Canada. Chapter 3 concerns the provincial lieutenant-governorship and its relation to provincial autonomy and self-government. Chapter 4 explores the way in which the autonomists looked to imperial home rule as a model for their understanding of federalism. Chapter 5 discusses the autonomists' deep, liberal faith in the rule of law, and the way in which they used the principle of the rule of law to discredit the veto power of disallowance. And chapter 6 discusses the dispute over the division of powers in light of the autonomists' beliefs about law and the preservation of individual liberty.

CHAPTER 2

Confederation
and the Federal Principle

If the Canadian Fathers of Confederation[1] held any truth to be self-evident, it was that the architects of the U.S. Constitution had made a fundamental constitutional mistake in 1787, the terrible consequences of which were being played out at that very moment—the mid-1860s—on the battlefield. John A. Macdonald, the central figure of the Confederation movement, argued bluntly that the Americans, in declaring "by their Constitution that each state was a sovereignty in itself," had begun "at the wrong end." Macdonald was not alone. As Peter Waite argues, "no understanding of Confederation is possible unless it be recognized that its founders, many of its supporters, and as many of its opponents were all animated by a powerful antipathy to the whole federal principle."[2] Yet what Macdonald conceived as an express attempt to overcome the "errors" of the U.S. federal constitution ended in the creation of a basic law, the British North America (BNA) Act,[3] which, within a generation of its passage in 1867, had come to be viewed by many as the legitimate source of provincial autonomy and the embodiment of the federal principle.

The burden of this chapter is to explain the constitutional bases of the Confederation settlement of 1867 with a view to understanding the apparent transformation that occurred thereafter. I say *apparent* transformation because I want to distance myself to some extent from the conventional view, encapsulated above, that generalizes from Macdonald's example and concludes that "the Fathers...distrusted pure coordinate or classical federalism."[4] As K. C. Wheare put it in a now-famous formulation, the original constitution can best be described as "quasi-federal" because the constitutional framers included a number of provisions (like the veto power of disallowance)

15

which rendered the regional governments "subordinate to the general government and, not co-ordinate with it."[5] The fundamental problem with the conventional view, I will argue, is that it underestimates the extent to which the meaning of federalism was in flux during the period 1864–1867. It is true that the Canadian political elite was horrified by the Civil War, and it is equally true that many of the Confederationists inferred from their reading of the causes of the war that the federal principle is inherently unstable. But for a significant number of Confederationists—drawn especially from the ranks of the Reform party of Upper Canada (Ontario) and the conservative Bleus of Lower Canada (Quebec)—the Civil War did not discredit the federal principle so much as it issued a challenge to place federalism on a more secure constitutional footing. The irony is that, having rejected one model of American federalism, these Canadian reformers came in their own way and on their own terms to reconceptualize federalism in a way that is strongly reminiscent of another American precedent—the Federalists' classic exposition of constitutional federalism.

These other Confederationists usually did not acknowledge explicitly the similarity between their own ideas and those of the Federalists; indeed, it is by no means clear that they appreciated the extent to which they were retracing the steps of James Madison and James Wilson. The parallel is nonetheless striking, and it suggests that the roots of constitutional federalism in Canada were put down somewhat earlier than is usually thought. While the provincial rights movement did not blossom until the 1880s, the seeds of provincial autonomy were sown in the BNA Act of 1867. It is therefore with the debate leading up to the Confederation settlement of 1867 that an account of provincial autonomy must begin.

II

Confederation came about in 1867 because the leaders of three of the four largest factions in Canadian politics at the time, George-Etienne Cartier, George Brown and John A. Macdonald, had agreed in 1864 to dedicate themselves to the establishment of a federal union in British North America.[6] The Great Coalition of 1864 is surely one of the most curious alliances ever forged in Canadian politics. The Reformer Brown and the Conservative Macdonald had been engaged in a longstanding political rivalry, the bitterness of which had been deepened by the rhetorical exigencies of party politics and the partisan press. Brown was relentlessly anti-clerical, Cartier was associated with clericalism. Brown and Macdonald were Upper Canadian and Scots, Cartier was Lower Canadian and French. Yet whatever their differences, each had come to the conclusion that it was in his interest to support a federal union. For this brief, but crucial, moment they were united by their common desire to form a federal union. That desire brought them, and held them, together.

A number of factors combined to make a union of the British North American colonies possible and perhaps even urgently necessary. The dismantling of the British mercantile system, the fear that the U.S. would abrogate the Reciprocity Treaty of 1854, and the prospect of turning the West both into a market for eastern goods and the supplier of raw materials made union an attractive economic option —especially for politicians with strong connections to crucial economic elites. The notion that some sort of coordinated defense was necessary to protect the colonies from American expansionism carried some weight; it probably did not hurt the cause to suggest that the real enemy was that "warlike power" to the south which, "under Mr. Lincoln" was ready to force "this universal democracy doctrine" on the rest of North America.[7] Moreover, it was patently clear to the members of the Great Coalition that the present union between Upper and Lower Canada (the forerunners of Ontario and Quebec respectively) was not working. The basic political institutions were deadlocked, ministries were created and fell with almost predictable frequency, and the tone of politics was deeply and unhelpfully confrontational. Given all of these things, some sort of basic constitutional reform appeared to Cartier, Brown and Macdonald to be necessary. The interesting question, therefore, is less why the Great Coalition came together than why they joined together to create a specifically federal form of union.

For Cartier and his Bleu party, federalism recommended itself as the best means to cultural survival. As A. I. Silver has argued, French Canadians in the 1860s "generally considered French Canada and Lower Canada to be equivalent."[8] That is, they equated their distinctive identity as a people with a specific territory in which they formed a majority. This was, admittedly, a somewhat false equation. There were, even in the mid-1860s, francophone populations beyond the borders of Quebec, in Manitoba and New Brunswick for example, but at the time of Confederation they figured only slightly in the political calculations of the French-Canadian political elite.[9] As Silver argues, most French Canadians at the time, whether for or against Confederation, considered that the future of French Canada depended on what happened in and to Lower Canada.[10] That said, it was quite natural to think that the distinctive institutions, laws and cultural values of French Canada could best be protected if decisions affecting them were made in the provincial legislature of Quebec, the one legislature in which French Canadians would be sure to dominate. Questions of importance to the country as a whole could safely be consigned to a central legislature in which French Canadians were represented but which they did not control as long as the distinctive, local subjects were left to the disposition of the provincial legislature which they did control. If there had to be constitutional change, then some form of division of powers between a national and a series of provincial legislatures was the best hope for cultural survival.[11]

George Brown's support for Confederation is slightly less self-explanatory, and must be understood in the context of the Reform party in Upper Canada. The Reform party grew from the Union Act of 1840, under the terms of which Upper and Lower Canada were given equal representation in a common legislature. This initially favored Upper Canada, which had the smaller population, but within a short time the demographic balance had shifted such that Upper Canadians found themselves proportionately underrepresented in the combined legislative assembly. What made matters worse, according to the Reformers, was that a solid phalanx of Lower Canadian Conservatives (or Bleus), together with a small number of Upper Canadian Conservatives, had been able to control the assembly without interruption since the early 1850s. Together, the Reformers claimed, this coalition legislated at the expense and against the wishes of the majority of Upper Canadians. Some Reformers protested that Lower Canada had forced sectarian schools on Upper Canada.[12] Others complained that they had been "fleeced" by Lower Canada, forced time and again to pay for what they believed was Lower Canadian profligacy.[13] Still others blamed the underdevelopment of the West on Lower Canadian indifference to the rich rewards to be won there.[14] All agreed with their leader, George Brown, that a great injustice had been visited upon the citizens of Upper Canada, and all agreed that some basic constitutional reform was necessary to redress these grievances.

At the fringes of the Reform movement, this indignation at Lower Canadian "domination" lapsed into crude bigotry. The Orange Association of Ontario was incorrigibly and militantly anti-Catholic; George Brown's newspaper, the Toronto *Globe*, was usually not far behind. Yet even at its most respectable, the Reform party insisted on viewing virtually every important question in Canadian politics through the prism of cultural "domination" and "injustice." One of the clearest statements of this sort was made before the Reform Convention of 1859 by Oliver Mowat, one of the most respected members of the Reform party before Confederation, and premier of Ontario and a leader of the provincial rights movement thereafter. The problem with the existing constitutional arrangement, Mowat insisted, was not merely that it effectively allowed a minority to rule the majority. The deeper problem was that it permitted a French, Catholic minority to rule an English, Protestant majority. It allowed those "of another language, another race, another country" to rule Upper Canada.[15] The fear for cultural survival dominated Lower Canadian politics before Confederation. Ironically, it dominated Upper Canadian politics as well.

Thus George Brown, leader of the Reform party, found the Confederation proposal attractive because it met both of the longstanding conditions set out by his party. First, the Confederation proposal was "a great measure of representative reform"[16] inasmuch as it provided that representation in the House of Commons would reflect population. It would simply be much more difficult for Lower Canada to "fleece" its neighbor when the latter would suddenly have "seventeen additional members in the House that holds the purse."[17] Beyond this, the Confederation plan embraced the principle that "local governments are to have control over local affairs."[18] This, too, would protect Upper Canada, for it meant that "if our friends in Lower Canada choose to be extravagant, they will have to bear the burden of it themselves."[19] Confederation thus held out the promise that Ontario would both dominate national politics and control its own affairs. It thereby offered Ontario a double indemnity against past "injustices." It is small wonder that Brown, speaking in 1865, could accept the Confederation plan "without hesitation or reservation."[20]

Macdonald's reasons for endorsing a specifically federal union were more narrowly political and his support less enthusiastic. He cheerfully admitted in the course of the debate on the Confederation proposal, held in the Canadian assembly in 1865, that he preferred a unitary to a federal government because he believed that what the country most needed—a strong defense, a continental outlook and material prosperity—could best be provided by a highly centralized regime. But he realized equally well that the various sections comprising the union would not agree to a plan that would destroy their "individuality." By 1864, he had reconciled himself to the impracticability of complete union and had given his support instead to a proposal that, he believed, would produce the next best thing: a highly centralized, but still federal, union.

III

Macdonald, Cartier and Brown are as central to the Canadian creation myth as Publius, the collective author of *The Federalist*, is to the American.[21] These were the "Fathers" who, at a decisive moment, joined together to seize the opportunity of "founding a great nation" by giving it a "Constitution."[22] However, as mythic figures the Fathers of Confederation have never been as successful as their American counterparts. Despite their best efforts to portray themselves as heroic legislators, they have never been idolized and revered in the way Madison, Hamilton, Jefferson and others have been in the United States. One reason for the difference is that the Canadians were engaged in an enterprise that was simply less amenable to myth-making. Notwithstanding their own conceits, the Fathers of Confederation were not "founding" a political state in the way it is often said the American constitution-makers were "Founders." In the Canadian case there was no self-conscious break with the past and certainly no revolution; indeed, the Fathers of Confederation went out of their way to emphasize that Confederation represented continuity and had been achieved "under the fostering care of Great Britain, and our Sovereign Lady, Queen Victoria."[23] There was, therefore, no need to expound first political principles or to weave together a set of authoritative public values in the way Publius did. It was enough to say that as Canadians they wanted to inherit a "constitution similar in principle to that of the United Kingdom."[24] For much the same reason, there was no need to develop a new approach to understanding politics, a new political science if you will, to provide a new perspective on these first principles. Fundamental questions about the purposes and organization of government, with which Publius had concerned himself and on which his mythic reputation is based, simply were not raised in the debate over Confederation. The fundamental political choices had already been made, and with those implicit decisions went the best opportunity for the Canadian framers to establish themselves as self-conscious, deliberate founders.

Yet as a number of the critics of the Confederation proposal noted, the Confederation coalition was even reluctant to explain and clarify the features of the plan that were novel—especially those concerning federalism.[25] This reluctance was in part strategic. Macdonald, Cartier and Brown understood perfectly well that their coalition ran clearly against the grain of Canadian politics, and they knew that their opponents were waiting for an opportunity to rekindle the rivalries that had been set aside temporarily. They therefore went out of their way to exaggerate what they had in common and to abstract from or simply ignore their differences. Given the imperative to maintain the unity of the coalition, it was crucial to confine the discussion as much as possible to the most general level where agreement could be assured, rather than descending to a detailed examination of the proposals, where disagreement almost certainly would have surfaced. Moreover, since the Quebec Resolutions were presented to the Canadian assembly as a fait accompli to be voted up or down, it was doubly necessary to create the impression of unity. Had the Quebec Resolutions been placed before the electorate for ratification, it might well have been in the coalition's interest to stress that this was a collaborative effort that was democratically heterogeneous and that invited a wide variety of views and interpretations. As it was, the resolutions were placed before the Canadian Legislative Assembly more in the form of a governmental measure in which differences had to be suppressed in favor of cabinet solidarity.

The debates on the Confederation proposal that were held in the Canadian Legislative Assembly in 1865 betray this strategic circumspection particularly clearly. At the most general level, the tripartite coalition agreed that federalism was the only acceptable constitutional remedy for the various ills besetting British North America. They agreed, further, that federalism meant dividing legislative jurisdiction between a national parliament, which would legislate on those matters of "general" or "national" interest, and several provincial legislatures, which would have the authority to pass laws on matters of "local" significance. But most supporters of the Confederation proposal did their best to avoid giving these general propositions substance. Most speakers were little inclined to explain how precisely the local was to be distinguished from the general; how conflicts of jurisdiction were to be resolved; whether federalism was compatible with the protection of minority rights, or other crucial matters of substance in a federation. In some cases the dogged refusal to examine the substance of the Confederation proposals became comical. C. B. de Niverville, a Bleu (or Conservative) member from Trois-Rivières, spoke in favor of Confederation even though he had not read the resolutions and even though, lacking English, he had been unable to follow the debate in the assembly.[26] Nor was the flight from substance confined to the back benches. John A. Macdonald himself avoided confronting the possibility of federal-provincial conflict by stating unequivocally (and quite absurdly) that the constitutional architects had managed to avoid "all conflict of jurisdiction and authority."[27]

It is not as if the Confederation proposal was crystal clear. The coalition's unwillingness to discuss matters of substance in any detail was especially noticeable and unsatisfying because the text of the proposal itself seemed to contradict the very federal principles that it was meant to embody. The coalition agreed, for instance, that in the proposed federation the provincial legislatures would enjoy full, indeed "exclusive," control over local affairs.[28] Yet the text that, read one way, seemed to guarantee local self-government could be read with equal ease as a massive hedge against local control. The federal government was given a general, residual power to legislate for the "peace, order and good government" of the country, a potentially vast power illustrated, but apparently not limited, by an additional, enumerated list of legislative powers.[29] The provinces were not given the fiscal capacity to match their constitutional responsibilities; from the start they depended on federal subsidies.[30] The federal government was given the power to claim jurisdiction over "local works and undertakings" by declaring them to be "for the general advantage of Canada."[31] The power of disallowance gave the federal government the right to veto any act of a provincial legislature within one year of the act's passage.[32] The federal government was expected to appoint a lieutenant-governor in each province, which officer had the power to reserve assent from (or effectively prevent the passage of) provincial legislation.[33] Even in the crucial area of sectarian education, the constitutional settlement deviated from the principle of complete provincial control. By section 93 of the BNA Act the federal government was given the power to oversee minority educational rights in any province in which a system of separate schools existed by law at the time the province entered Confederation. Section 93 further provided that, if necessary, the federal government could impose remedial legislation upon an offending province.[34]

None of these provisions could be reconciled easily with the official claim that under the terms of the Confederation settlement each province would be utterly free to legislate on all matters of peculiar importance to it—something the many critics of Confederation repeatedly pointed out. The most perceptive and spirited of these critics were Antoine-Aimé and Jean Baptiste Eric Dorion, Rouge representatives from Quebec, who insisted that Confederation would become for all intents and purposes a unitary government because the provinces would be both too weak and too vulnerable to defend themselves against the imperious and meddlesome designs of the federal government. What the Dorions had wanted was a "real Federal system" in which the member states "retain their full sovereignty in everything that immediately concerns them, but submitting to the General Government questions of peace, of war, of foreign relations, foreign trade, customs and postal service."[35] What had been proposed instead was "a Legislative Union in disguise" in which "the Federal Parliament will exercise sovereign power inasmuch as it can always trespass upon the rights of the local governments without there being any authority to prevent it."[38]

The great force of the Dorions' criticism was that it related the new and unfamiliar proposals for Confederation to one of the basic concepts of Anglo-American political discourse—sovereignty. Gordon Wood has shown how the debate leading to the ratification of the American Constitution was informed by Blackstone's axiom that there must be in every political system "a supreme, irresistible, absolute, uncontrolled authority, in which ... the rights of sovereignty reside."[37] And he has described brilliantly how this assumption that sovereignty is indivisible became "the most powerful obstacle" to the acceptance of the federal constitution.[38] Blackstone's axiom was no less important in the debate leading to Confederation and no less powerful an obstacle to its coherent defense. For the Dorions, as for most educated Canadians, the idea of sovereignty served as an anchor for political analysis, even if they were typically less inclined than Americans to identify this foundation explicitly.[39]

In making sovereignty the focus of their analysis of the Confederation scheme, the Dorions immediately clarified the choices and hardened the alternatives. For if Blackstone was right that sovereignty is indivisible, then, as the Dorions showed, there could really be only two ways of forming a broader political association in British North America. At one extreme, sovereignty could be lodged in some central authority which had the legislative power to make laws for all the colonies or provinces; this was what was meant by a legislative union. At the other extreme, each member of the association could remain sovereign or supreme; this was the legal description of what the Dorions called a federal union. In either case the sovereign power could "delegate" law-making authority to some "subordinate" body. In a legislative union authority could be delegated to provincial legislatures in much the same way that authority was traditionally delegated to municipal or county councils or in the way that the imperial Parliament "delegated" power to the colonial legislatures. Conversely, in a federal union authority could be delegated in various ways from the individual sovereign states to a common congress. But in either case, the delegated power ultimately existed at the sufferance of the sovereign. Power could be withdrawn, supervised, influenced and controlled by the one supreme authority.

Judged by the criterion of sovereignty, it was clear to the Dorions that the Confederation proposal was misnamed. This was not a "real confederation, giving the largest powers to the local governments, and merely a delegated authority to the General Government."[40] Rather, the various elements of the Confederation plan, taken together, established a clear pattern of national hegemony. The extraordinary, potentially limitless power to legislate for the peace, order and good government of the country; the veto powers lodged in the federal government; the creation of federally appointed governors in each province; the power to declare local works in the national interest—all of this was incontrovertible evidence that the provincial legislatures would have no real control over local affairs because they were not sovereign. In the Confederation plan "all the sovereignty is vested in the General Government"[41]; conversely, "all is weakness, insignificance, annihilation in the Local Government."[42] As another member put it, under the Confederation scheme local governments would be "nothing more than municipal councils," which, in the case of jurisdictional collision, would be "completely at the mercy of the hostile Federal majority."[43]

What was yet more damning was that the supporters of Confederation co-operated in their own indictment. Macdonald was of course particularly vulnerable to the charge of false advertising. He openly admitted that he had only grudgingly accepted the proposal to create a specifically federal union, and even then his conversion was half-hearted. Federalism was a practical or political necessity for Macdonald, not something desirable in itself, and he did his best to limit this concession by ensuring that the federal government would always be able to judge and control precisely how much "individuality"[44] the provinces should be allowed to display. For Macdonald, the constitutional model from which the Canadian proposal was derived was not the American federation (which, after all, had been discredited by the Civil War)[45] but the British empire. Expressed in the language of sovereignty, Macdonald argued that the relation between Ottawa and the provinces would replicate the relation between the sovereign imperial Parliament and the colonial legislatures; "all the powers incident to sovereignty," he argued, would be vested in the federal government while "the local governments and legislatures" would be "subordinate to the General Government and Legislature."[46] The extent of provincial autonomy or liberty would depend on the judgment of the federal government just as the extent of colonial freedom depended on the judgment of the imperial authorities. The provinces, like the colonies, might be allowed considerable room to legislate freely on those matters local in nature. But there could be no mistake, according to Macdonald, that in the final analysis the federal government was sovereign over the provinces just as the imperial Parliament was sovereign over Canada. Thus, it is no coincidence that much of the apparatus of imperial supervision—the vetoes of reservation and disallowance and the office of lieutenant-governor, for example—found their way into the Canadian constitution as tools of federal supervision. This was to be federalism on the imperial model; this is what I will call "political federalism."

The position of the Upper Canadian Reformers[47] is rather more difficult to categorize and describe, but here too there was considerable grist for the Dorions' mill. The Reformers in general and George Brown in particular were well aware of the advantages of a strong central government.[48] They were eager to develop the West, build industry and promote trade. They realized that such development would require greater central co-ordination than a weak, state-centered federation could provide, and they understood perfectly well that Ontario, by virtue of its greater political and economic power, would be able to dominate national affairs. Moreover, the Reformers appreciated the disadvantages associated with traditional, state-centered federalism. For most of the Upper Canadian Confederationists, traditional federalism was synonymous with American federalism—a model which in 1864 hardly invited imitation. In light of the Civil War, most Reformers simply concluded that to confer sovereignty on the states was tantamount to sowing the seeds of national dissolution. The most prominent Reform newspaper, George Brown's Toronto *Globe*, put it this way:

> The civil war...has afforded an excellent opportunity of judging of the weak points and defects in the United States constitution. It has especially shown the evil which the "States-rights" doctrine involves. The idea of the United States constitution is that the central government is a delegated government, deriving its powers from the "sovereign" States which go to make up the Union. The constitution provides that the President and Congress shall have certain powers which the States have covenanted to give up to it. All others are vested in the States. This idea, pushed to the extreme, lies at the basis of what is known as the Calhoun doctrine, and was held thirty years ago, to justify the attempt of South Carolina to "nullify" a certain Act of Congress. The same thing is now relied upon by the secessionists to justify their efforts to withdraw their States from the federal compact.[49]

The *Globe* recognized that the Civil War could not be explained in terms of these constitutional defects alone. But it had to admit that Calhoun's radicalization of the constitutional principle of state sovereignty had "served to weaken the authority of the general Government at Washington" and had furnished "the secession leaders with an exceedingly plausible argument."[50] This was not, therefore, an example to be followed.

The Reformers' aversion to state sovereignty forced a good many of them to concede that the only alternative to this state-centered federalism was to vest sovereignty squarely in the central government. As long as they remained loyal to the language of Blackstone, they had no choice but to think of federalism as "an extension of our municipal system" in which the provincial legislatures would be "subordinate" to the federal government, their powers "delegated" by the central government.[51] Indeed, lacking the attributes of sovereignty, George Brown's *Globe* argued that it would be advisable to keep "the local governments as simple and inexpensive as possible."[52] It clearly would be unnecessary to have two legislative chambers in each province, and the *Globe*, in October 1864, even cast doubt on the necessity of bothering with a truly responsible government. After all, the federally appointed "Governor" of each province would probably have a veto on the legislature's acts, and "a responsible ministry in each province would certainly not be the cheapest system which could be adopted."[53]

The Reformers put the best possible face on this situation. They argued valiantly that the federal government would understand that it was not in its interest to become embroiled in local affairs, and they maintained that the Senate would protect the smaller provinces from being bullied.[54] Yet at base these were guarantees, like Macdonald's, that depended on the good graces of a central government that was sovereign over provincial governments that were legally subordinate. The critics of Confederation could see no difference between the Reformers' understanding of "political federalism" and Macdonald's, and this remains the conventional scholarly view of the Confederation settlement as well. It seems fair to say that most scholars agree with J.C. Morrison's conclusion that the Reformers "recognized the true nature of the system which it was proposed to establish"; that they "committed their party to the support of such a Government"; and therefore "(t)here seems no basis whatsoever for the subsequent cry, raised first in Ontario, that the intention of the Fathers of Confederation" was to create "a truly federal system."[55]

What this view ignores, however, is that the Reformers were clearly uncomfortable with this conception of federalism because they, too, realized that it offered insufficient protection for the autonomy of local governments. The Reformers, after all, were committed by ideology and tradition to some form of decentralized government.[56] The roots of that tradition can be traced at least as far back as the 1820s, and it had been given special force in the 1860s by their francophobia.[57] Thus, while it is perfectly true that the Reformers wanted a strong central government, especially one in which Ontario would dominate, they simply did not see that the achievement of "Rep. by Pop." and strength at the center were incompatible with their traditional goal of local control over local affairs. What the Reformers really wanted to create was a federal system that would provide both strong, united direction at the center together with clear constitutional protection for local government at the periphery. As the *Globe* put it: "We desire local self-government in order that the separate nationalities of which the population is composed may not quarrel. We desire at the same time a strong central authority. Is there anything incompatible in these two things? Cannot we have both? What is the difficulty?"[58]

The difficulty was with the traditional understanding of federalism, and as long as the Reformers accepted the doctrine of undivided sovereignty, these desiderata—central power and provincial autonomy—were indeed incompatible. But as the Reformers were pressed, especially by Lower Canadians, to provide a more solid constitutional foundation for provincial government, they began to wonder aloud whether their choices were quite as limited as traditional federal theory seemed to suggest. The Reform supporters of Confederation were neither sufficiently presumptuous nor sufficiently sophisticated to reject the conventional understanding of sovereignty outright. But in the period preceding Confederation they did begin, albeit tentatively, to offer a second description of Confederation that differed in subtle, but important, ways from Macdonald's conception of "political federalism" that I have already described. While on the one hand the Reformers cleaved to the traditional language of legislative and federal union, they asserted on the other that they were creating a new form of political organization that could be described neither as a legislative nor as a federal union but which was a "happy medium" between them, a "compromise" that would allow both for a powerful central government and legally secure provincial legislatures.[59] This is what I will call "constitutional federalism."

IV

The Reformers' attempt to reach an acceptable constitutional compromise can best be understood in light of the American precedent that anticipated both their problem and their solution. To be sure, there is little evidence that the Confederationists explicitly patterned their understanding of federalism on the American model, and I do not mean to suggest that they did. What is nonetheless striking is that the Reformers defended a constitutional position in 1865 that was in many ways similar to the Federalists' defense of the American Constitution some eighty years before, and it will prove helpful for understanding the pre-Confederation debate to bear in mind the American model. Like the Reformers, the Federalists were accused of creating a constitutional system that pretended to reserve an important place for the states but which in fact would lead ineluctably to their annihilation. Like the Reformers, the Federalists were told that there could be no middle ground between the loosest form of confederation and outright consolidation. And like the Reformers, only more forcefully and clearly, the Federalists attempted to demonstrate that it was possible to dissolve the tension between these two forms of political organization, to create a constitution that was a defensible, principled compromise between them. In James Madison's famous phrase, the Constitution of 1787 was "in strictness neither a national nor a federal constitution; but a composition of both."[60]

Madison's explanation of this constitutional compromise is now taken to be the first and authoritative definition of modern, "classical" or constitutional federalism.[61] This definition turned on a reformulation of the idea of sovereignty and a qualified rejection of Blackstone's authoritative teaching. For Blackstone, the two great threats to liberty were anarchy on the one hand and kingly prerogative on the other. By defining sovereignty as the power to make laws, Blackstone provided an alternative to the traditional identification between sovereignty and the monarch's will. By locating this sovereign law-making power in one body, even one as complex as Parliament, he provided some final, ultimate political authority that would thereby foreclose the possibility of anarchy.[62] For both reasons a Parliament which could make laws, delegate limited authority to other bodies (or rescind that authority), and enforce the laws, became for Blackstone and those who followed him the central institution of British politics.

For the Federalists (as indeed for the revolutionary generation of 1776), this identification of sovereignty with legislative will was inadequate either to protect liberty or maintain stability. Put bluntly, the pre-Revolution experience with Parliament suggested to the Americans that they could hardly count on Parliament to protect their liberties. Indeed, as the authors of the Declaration of Independence understood very well, Parliament had actually co-operated in the oppression of America. Nor was this all. American experience under the Articles of Confederation suggested the still more sobering lesson that even indigenous, democratically representative legislatures could not be counted on to protect liberty—especially, but by no means exclusively, the right to accumulate and dispose of property. If Parliament, or representative assemblies more generally, threatened liberty, it would not do to allow them to be sovereign. This problem led many Americans to rethink Blackstone's doctrine and to relocate the locus of sovereignty outside of government altogether—in the people-at-large.

The Federalists were particularly quick to seize on this novel understanding of sovereignty because it helped them to see how they could create a constitutional system that would purge the "ill humours" they associated with excessively democratic government without actually abandoning democratic principles.[63] Thus, while a state legislature or the Congress might be called sovereign in some "lower" or "secondary" sense of legislative power, the source of this power, sovereignty in the "higher" sense, rested with "the people." The people, Publius argued, are "the only legitimate fountain of power." They are the "ultimate authority" by which governments are constituted and "the common superior" to which all duly constituted governments are answerable.[64]

This transfer of sovereignty from law-making bodies to the people-at-large had enormous implications for the theory and practice of American politics because it made it possible to conceive of a government that was derived from, but not in any immediate way controlled by, the people. As Judith Shklar has pointed out, the effect of this transfer of sovereignty was to make the people the only legitimate source of authority; but the effect was also to replace the unmediated will of the people—their sovereignty—with a complex set of political and legal processes, federalism included, that could operate without constant popular initiative.[65]

This transformation of the locus (and understanding) of sovereignty was especially important in the case of federalism because it made it possible to contemplate what had previously been unthinkable—the existence of two independent, fully constituted, sovereign governments within the same political system. The people, acting in their original, primal, constituent capacity could create two levels of government, empowered and limited by a constitution. It was no longer necessary to ensure that one level could control, and if necessary destroy, the other because both would be controlled by their "common superior," the people or the constitution framed by the people. Sovereignty remained indivisible. It was vested, in this constituent sense, in the people. But at the same time, federal and state governments could be understood to be "coequal sovereignties," as legally equal, independent governments which derived their authority from, and were protected by, a constitution; governments which were sovereign in the sense that they had full or supreme power to act within the sphere defined by the fundamental law.[66]

Madison described this new understanding as a compromise between outright nationalization and confederalism, and although it was later challenged we recognize it quite clearly as the first description of classical or constitutional federalism. The members of the Canadian Confederation elite, however, did not recognize the Federalists' project this way. They interpreted the federal provisions of the American Constitution largely in the manner of John Calhoun, and to that extent they continued to believe that the American understanding of federalism, based on the sovereignty of individual states, was misguided beyond remedy. Yet while the Canadians were doing their best to distance themselves from Calhoun's doctrine of state-based confederalism, they were simultaneously groping towards something that in crucial ways resembled the Madisonian understanding of constitutional federalism; and, as with Madison, this search began with a reconsideration of the idea of sovereignty.

The Canadians of the 1860s took Blackstone's understanding of sovereignty as their base. For them, as for Blackstone, sovereignty meant parliamentary sovereignty, and they therefore typically identified sovereignty with legislation, the power to makes laws. Yet as the citizens of a largely self-governing colony, the Canadians came in their own way and through their own experience to appreciate the ambiguity of Blackstonian sovereignty. For while the imperial Parliament was sovereign over Canada, the Canadians well understood that this sovereignty did not express itself as directly or with the same bite as in Britain. At least since the time of Lord Durham, it was understood to be in the interest both of the colonies and of Britain to leave British North America to govern itself on those matters that did not directly compromise or conflict with imperial interests. By 1864, Durham's suggestion had become the basis of a well-established, if informal, proto-federal arrangement. To be sure, Parliament passed the basic laws by which the various colonial legislatures governed; it served as the ultimate appeal from colonial legislation; and it reserved the right to involve itself in Canadian affairs when its own interests—as it defined them—were at issue.

Still, by 1864 the Canadian colonists had come to expect that Britain would not as a rule interfere in colonial politics. The Canadians thus understood quite well that sovereignty and legislative power, the source of legitimacy and actual governance, need not be identical. The Toronto *Globe* insisted, as Madison had, that it would be a mistake in framing or interpreting a constitution to assume that sovereignty and legislative power were simply synonymous. As the *Globe* noted, one could easily conceive of a government that was sovereign but which exercised little legislative power, having delegated "a very wide range of duties" to some other authority.[67] Conversely, one could imagine a local government that legislated on a host of subjects even though it was not nominally sovereign. This was, after all, basically how the empire worked, and in Canadian eyes it provided a useful model.

The conceptual wedge having been driven between sovereignty and legislative power, the debate over Confederation allowed (or perhaps forced) the supporters of the proposal to push the distinction still further so as to defend the Confederation proposal against those who believed it would lead to the destruction of local governments. In this respect the distinction between sovereignty and legislative power was important to the *Globe* for much the same reason that it was important to Madison: it allowed the supporters of Confederation to break out of the familiar pattern of federal thinking, to find a "middle ground" which would secure a firm constitutional foundation for provincial legislation without sacrificing vigorous central leadership.

The Dorions, to recall, had argued that under the terms of the Confederation proposal the federal government would be able to legislate on virtually any matter, no matter how local, and override any provincial legislation, no matter how innocuous. Armed with the distinction between sovereignty and power, the advocates of Confederation were able to respond that this misrepresented the sovereign basis of Confederation and therefore underestimated the extent of provincial security. True, the federal government would be a powerful government, but it would not be a sovereign government in the full Blackstonian sense of the term. It did not create the provincial governments and could not destroy them; it could not unilaterally change the terms of the agreement and was not the final authority to which an aggrieved party could turn for redress. Only the imperial Parliament would be sovereign in this fundamental, constituent sense of the term. In the Canadian scheme, therefore, the imperial Parliament performed much the same function and was sovereign in much the same way that the people were sovereign in the United States; it would be the source and ultimate authority over the legitimate exercise of political power. By precisely the same reasoning, the BNA Act would do in Canada what the Constitution did in the United States: it would empower and limit the various governments by law.

Of course the substance of the Reformers' understanding of sovereignty was not identical to the American, and they did not intend it to be. The Reform view maintained a world of difference between vesting ultimate sovereignty in the people and vesting it in the imperial Parliament, and guarded the difference jealously. The real beauty of the Reformers' argument, therefore, was that it allowed them to adapt their comfortable loyalty to British imperialism to the new categories of American political science, to combine the substance of British political culture with the forms of American government. Thus did the Reformers use their experience of British colonial politics to create a legal structure that in this crucial way resembled American constitutional federalism.

Already by 1864 the Reform press (and even a few Conservative papers) had begun to put together the pieces of this novel federal understanding. A month before the Quebec Conference was convened to discuss federal union of the British North American colonies, the Toronto *Globe* attempted to reassure its public, especially in Quebec, that if a federation were created it would provide adequate protection for the integrity of local government:

> When we speak of local provinces under a federal form of government, we do not mean mere County Councils, but legislatures empowered by the Imperial Legislature and the Crown to deal with specified matters, and enjoying a prescribed authority, with which "Congress" will not be allowed to interfere. Such legislatures would be beyond the control of the central power, set apart from it, untouchable by it.[68]

Untouchable, the *Globe* pointed out, because provincial jurisdiction would be protected by what Americans—and increasingly Canadians[69]—called a constitution, a fundamental law over which neither federal nor provincial governments would have control:

> The Lower Canadians who have been apprehensive that their rights would not be fully secured will be glad to see the proposition that the distribution of power between the local and general governments shall be clearly fixed by an act of the Imperial Legislature, and shall not be the work of the federal Parliament. This removes all fear of local privileges being tampered with.[70]

Reporting on the Quebec Conference itself, the Hamilton *Weekly Times* concluded that "the functions of the general and local governments, and the subjects delegated to each, must be clearly defined in the constitution, so as to prevent collision and leave security for local interests, the whole to be embodied in an act of the Imperial Parliament."[71] For its part, the Toronto *Leader* noted that while the powers of the local government would be "defined and limited," they would be "conferred by Imperial authority" and so "practically" would not be "subject to recall."[72] The imperial Parliament, being the source of governmental power in Canada, was thus truly sovereign in the constituent sense of the term, and the BNA Act was, as in the United States, a fundamental law by which federal and provincial governments were both empowered and limited. So conceived, the *Globe* could conclude that under the Confederation scheme the federal government would be "precluded from any interference with the legislation of the local bodies, so long as they keep within constitutional limits, and we shall all be quite safe."[73]

By 1867, the view that under the Confederation scheme the provinces would be able to legislate without interference from the federal government had become a standard part of Reform rhetoric. At the Reform convention held only days before the BNA Act came into effect, the first resolution recorded the delegates' "high gratification that the long and earnest contest of the Reform party for the great principles of Representation by Population and local control over local affairs, (had) at last been crowned with triumphant success."[74] Several of the delegates, in speaking to the resolution, seized on the importance of constitutionally protected non-interference. Aemilius Irving reminded the delegates of the editorialist who, at the time of the 1859 Reform Convention, had called for the creation of a federal system that would give the local legislatures "entire control over every public interest, except those and those only that are necessarily common to all parties." The BNA Act, Irving concluded, represented "the most satisfactory fulfilment of the prophecy."[75] George Brown reiterated his now well-worn view that "this Constitution gives us entire control over our own local affairs."[76] The St. Thomas *Journal* came to the same conclusion in its pre-Confederation analysis.[77] And the Toronto *Globe*, in its pre-convention exhortation to Reform delegates, interpreted the impending constitutional change thus: "The people of Ontario have got the absolute control of their local affairs, and they have a just representation in the Parliament which deals with the affairs of the Dominion. So far as these cardinal points in the Constitution are concerned, we have all that we asked or could ask."[78]

Many of the Quebec supporters of Confederation arrived at much the same conclusion and drew out the implications more clearly. A. I. Silver has shown through an exhaustive analysis of Bleu pamphlets and newspapers that the "moderate majority was firm in maintaining that the provinces would be in no way inferior or subordinate to the federal government, that they would be at least its equal, and that each government would be sovereign and untouchable in its own sphere of action."[79] As Joseph Blanchet put it to the Canadian Legislative Assembly: "I consider that under the present plan of Confederation the local legislatures are supreme in respect of the powers which are attributed to them, that is to say, in respect of local matters."[80]

Stung by the Dorions' criticism that the provincial legislatures would have no protection against a central government holding supervisory powers, several of the Bleus were finally moved toward the end of the Confederation Debates to demonstrate that Lower Canada would in fact have nothing to fear. Cartier interrupted A. A. Dorion's attack on the Confederation plan to explain that in the case of jurisdictional collisions the federal government would not be able to run roughshod over the provinces, but that disputes would be resolved by a third party—although he was not quite sure whether this responsibility would devolve upon the imperial authorities or the courts.[81] His colleague Paul Denis argued that the federal government would not have the unilateral power to abolish the use of French by noting that "the Imperial Act will guarantee to us the use of our language."[82]

The clearest defense of the plan, however, was provided by Joseph-Edouard Cauchon. By the time of Confederation, Cauchon was one of the most powerful Conservative figures in Quebec. He had been in public life for some twenty years, having first been elected to the combined Legislative Assembly in 1844. He had held various governmental posts in the intervening years, most notably minister of public works, and enjoyed a high public profile as the editor of the Quebec daily *Le Journal*.

Cauchon's views on federalism were complicated. When the idea of a British North American union was first discussed in the late 1850s, he opposed it because he saw no reason to shake the stability of the established order. By 1864, he had reached the conclusion that something had to be done to meet the challenge presented by American expansionism on the one hand and Anglo-Saxon preponderance on the other. The difficulty, from Cauchon's perspective, was that these threats required quite different reactions. To meet the American threat, Cauchon argued, unity was absolutely necessary; to preserve the French-Canadian nation, some form of separation was needed. The solution, therefore, was to create a centralized federation that also respected the autonomy of the provinces, and it was on this understanding that Cauchon became one of the most vigorous supporters of the Confederation proposal. The Dorions maintained that the central government would have "sovereign power ... over the legislatures of the provinces." Cauchon denied it:

There will be no absolute sovereign power, each legislature having its distinct and independent attributes, not proceeding from one or the other by delegation, either from above or from below. The Federal Parliament will have legislative sovereign power in all questions submitted to its control in the Constitution. So also the local legislatures will be sovereign in all matters which are specifically assigned to them.[83]

In the case of conflict, matters would be settled by "the judicial tribunals,... charged by the very nature of their functions to declare whether such a law of the Federal Parliament or of the local legislatures does or does not affect the Constitution."[84] And he understood that, as the ultimate source of both federal and provincial power, the Imperial Parliament—not one of the constituted governments—would have the final authority to judge on questions pertaining to the Canadian constitution.[85] This was pure Madisonian logic applied to the Canadian case.

To be sure, the Reform and Bleu understanding of federalism as it was expressed in the years 1864–1867 was inchoate, often expedient and frequently confused. Grappling with a new way to think about federalism yet unable to jettison the older conception altogether, they would often move casually from the older to the newer discourse apparently without fully realizing their incompatibility. Yet it would be wrong to dismiss their contribution to the Confederation debate simply because their thought was often obscure, self-interested or even contradictory. For one thing, if these supporters sometimes described federalism in a way that was more compatible with John A. Macdonald's vision, so Macdonald conceded something to them and, in so doing, rendered his own conception deeply ambiguous. It is an indication of the force of the new constitutional conception of federalism that despite all of the centralizing mechanisms even Macdonald was forced to accept its core principle: the principle that, within its sphere of jurisdiction, each province has the "exclusive" power to legislate. That is how he presented the proposal publicly, and that is how the BNA Act was drafted and passed.[86]

Moreover, however imperfectly the federal principle was understood in 1865, it provided a foundation on which to build a more impressive and coherent constitutional doctrine. The discovery of federal theory in the years preceding Confederation played a crucial part in the subsequent struggle for provincial rights because it allowed the provincial autonomists to treat Macdonald's centralizing mechanisms as if they were impurities that had to be removed from the constitutional system. They could thus claim that, in attempting to secure the real autonomy of the provinces against Macdonaldian centralism, they were fulfilling the spirit of the constitution of 1867, not undermining it—a difference of real rhetorical importance. In short, the discovery of the federal principle allowed the autonomists to create their own founding myth around the Confederation settlement, to prosecute their political goals in the name of constitutional principle, and to dictate the terms in which the debate was carried on. As we will see, this creation of a new language of federalism in Canada was enormously advantageous to the provincial rights movement and deeply significant for Canadian constitutional discourse.

V

It did not take long before the language of constitutional federalism—of inviolable spheres of legislative autonomy—became the *lingua franca* of constitutional discourse in Canada. Before 1867 the disagreement about the role and status of the provincial governments remained latent and inoffensively general. Once the ink was dry on the BNA Act, however, these differences came into the open while the meaning and implications of the federal principle were refined into a versatile and powerful constitutional doctrine. It cannot be overstressed that the most serious and damaging criticism of John A. Macdonald's centralism came not from those who actively opposed Confederation, but from those who had been part of the coalition that engineered its passage. Three episodes—involving the privileges and immunities of the legislatures, the dual mandate and better terms for Nova Scotia—set the tone for what was to come.

In 1869, the Ontario legislature passed a bill that conferred the traditional privileges and immunities associated with parliamentary government—immunity from prosecution for slander, for example— on members of the Legislative Assembly and its employees.[87] Upon review by the federal government, however, the act was struck down (that is, "disallowed") for being beyond the power of the provincial legislature. John A. Macdonald, who served both as prime minister and attorney general in the first federal cabinet, explained that while the BNA Act expressly conferred the power to define "the privileges and immunities of the Senate and House of Commons" on the Parliament of Canada, it said nothing about the provincial legislatures. Even in the absence of such clear authorization, the federal government could still argue that the definition of parliamentary privileges pertained to the "peace, order and good government" of the country. But the provincial legislatures, he noted, had no corresponding general power to legislate "for the good government of the provinces" as a whole. It must, therefore, be assumed that the Ontario act was "in excess of the power of the provincial legislature."[88]

As in many of the subsequent disputes, this formal explanation of the constitutional issue barely hints at the larger, symbolic significance of the provincial action. The first premier of Ontario, John Sandfield Macdonald, was not known as a champion of provincial rights. Though of Reform stock, he had opposed Confederation and had been persuaded by John A. Macdonald to head a coalition government in Ontario.[89] Yet even Sandfield bridled at the suggestion that the provincial legislatures could not define the rules by which they governed themselves. It was "singular," Premier Macdonald wrote in reply to the disallowance report, that the provincial legislature should be allowed to "confer such privileges upon any court or municipal body" but that it "should not be able to grant them to itself."[90] More seriously, it was an affront to the "dignity" of the provincial legislature, rendering it "more feeble than a justice of the peace, who has a right to punish contempt committed at his petty sessions."[91] This was the crux of the issue, and this is why the premier took it so seriously. From John Sandfield's perspective, the disallowance of this apparently innocuous legislation conveyed the clear message that the federal government considered the provinces to be less independent, less sovereign, in short less worthy of respect even than municipal councils. What Ontario affirmed, and what the federal government apparently denied, was that the provincial legislatures were full-fledged parliaments, not municipal councils or local corporations: independent, sovereign, and as deserving of respect as any other parliament, the one in Ottawa included.

In the end and despite the veto, Ottawa acquiesced. Having disallowed both the Ontario law and a similar Quebec law in 1869, the federal government declined to strike down a repackaged version of the parliamentary privileges act when it was passed by the Quebec legislature in 1870.[92] Macdonald still had "great doubts whether the legislature had jurisdiction." But he ultimately judged it "inexpedient to interfere" when the act was thought necessary "to uphold the authority and dignity of the provincial legislature."[93] Several years later, with a Liberal administration in power federally, the Ontario legislature repassed its parliamentary privileges bill without incident.

Of greater substantive importance was the abolition of the "dual mandate," the practice which allowed the same person to represent a constituency simultaneously in the provincial legislature and the federal parliament. In Ontario, for example, John Sandfield Macdonald was both premier of the province and a federal member of Parliament, while on the other side Edward Blake both led the Liberal party in the Ontario legislature and sat on the Liberal side in the House of Commons. As W. L. Morton has observed,[94] the practice of dual representation "was in many ways a continuation of the Union" that had preceded Confederation, for it supposed that "local" and "national" issues could be, and in the interests of harmony ought to be, deliberated upon by the same people. Brown Chamberlin, one of John A. Macdonald's closest political allies in Quebec, explained the purpose of dual representation this way:

> Every man who has studied history carefully, especially the history of Federal Governments, knows that the greatest danger to their stability lies in the amount of jealousy and friction likely to grow up between the Local and the General Governments. This is especially seen in the history of the United States. That country has suffered in consequence of the powers exercised by the Local and the General Governments being ill defined, and it has resulted in imposing upon that people a constitution that their forefathers would never have assented to. We should avoid this jealousy rising up against the General Government. By having some members in the Local Legislatures, we will promote a spirit of harmony between them and the General Government. They will carry our views into the Local Legislatures, and they will bring us back some ideas acquired by mingling with their orators.

The ultimate, and salutary, effect of dual representation would thus be "to ward off continual collision between the Local and the General Governments."[95]

Chamberlin's defense of dual representation was transparently centralist; the object, as the foregoing quotation says directly, was to protect the central government from jealous provincial governments, not the other way around. The opposition to dual representation was led by David Mills (1831-1903), the Liberal MP for the southwestern Ontario constituency of Bothwell. Mills is one of the most remarkable, and least known, figures of late-nineteenth-century Canadian politics. Member of Parliament for some thirty years, newspaper editor, law professor, minister of justice under Laurier, associate justice of the Supreme Court—Mills was in all of this one of the leading defenders of provincial rights in the formative period of Confederation. Mills's background was quite typical of the Reform movement to which he belonged. He was born in Canada, grew up in rural, southwestern Ontario, and was given a strong religious education. Upon graduating from the local common school, Mills apparently received further private tuition, worked as a school inspector for almost a decade, then, in 1865, left the family farm to attend law school at the University of Michigan.

Mills's views about law, especially the constitutional basis of federalism, were decisively shaped at Michigan by Thomas Cooley. Cooley was one of the dominant legal minds in the U.S. in the latter part of the nineteenth century.[96] His treatise on the "Constitutional Limitations which Rest Upon the Legislative Power of the States of the American Union"[97] is considered one of the classic expositions of the period and one of the leading mid-century attempts to fashion American law into a systematic whole. Cooley's treatise was adapted from his lectures on the same subject at Michigan, lectures which Mills attended. For a Canadian, they were of special value in explaining with great clarity the sovereign basis of American federalism. Mills's notes record Cooley's words thus:

> In every country sovereign power is recognized as resting somewhere, and wherever that power is lodged there too reposes the power to amend or change the constitution. A constitution is expressive of the present will of the sovereign power. The power to change the constitution rests with the person or body that is sovereign. Here the sovereign power is with the people, not with the law making power. The legislature of the state or nation derives its power from the constitution and is subject to it.[98]

From this it followed, according to Cooley, that "both the state and national legislature are sovereign in a qualified sense." Each is sovereign in that each has "complete jurisdiction over the persons and property within its territorial limits." But this sovereignty is qualified in that this authority is limited to "a certain class of subjects"[99] as defined by the Constitution. Here, succinctly, was a description of the federal principle towards which the Reformers groped their way in the years preceding Confederation.

Cooley provided much more than a formal framework for understanding federalism, however. Cooley's legal universe was informed by a fundamental tension between legislative will and constitutional limitation. The object of government, Cooley stated, is "to give each person the greatest amount of security with the least curtailment of liberty." Government is necessary, but unrestrained it threatens to overwhelm the liberty or independence of those less powerful than it. It is consequently necessary, Mills recorded, to keep government from going "beyond its own legitimate province," and to keep governmental power within "its prescribed limits."[100] Specifically constitutional governments, including federal governments, "are such as not only locate the sovereign power but define the power of individuals and bodies and limit the exercise of this power with a view to protect individual rights and shield them against arbitrary action."[101] Power and the limitations on power to secure liberty—this was the theme, indeed the title, both of Cooley's course and of his treatise.

This was the understanding of federalism as a form of constitutional government that Mills applied to the question of dual representation. As Mills understood it, the BNA Act "called into existence a number of independent Legislatures with limited powers... each having exclusive jurisdiction within the sphere assigned to it by the Constitutional Act."[102] Like Cooley, however, Mills assumed that neither federal nor provincial legislatures could be trusted to stay within the jurisdictional boundaries that were meant to separate them:

> It was a matter which the experience of men in every department of life fully justified, and one resulted from the imperfections of human nature, that if a man was placed in any position he would always attempt to arrogate to himself more power than was necessary for the discharge of the duties which devolve upon him.[103]

Considering the evident weakness of the provincial legislatures, it was especially important to ensure that the "barriers erected by the Constitution"[104] were respected by the federal government.

Federalism, like all social relations, was essentially competitive. The only way to regulate the competition, therefore, was to give both governments, but especially the provinces, the defensive capacity to "mutually check each other."[105] This competitive premise left no room for co-operation, alliance or even divided loyalties among federal and provincial representatives. Mills explained the implications of his understanding to Parliament as follows:

> A gentleman having a seat in this House as well as in a Local Legislature was like a person who was a partner in two firms, one of which could not gain except at the expense of the other. When he found the house trespassing on the powers of the Local Legislatures, it was not his interest to object, because as a member of this house he would share in the advantage of the powers thus usurped.[106]

The object of the constitution, in other words, was quite different from what Brown Chamberlin suggested. It was not to create harmony or alliances. Rather, the object of the "federal principle" was "to enable the different Governments to carry on their functions independent-ally (sic) and without interference."[107] To protect this freedom within the limits of law (what Mills and others variously called independence, autonomy or sovereignty), "it is necessary that the Local Legislature be composed of persons entirely distinct from the general Govern-ment, in order to prevent the Parliament of Canada from making encroachments upon the Local Government."[108]

In 1873, after several unsuccessful attempts, Mills managed to shepherd his bill prohibiting dual representation through Parliament. One by one the provincial legislatures that had permitted the practice passed similar legislation, with the result that by 1874 dual represen-tation had disappeared in Canada. Thereafter, as W. L. Morton has astutely observed, "two separate kinds of politicians developed, the national and the provincial,"[109] and from that ensued the very sort of competition that Mills had said was the normal state of affairs in a federation.

In the attempt to block increased subsidies to Nova Scotia, the third major federal-provincial issue that came before Parliament in the years immediately following Confederation, the provincialists were less fortunate.[110] Nova Scotia had not so much entered Confed-eration as it had been brought in. The Nova Scotian legislative assem-bly, like the Canadian, had approved the Quebec Resolutions, but it was widely believed that the legislators were not representative of the Nova Scotian population generally. A movement to repeal the Confed-eration settlement grew quickly and produced impressive electoral strength. In the elections of 1867 the anti-Confederationists claimed thirty-six of thirty-eight seats in the provincial assembly while, under the leadership of Joseph Howe, they won eighteen of nineteen federal constituencies.

The agitation for the repeal of the BNA Act was by all standards a polite protest, the object of which was to return to the colonial status quo. Joseph Howe, for instance, objected to Confederation because he believed that Nova Scotia was better off, both politically and economically, as a self-governing colony of Britain than as a small province in Canada. As the name suggests, this was a repeal movement, not an independence movement, much less an annexation movement. What he wanted "was the continuance of Imperial stewardship."[111] Thus, fresh from the electoral triumphs of 1867, the Nova Scotians headed to London to press their case for repeal before the British Parliament. Predictably enough, Parliament paid little heed to their protests. A united Canada was part of imperial policy, and the colonial secretariat was not about to sacrifice the advantages of a united Canada to satisfy the complaints of the Nova Scotians.

The British reaction left the Nova Scotians without a clear strategy; it also provided John A. Macdonald with an opportunity to reconcile the Nova Scotians to Confederation by offering them "better terms" than those originally negotiated. Macdonald's strategy was shrewd. He refused to deal with the provincial government of Nova Scotia, preferring instead to negotiate with Howe and other members of the Nova Scotian delegation to Parliament. This divided the repeal movement, isolated the provincial government, and left Macdonald to bargain with those, like Howe, who were less truculent. The federal government promised to increase its annual subsidy to Nova Scotia, increase the province's debt allowance and protect it from discriminatory tariffs. Howe agreed, he was given a post in the cabinet and, at least for the moment, the crisis passed.

Parliamentary ratification of the "better terms" would have been routine had not the Liberal-Reform opposition challenged the constitutionality of the federal government's action. The constitutional objection touched two subjects that remain controversial to this day —constitutional amendment and the federal spending power. When the BNA Act was negotiated, it included a complicated financial settlement. One part of the settlement involved the provision of a provincial subsidy at the rate of eighty cents per capita; another was the federal government's assumption of provincial debts. All of this was to be "in full settlement of all future demands on Canada."[112] In this context, the Liberal-Reformers argued, the better terms arranged for Nova Scotia could not be construed simply as a routine national expenditure. The settlement with Howe and his colleagues, rather, had to be understood as a revision of the original terms of Confederation. It was, in effect, an amendment to a federal constitution made unilaterally by the Parliament of Canada for which even the consent of the Nova Scotia legislature had not been sought.

The BNA Act of 1867 did not contain an "amending formula" as such, that is, clear rules according to which the terms of the basic law itself could be changed, but this did not deter the Reformers from manufacturing their own rules from deeper constitutional principles. The Reformers maintained that as a matter of principle Parliament could not itself change the terms of the constitution in a way that would affect the several provinces because Parliament, while sovereign within the sphere allotted to it, did not possess sovereignty in the formative, constituent sense of the term. It had not made the constitution; it was therefore inappropriate for it unilaterally to revise basic constitutional decisions. Edward Blake, David Mills's friend and ally, argued that only the British Parliament could change the terms of the constitution, and he and Mills both sponsored motions to have the matter of Nova Scotia's financial complaints shelved until the British Parliament had approved the changes.[113] The maverick Luther Holton did them one better. While it was true, Holton argued, that the imperial Parliament was formally sovereign, in that it had passed the BNA Act, it was really "a compact between the Provinces" that "could only be violated, disturbed, changed or modified with the consent of all the contracting parties."[114] According to this argument, Ottawa should have nothing to do with the better terms at all. Instead, they should be submitted to the provincial legislatures for approval.

In either form this was a procedural objection to the government's action and perhaps the first important appearance of the "compact theory" of Confederation. But the opposition to the "better terms" resolution was also inspired, like Mills's attack on dual representation, by the perceived need to maintain provincial "independence." As a result, it produced what is perhaps the first sustained attack on the federal spending power. It was one thing, in the Liberal-Reform view, for the constitution to contain a financial settlement between the former colonies and the newly created Dominion government. It was quite another, they argued, for the federal government to make the subsidization of the provincial governments an ongoing matter of governmental policy. As independent legislatures within a federal system, the Liberal-Reformers argued, each level of government was meant to pay its own way. A provincial legislature "might fling its money into the lake if it liked, but it could not devote any of it into a channel which was within the jurisdiction of this Parliament."[115] Conversely, Blake continued, "this Parliament had no right to devote, from the service of Canada, for the support of the local governments, any money whatever, except those (constitutionally) specified sums."[116]

Any policy that allowed the federal government to spend money on matters over which they had no jurisdiction encroached on this independence and so contradicted the federal principle; and this encroachment, in turn, would inevitably produce mischievous political consequences. If the Nova Scotian precedent were allowed to stand, Blake argued, it would open "the flood gates"[117] to requests from other provinces who claimed that they had been unjustly treated by the federal government. The weaker provinces would seek bailouts; the stronger provinces would use their superior economic and political position to negotiate their own subsidies. All of this would lead "to a general scramble for more money and increased subsidies by the other Provinces,"[118] which in turn would create the very sort of inter-regional discord that Confederation had been intended to overcome. The practice of federal subventions, in short, would "shake the stability of the Constitution."[119] Better to honor the principle of strict independence in financial matters and to require each level to pay its own way than risk instability; "better to leave injustice if injustice there were, untouched, rather than meddle with the principle underlying the whole structure."[120]

This constitutional argument was easily rebuffed. George-Etienne Cartier argued that the additional federal subsidy sought to keep Nova Scotia in Confederation and thus meant to "promote order and good government in the Dominion,"[121] an obvious allusion to the federal government's broad power to act for the "peace, order and good government" of the country. There could not, therefore, "be a more correct appropriation."[122] For his part, John A. Macdonald simply argued that the federal government had the right to spend the money in its "public fund"[123] as it pleased, a view of the spending power which to this day remains dominant.

The greatest weakness in the Liberal-Reformers' argument, however, was that it alternately ignored and denied the justice and necessity of the case at hand. As Blake saw it, the Nova Scotian case could and should be settled simply as a matter of constitutional principle "abstracted altogether from the merits of the proposition."[124] But as the debate on the better terms wore on, the artificiality of this distinction became increasingly apparent. Most of the participants in the debate simply could not credit the argument that they should be guided solely by the abstract constitutional principle sketched by Blake, or that the justice and necessity of federal action should play no part in their votes.[125] In the event, the "better terms" resolution passed easily.[126]

These three episodes suggest an important lesson. The immediate post-Confederation period was crucial for the development of Canadian federalism because it proved conclusively that the Confederation settlement, far from settling matters, had in fact lent legitimacy to two quite different visions of Canada, the one represented by the relentless centralism of Macdonald, the other dedicated to the establishment of provincial governments which were legally autonomous and independent—supreme within the sphere allotted to them by the constitution. But these episodes demonstrate as well that this constitutional quarrel over the status and place of the provincial governments, while frequently expressed in the technical and arcane language of lawyers, drew heavily on the larger political values that were perceived to be at issue—dignity, liberty, and justice among them. The supporters of provincial autonomy sometimes forgot, or what is more likely, tried to deny the association between their constitutional agenda and the larger values that gave their federal principles substance and weight—witness the debate over the pacification of Nova Scotia. But as we will see in the next four chapters, the Nova Scotian episode was the exception rather than the rule. Between the time John A. Macdonald became prime minister in 1867 and his death in 1891, the provincial autonomists succeeded remarkably in blunting, derailing or in otherwise forcing the abandonment of his most prized centralizing mechanisms. In so doing the provincial autonomists did more than fashion a successful constitutional doctrine—they created a provincialist ideology.

CHAPTER 3

Provincial Autonomy
and Self-Government

The provincial lieutenant-governorship is now widely perceived to be a largely ceremonial and symbolic office. It was not always so. Centralists like Macdonald supposed that the lieutenant-governor would act as an agent of the federal government in Ottawa's efforts to control the provinces. So conceived, the lieutenant-governorship was one of the essential centralizing mechanisms of the Macdonald constitution. So realized, the office of lieutenant-Governor became the focus of a series of controversies in the years following Confederation in which the provincial rights movement challenged Macdonald's design as an affront to the basic, liberal principles of self-government. As we will see in detail in this chapter, the provincial autonomists sought to neutralize the lieutenant-governor as a federal officer by underscoring the powerful connecton between the doctrine of provincial autonomy and the ideal of parliamentary self-government. Stated baldly, the autonomists argued that to permit the lieutenant-governor to use the veto power of reservation, or to view prerogative as a discretionary power, was in effect to sustain the very sort of arbitrary executive power that earlier generations of constitutional reformers had struggled against. To support provincial sovereignty and autonomy over its own affairs, on the other hand, was to stand foursquare behind the sort of popular, parliamentary self-government that distinguished the British constitution, the deepest symbol of colonial political life. To the autonomists, therefore, the lieutenant-governorship represented more than a meddlesome federal agency; it represented a challenge to the deepest stratum of their self-conception. That is why they took the lieutenant-governorship so seriously, and that is why at every turn the leaders of the provincial rights movement sought to draw on the deeper, cultural symbols associated with self-

47

government and political liberty to consolidate their constitutional position.

The office of provincial lieutenant-governor was important to Confederation's designers because ti was associated with, and actually reproduced the tension between, two basic threads of British political practice: imperialism and responsible government. On the one hand, the lieutenant-governor was intended to act as a "federal officer" within each provincial government in much the same way that the colonial governors had been imperial agents on behalf of Westminster. Like the colonial governor, the lieutenant-governor was to be appointed, paid and in the event of misconduct, dismissed by the "senior" government. Like the colonial governor, the lieutenant-governor was meant to be a permanent lobbyist for the interests of the central government and a source of information about the activities of the provincial government. And like the colonial governor, the lieutenant-governor was supposed to ba a thinly disguised mole, "a possible traitor,"[1] who was meant to ensure that the provincial governments remained just as subordinate as the federal government wanted them to be.

At the same time and on the other hand, the lieutenant-governor was held to be the formal and compliant executive branch of a responsible government. There was, as we will see, some dispute in the early days as to whether the provincial lieutenant-governor was a direct representative of the monarchy or simply a representative of the governor general and, hence, at best an indirect representative of the queen. There was no dispute, however, as to the place of the lieutenant-governor within the parliamentary process. The Canadians, like most of the other colonists, identified the genius and progress of the British constitution with the institution of self-government in general and in the historical elevation of the Commons and electorate over the Crown and Lords in particular. The most basic rule of responsible government, which the Canadians had won in the 1840s, was therefore that "the Representative of the Sovereign, can act only on the advice of his ministers, those ministers being responsible to the people through Parliament."[2] This was the standard understanding in 1865 and remained the most basic constitutional principle throughout the period. As John A. Macdonald himself put the matter in a speech before Parliament in 1882:

> ...the Queen...cannot refuse a Bill which has been passed by both branches of the legislature. If a bill containing, in fact, her death warrant was placed before her she would be obliged to give her consent to it, and the hon. Minister would be obliged to proffer that Bill for the

purpose of getting the Royal Assent. The same principle applies here.
The Governor General is obliged to pass any bill that has passed this
House and Senate.[3]

As it is with the queen and the governor general, Macdonald concluded, "so it is with the Lieutenant-Governor."[4]

The difficulty, of course, is that the lieutenant-governor, who was
expected to be a compliant chief executive officer of a responsible
government, was simultaneously meant to be an active representative
of the federal government. The former function required that the
lieutenant-governor not block the legislative will; the latter required
that federal interests be protected, even if that meant blocking the
legislative will. There was, in short, a fundamental tension, even self-
contradiction, in the lieutenant-governorship which became the
source of almost immediate difficulty after Confederation.

In his various speeches in the Confederation Debates, Macdonald
did not even admit, much less attempt to resolve, this tension. In part
this probably reflects his aversion to substance, already referred to. In
fairness, however, it probably also reflects his judgment that this tension between the executive and imperial functions of the lieutenant-
governor had already been worked out in the previous two decades of
colonial practice. If the office of provincial lieutenant-governor was
inherited from the colonial system, so too was the tension between
imperial and responsible functions. And if the tension had been inherited from imperial practice, so too did that practice provide an
apparently workable solution to it.

In the two decades that preceded Confederation, the imperial
authorities had attempted to accommodate the contradictory demands of legislative responsibility and imperial supervision by distin-
guishing as sharply as possible between local matters (upon which
governors should allow their legislatures the freedom to legislate as
they pleased) and imperial matters (upon which they should be vigilant in their supervision). Lord Durham, whose defense of responsible
government was crucial to the political development of Canada, was
among the first to propose such a division of power. In his famous
Report of 1839, Durham wrote as follows:

> Perfectly aware of the value of our colonial possessions, and strongly
> impressed with the necessity of maintaining our connection with
> them, I know not in what respect it can be desirable that we should
> interfere with their internal legislation in matters which do not affect
> their relations with the mother country. The matters, which so con-
> cern us, are very few. The constitution of the form of government,—

the regulation of foreign relations, and of trade with the mother country, the other British Colonies, and foreign nations,—and the disposal of the public lands, are the only points of which the mother country requires a control.[5]

If it were not possible simply to dissolve the tension between legislative responsibility and imperial supervision, one could still mitigate its worst effects. Durham's proto-federal distinction between local and imperial matters attempted to accomplish just that.

Yet this proto-federal arrangement proved no more satisfactory in dealing with Canadian affairs than it had almost a century before in satisfying American grievances. It provided no principle by which to distinguish the local from the imperial, and so begged the crucial question of the size of each sphere, and who might decide which is which. What is more, it did nothing to ease the delicacy of the governor's position. It was one thing for the Foreign Office to intervene in Canadian politics, to direct its foreign policy, to supervise its negotiations with foreign nations or even to strike down (or "disallow") acts that interfered with "imperial interests." It was quite another thing, even for those who supported active imperial intervention in colonial affairs, to make the governor, whose compliance with the legislature's will was such a powerful symbol of self-government, the agent of this intervention.

The difficulty of the governors' position was reflected in the actual practice of imperialism; in no instance was this difficulty more striking than in use of the power of reservation. The colonial governor possessed the power to "reserve" assent from questionable legislation until it had been examined by the imperial authorities. Reservation thus acted as a suspensive veto, for in the absence of gubernatorial assent, a bill could not become law. To make the governors' task easier, Whitehall furnished them with a set of "Instructions" which listed those subjects, ranging from coinage and currency to the imposition of differential duties, that ought to be reserved and passed on to the imperial authorities.[6] Once vetted by London, assent was either given by the queen or withheld permanently. As such, it was one of the more useful instruments of maintaining control over the colonies, including those in British North America. Between 1836 and 1849, the governors of the four colonies which comprised the original Confederation together reserved an average of sixteen bills a year. In one year, 1837, they reserved as many as twenty-eight. Yet by the time of Confederation, the use of reservation had decreased sharply. Thus between 1852 and 1864, the number of bills reserved averaged but two per year.[7] Confederation only served to deepen the trend, and when the Royal

Instructions were amended in 1878 to eliminate most of the usual subjects on which the governor general was meant to act, the power passed into virtual desuetude.[8]

The driving force behind the reforms that led to the disappearance of imperial reservation was Edward Blake (1833–1912). Blake was one of the two or three leading Canadian constitutionalists in the generation after Confederation. He was variously provincial leader of the Reform party in Ontario, minister of justice for a time in the Mackenzie administration, leader of the federal Liberal party and, in the years before his death, member of the English House of Commons. It was one thing, Blake argued in his memorandum on the subject of imperial reservation in 1876, for the colonial governor to reserve legislation in one of those colonies that was "in a less advanced condition of a lesser measure of self-government." It was quite another for reservation to be allowed in a dominion which "expressly recites that her constitution is similar in principle to that of the United Kingdom," which possesses "representative institutions," enjoys "responsible government," and which the imperial authorities themselves said was "invested with 'the fullest freedom of political government'."[9]

It should be stressed that those Canadians who requested the abolition of reservation, Blake chief among them, did not think of themselves as being in any way disloyal to the empire or legitimate imperial interests. Quite the opposite. Blake was only too willing to concede that while Canada ought to be largely self-governing, there were still some matters on which imperial policy ought to prevail. He entertained the hope that imperial interests would be secured "by mutual good feeling, and by proper consideration for Imperial interests on the part of Her Majesty's Canadian advisers."[10] But he admitted that in the case of disagreement, the imperial authorities were perfectly within their rights to exercise the blunt veto power of disallowance to strike down a Canadian act that offended imperial policy. What Blake would not tolerate was that the governor general should be made the routine agent of imperial policy, even if the governor general's power to reserve legislation for London's consideration, being only a suspensive veto, was actually milder than disallowance.

Blake's view on this matter seems less strange when one considers the symbolic importance of the governor as the compliant executive branch of a responsible government. Responsible government implies self-government. As Blake and many others were fond of pointing out, the great contribution of the British empire to civilization was the gift of "constitutional freedom," of legislative self-government, to its colonies. It would have been profoundly ironic to say the least had this self-government, this "constitutional freedom," been routinely stymied by an agent of the Crown wielding the sort of arbitrary regal power against which the whole tradition of British constitutional reform was defined. Nor was this some abstract, distant claim. One part of the Canadian claim both to its distinctiveness and its superiority, after all, was that the British constitution, unlike the American, did not concentrate power in an executive that was largely independent of the legislature. The common Canadian view was that the president was "in a great measure a despot, a one-man-power,"[11] who exercised a form of executive tyranny in part with the help of the veto power over Congress. It would have been particularly ironic, indeed devastating to the argument, had the Crown's representative in Canada been allowed to disregard the legislature's will in the way the president could veto congressional legislation. The Canadians, in short, saw themselves as the inheritors of a form of self-government second to none. The power of reservation simply could not be squared with this self-image.

II

The imperial analogy which informed Macdonald's conception of the office of lieutenant-governor was for this reason not merely anachronistic, it was positively threatening. To the defenders of local control over local affairs, the danger of the imperial analogy consisted precisely in its inaccuracy, for it suggested that Macdonald expected the federal government to treat the provinces more "colonially" than the imperial authorities had latterly treated the colonies. That is what the creation of the office of lieutenant-governor and the power of reservation seemed to portend, and that explains the provincial autonomists' opposition to them once Confederation was formed. Put slightly differently, in modeling the office of lieutenant-governor after this anachronistic conception of an interventionist colonial governor, Macdonald had been compelled to distort the historical record. More seriously, in implying that provincial lieutenant-governors might reserve bills that interfered with federal interests, he had re-opened a constitutional wound which, in the case of the governor or governor general, had already healed.

For these reasons, the questions that had dominated constitutional debate in the decades before Confederation, namely how to reconcile responsible self-government with some sort of wider supervision, came to dominate it in the decades after Confederation as well. The terms of the debate had changed, it is true. Before Confederation the rallying cry had been colonial self-government; after 1867 it was provincial autonomy. But the principle—self-government—was the same, and precisely because it was the same, the debate assumed a familiar form.

Macdonald's understanding of the provincial lieutenant-governor both as executive and federal officer seemed to perpetuate the self-contradiction inherent in the office of colonial governor. To this extent it was vulnerable to precisely the same objections that had forced the imperial authorities to shrink from direct gubernatorial supervision of colonial legislation. Like its pre-Confederation model, the federal power of reservation raised fundamental questions about the nature of responsible government. Like the earlier debate, the provincial autonomists drew out the implications of responsible government uncompromisingly. And like the earlier episode, the logic of responsible government was instrumental in forcing the abandonment of reservation as a supervisory power.

The evident difficulties with the imperial analogy notwithstanding, Macdonald meant it, and in the years immediately following Confederation he came to rely heavily on his lieutenant-governors to enforce federal discipline in Canada. The quality of the first appointments was high. It had to be. Macdonald expected his provincial lieutenant-governors both to lobby the provincial governments on Ottawa's behalf and to keep the federal authorities abreast of provincial developments. In the absence of instantaneous communications, these duties inevitably carried with them a large amount of discretionary authority.

In the case of reservation, the discretion had an additional constitutional justification. The BNA Act provided that a lieutenant-governor could reserve a bill either subject to instructions from the governor general or according to discretion.[12] Although Macdonald had quickly established rules governing the use of the other federal veto power, disallowance, for some unexplained reason he provided no explicit rules to guide the lieutenant-governors in their use of reservation. General instructions were sent to each province, but these were imperial hand-me-downs which provided little guidance in federal-provincial affairs.[13] The individual orders which accompanied each appointment, moreover, were usually so general as to be of little help. Thus, what the lieutenant-governors reserved in those early years, they reserved on their own, that is according to their discretion.

This discretion was by no means unlimited, however. Since the office of lieutenant-governor was modeled after that of the governor or governor general, it is reasonable to suppose that in the absence of clearer guidelines the first lieutenant-governors would have taken their bearings from past, imperial experience. Imperial practice, after all, provided relatively clear rules on the matter: convention taught, and the Royal Guidelines confirmed, that the governors were bound, at least after the 1840s, to protect imperial interests and only imperial interests. Governors might consider legislation unwise, imprudent, unjust, in a word "unconstitutional"; but they could properly reserve only those bills which exceeded the jurisdiction granted to the colony in question or which otherwise interfered with imperial interests. No larger role could be squared, even minimally, with the logic of responsible government. As I noted above, by the time of Confederation the number of matters justifying direct, gubernatorial intervention were few indeed. But the rule, hollow as it had become, remained. As governors could act only to protect imperial interests, so the provincial lieutenant-governors, *mutatis mutandis*, would intervene directly in the provincial legislative process only to protect federal interests.

The first lieutenant-governors must have been influenced by the imperial analogy, for it is otherwise difficult to account for the consistent pattern established during the first Macdonald administration, 1867–1873. In a nutshell, reservation was exercised by the first lieutenant-governors as it had been by the colonial governors after the establishment of responsible government: as a jurisdictional veto whose object was to bring to the attention of the federal minister of justice those provincial bills which seemed to exceed provincial authority.

Thus bills were routinely reserved in the years 1867–1873 because they trenched upon the federal Parliament's exclusive jurisdiction over matters enumerated in section 91 of the BNA Act. A New Brunswick bill relating to marriage licenses was reserved because it seemed to infringe Parliament's authority in matters of "Marriage or Divorce" (91:26).[14] A bill of the Nova Scotia legislature was reserved for interfering with Parliament's exclusive power over matters dealing with the militia (91:7).[15] A Manitoba bill was reserved because it dealt with the subjects of navigation and shipping, matters upon which Parliament alone may legislate (91:10).[16] In all, some twenty-four bills were reserved between 1867 and 1873, more than during any comparable colonial period going back to the mid-1850s.[17]

The force of the reservation power is all the more striking when one considers that the lieutenant-governor's constitutional judgment was usually vindicated. Assent was ultimately withheld by the minister of justice on sixteen of the twenty-four bills reserved during the first Macdonald administration—usually for the same reason given in the first place. In those cases in which the lieutenant-governor's judgment was overturned and assent given by the federal government, Macdonald ordinarily pointed out that his provincial representative had simply misinterpreted the terms of the bill in question, the meaning of section 91 or 92, or both.[18] Thus even in those few instances in which Macdonald disagreed with his lieutenant-governors' application of the reservation power to particular cases, the prime minister confirmed the general rules which should govern its use. Reservation was essentially a jurisdictional veto, the lieutenant-governors were not afraid to exploit it, and Macdonald was quick to uphold it.

The exceptional case, Manitoba, confirms this reading. In Manitoba, the first lieutenant-governors, Adams Archibald and Alexander Morris, exercised the power of reservation rather more liberally than their colleagues in the other provinces. While they did not hesitate to strike down legislation on jurisdictional grounds, on at least two occasions Archibald and Morris reserved bills that were clearly within the competence of the provincial legislature yet which, in their opinion, were unjust or unwise. The first, a bill to incorporate the Law Society of Manitoba, was reserved on the grounds that it was unwise to place "obstacles in the way of any person in good standing at the bar of other provinces to practice law in Manitoba" when good lawyers were in short supply. The second, a bill respecting land surveyors, was objectionable for some of the same reasons. In both cases Macdonald upheld the reservation despite the fact that the bills were clearly within provincial jurisdiction.[19] Indeed, he did them one better. In 1872, Lieutenant-Governor Archibald reserved a bill incorporating the Assiniboine and Red River Navigation Co. on the grounds that it was *ultra vires*, or beyond the jurisdiction of, the provincial legislature. Macdonald upheld the reservation, but he did so for a different reason. The matter, he reported, was in fact within the legislative competence of the provincial assembly. But the bill violated the "the first principles which govern the corporation of companies,"[20] and for this quite non-jurisdictional reason it could not be allowed to stand.

Yet Manitoba was arguably different from the rest of the provinces, and it was therefore subject to slightly different rules. The difference is that for the first four years of its existence, from 1870 to 1874, Manitoba did not enjoy fully responsible government. The first lieutenant-governors of Manitoba were more like governors under the *ancien régime* than provincial officers within Confederation. They were effectively both lieutenant-governor and premier, such that they both called the Legislative Assembly together and directed it. As Macdonald put it to Lieutenant-Governor Morris in 1872: "Although you have responsible government nominally, nevertheless you must be, for want of men, a paternal despot for some time to come."[21] Reservation understood as a jurisdictional veto was a way, albeit an imperfect way, of combining federal supervision with provincial self-government. Since Manitoba did not enjoy full self-government, reservation did not have to be so limited. And, indeed, once responsible government was fully established in 1874, the power of reservation was applied exclusively, as elsewhere, to jurisdictional questions. Far from being the exception to the rule, therefore, the case of Manitoba serves to underscore this characterization of the use of reservation.[22]

Yet, to say that reservation is a compromise between federal supervision and provincial self-government is already to hint at its fatal weakness; for surely if self-government is a fundamental liberty and the cornerstone of British constitutional practice, it should be enjoyed in some other measure than half. Such, at least, is the way Macdonald's opponents framed their case. It is ironic that the case against reservation was made most forcefully by two Ontario critics, Oliver Mowat and Edward Blake, for Ontario suffered the least from it. Indeed, no bill of the Ontario legislature was reserved until 1873, and then, as we will see below, the circumstances were rather extraordinary. Yet it is typical of the provincial rights movement that it should have been led on this, as on other occasions, by members of its Ontario branch. If nothing else, the jackal Mowat and the lion Blake (as Macdonald liked to call them) understood how to appeal, beyond the dry technicalities of formal constitutionalism, to the more fundamental principles which underlie them. This was the key to their success on this and other issues relating to provincial rights. Simply put, the power of reservation, even when limited to jurisdictional matters, violated the principle of responsible government. For Ontarians schooled in the triumphs of colonial self-government, there could be no graver indictment.

The matter which brought things to a head was the reservation, in 1873, of two Ontario bills incorporating the Orange Lodges of Ontario. Ordinarily, the enactment of these bills would have been a routine and uncontroversial matter. But in a province as deeply divided between Catholics and Protestants as Ontario was, the Liberal government led by Oliver Mowat (1820-1903) was well aware that its association with legislation to incorporate the symbol of Protestant chauvinism in Ontario was fraught with grave political risks. If the government sponsored the bills, it would offend Catholics who considered that the Orange Association had become "a standing actual menace against Catholics";[23] if it refused to sponsor the legislation, the Mowat government just as surely would offend Protestants who believed that Mowat was ready, for electoral reasons, to capitulate to Catholic pressure. Mowat's own cabinet was badly divided on the question. To avoid controversy it was therefore decided to have the bills introduced as a private member's bill rather than as a government measure. The bills passed, but the controversy did not give way. Mowat then recommended to the lieutenant-governor that he reserve the bills for the consideration of the governor general, hoping thereby to shift the burden of responsibility for the bills, and therewith deflect any criticism, to the federal government. The ploy worked, and when Lieutenant-Governor Howland accepted the premier's recommendation to reserve, the Macdonald administration found itself deliberating over a question of which it, like the Mowat government, wanted no part.

Mowat had laid a trap, but Macdonald would not let him spring it; he was, as he recalled later, "too old a bird to be caught with such chaff."[24] As Mowat had declined to take responsibility for a measure which he and a majority of the Ontario legislature supported, so now Macdonald refused even to report upon it. As he tersely summarized his constitutional position to a later Parliament: "'Gentlemen, this is none of our funeral. You may deal with your own measures', and we handed it back to them."[25]

The official report which Macdonald wrote on the subject, although appreciably less vivid than the parliamentary account just cited, is one of the more interesting constitutional documents of the immediate post-Confederation period. The report, in the absence of a general dissertation on the matter, stands as the most comprehensive examination of the power of reservation before 1882; it both sheds light on the earlier use of the power of reservation and attempts, albeit somewhat unsystematically, to provide clear guidelines for its future use. Interpreted in the light of the Orange episode, it also reveals the defects of reservation considered as an instrument of federal supervision of provincial legislation; defects which, though still only vaguely apprehended in 1873, soon enough made the power of reservation for all practical purposes expendable.

Macdonald's immediate purpose in writing the report was to defend his government's action, or inaction, on the Orange bills. The defense itself was straightforward and syllogistic: the Orange bills purported to incorporate two provincial associations whose object was the "holding of property, real and personal." By section 92 of the BNA Act, matters relating to property and civil rights "are within the competence of the provincial legislature." Such being the case, and since the lieutenant-governor "had no instructions from the Governor General in any way affecting these bills," he "ought not to have reserved these Acts...but should have given his assent to them as Lieutenant-Governor."[26] Accordingly, Macdonald had neither confirmed the judgment of his lieutenant-governor by allowing the bills to lapse nor overruled his lieutenant-governor by assenting to them. He had chosen a third course; that is, he refused to consider them at all.

Macdonald's objection to Mowat's action was simply that it had violated the basic principles of responsible government by attempting to find a way to circumvent, rather than to execute, the legislature's will. It was already bad enough that the cabinet, after discussion, had refused to sponsor this legislation as a governmental measure. The transparent purpose of this strategy had been to avoid legislative responsibility, and perhaps defeat—the very things responsible government was meant to exact. But the bills having passed, it was completely unacceptable for the premier then to instruct the lieutenant-governor to reserve his assent. Such a precedent, were it generalized, would make the real government (the cabinet) and the formal executive (the lieutenant-governor) superior to the legislature, for it would allow the executive to determine which bills passed by the elected representatives of the people would become law. And that simply contradicted the first principles of "the system of government that obtains in England, as well as in the Dominion and its several provinces." Responsible government, Macdonald concluded, means that "it is the duty of the advisers of the executive, to recommend every measure that has passed the legislature for the executive assent."[27]

There was, however, one crucial qualification to Macdonald's principle of ministerial responsibility and executive compliance. The lieutenant-governor could not be expected to assent to absolutely every bill that had been passed by the legislature because not every bill was within the power or jurisdiction of the provincial government to enact. The ministry having taken responsibility for a bill:

> It then rests with the Governor General, or the Lieutenant-Governor, as the case may be, to consider whether the Act conflicts with his instructions or his duty as an imperial or a Dominion officer,—and if it does so conflict, he is bound to reserve it, whatever the advice tendered to him may be; but if not he will doubtless feel it is his duty to give his assent, in accordance with advice to that effect, which it was the duty of his ministers to give.[28]

In a somewhat apologetic letter to the man who bore the brunt of the criticism, Lieutenant-Governor Howland, Macdonald explained what he considered this "duty" as a Dominion officer to entail:

> ... every Bill passed by a Provincial Legislature should be assented to
> unless the Lieutenant-Governor is satisfied that it is beyond the
> jurisdiction of the Local Legislature or if it be contrary to the instruc-
> tions received from the Governor-General.[29]

The principle was sufficiently important to merit reiteration. "Bills are
only reserved," Macdonald wrote, "when, in the opinion of the Executive, they are beyond the competence or jurisdiction of the Legislature,
or contrary to instructions."[30]

The power of reservation, in other words, was meant in Macdonald's view to be exercised in provincial matters as the governor
general (and before that the colonial governor) exercised it in imperial matters—to protect federal interests by keeping provincial legislatures within the limited jurisdiction granted to them. It was a
compromise between complete legislative responsibility on the one
hand and inappropriate federal and executive interference on the
other. The difficulty is that this compromise had not worked in imperial affairs; nor, ultimately, did it work in federal affairs.

As in the case of imperial reservation, Edward Blake led the
opposition to the use of reservation as an instrument of federal discipline. While he opposed Macdonald's understanding of reservation
throughout his career, Blake actually began from the same premise.
Blake agreed with Macdonald that a provincial ministry ought not to
recommend the reservation of a bill which had passed through the
legislature. And he agreed that if a provincial ministry nonetheless
attempted to disclaim responsibility by advising reservation, it was
the duty of the minister of justice to return the bill whence it had
come. "We want these matters discussed in the Local Legislatures by
the people who are responsible for their disposition."[31] Ministerial
responsibility to a representative legislature was as fundamental to
Blake's understanding of reservation as it was to Macdonald's.

The difference is that for Blake these principles of responsible
government were not only fundamental, they were well-nigh absolute.
Ministers had to abide by the decisions taken by the legislature; if they
disapproved of the legislature's action or if the legislature no longer
possessed confidence in them, they must resign. By the same token,
the principles of responsible government required that if a bill came
before the lieutenant-governor, assent had to be given. The lieutenant-
governor might try to persuade, influence or cajole ministers while a
measure was before the assembly:

> but when he permits the measure to pass through the Local Legis-
> lature and it comes before him for assent, he has no right to refuse

assent. He has no right to turn what would be a conflict between
himself and his Ministers into a much more serious thing, a quarrel
between himself and the Assembly by declining to assent to a bill
after it has been passed.

Blake, unlike Macdonald, would brook no compromise on this point.
Real legislative responsibility, he argued, depended on the recognition
that the lieutenant-governor "has no constitutional right as a rule to
reserve bills."[32]

Again it must be stressed that Blake was opposed to the use of
reservation as a form of federal supervision, not to federal supervision
as such. Disallowance, which unlike reservation does not depend on
the wholesale participation of the lieutenant-governor, was for Blake
a legitimate and useful veto power that is "sufficient for all possible
purposes."[33] Questions of jurisdiction could always be tested in the
courts. And Blake, who was never one to paint himself entirely into a
principled corner, even allowed for certain "exceptional cases"[34] in
which reservation might be legitimately exercised. Yet the principle
that the lieutenant-governor "has no constitutional right as a rule to
reserve bills" stood in the federal arena as it had in the imperial
one—and for precisely the same reasons. The growth of Dominion and
provincial autonomy were, after all, two chapters of the same story in
which the prerogatives of the Crown had gradually narrowed; in
which, "by slow degrees the balance of power changed, until we find
that now the government is in the House of Commons";[35] and in which
the Constitution had grown and developed "in favor of popular
rights."[36] The use of reservation, for whatever reason, cut squarely
against the grain of this march of political freedom. "It is said by
Bagehot," Blake explained, "that the people of England would be as
much surprised to find that an Act which had passed both Houses had
not been assented to, as they would be to look out some morning and
find a volcano on Primrose Hill."[37] The argument for self-government
that had been used so successfully by the colonial reformers in the
1840s and 1850s had, by the 1870s and 1880s, become part of the provincial rights arsenal as well.

After the defeat of the Mackenzie government in 1878, Macdonald
once again assumed the prime ministership, a position he did not
relinquish until his death in 1891. Whatever the merits of Blake's argument, Macdonald remained unpersuaded by it. Though Blake had
carefully and probably intentionally fashioned his argument upon
Macdonald's own premises, the Old Chieftain did not admit that the
same conclusions followed. To the end, he could see no constitutional
reason to renounce the use of reservation altogether, especially if it

were confined to flagging legislation that exceeded provincial jurisdiction. Yet despite this, the exercise of reservation continued to
decline steadily. To repeat, during Macdonald's first term (1867–
1873), over twenty provincial bills were reserved, and in two-thirds of
these cases assent was withheld by the governor general (in council)
—that is, effectively by the cabinet. From the time of the Conservative
victory in 1878 until Macdonald's death in 1891, by contrast, only half
that number were reserved, and in many of those cases the federal
government acted as if the reservation had not occurred and took no
action whatsoever.

Bearing the Orange episode in mind, and by all accounts everyone
involved did, it is not difficult to explain this decline. The liberal use of
the reservation power had rendered the federal government vulnerable to the sort of trap that Mowat had laid for it in 1873. The Orange
episode drew attention to the fact that reservation is by its nature a
political power; it is a power, in other words, which exacts responsibility. But the federal government, as Macdonald quickly came to realize, does not always want to accept the responsibility that reservation,
and more generally the supervision of the provinces, entails. It was
because Macdonald wanted to protect the national government from
the sort of embarrassment that the Orange bills would have forced
upon it, that he asserted the principle that the provincial government
must accept responsibility for bills passed by its legislature. And it was
for the same reason that he was forced to reduce sharply the discretionary powers available to the lieutenant-governor.

Judging from the record after 1878, it is fair to say that Macdonald
had learned his lesson. At the time of the Orange affair, Macdonald
had grasped one of the means by which to eschew responsibility for
legislation like the Orange Association bills. He laid down the rule, as
we have seen, that the federal government would simply refuse to
comment on bills which had been improperly reserved. But he had
also realized that ultimately the more effective tactic was preemptive.
The federal government could avoid the embarrassment of publicly
scolding its lieutenant-governors by providing them with more
explicit guidelines and less maneuverability in the matter of reservation. It might avoid embarrassment, in other words, by providing
fewer opportunities for the discretionary reservation of provincial
bills. This was what the letter to Howland, written after the Orange
Affair, was meant to accomplish.

When he came to write the first comprehensive report on the
exercise of reservation in 1882, Macdonald pushed this strategem a
step further. The report, distributed to all the lieutenant-governors,
was in many ways just a more systematic version of the report

accompanying the Orange bills in 1873. The principle of ministerial responsibility still applied and the implication drawn from it was stated unequivocally: "The Lieutenant Governor is not warranted in reserving any measures for the assent of the Governor General on the advice of his ministers."[38] As he had repeated the conditions under which a lieutenant-governor was not permitted to reserve bills, so he repeated the conditions under which reservation was permissible: "He should do so in his capacity as a Dominion officer only, and on instructions from the Governor General."[39]

But here followed an important qualification which had not been present in the 1873 report and which virtually eliminated whatever discretion lieutenant-governors might have interpreted their duty as Dominion officers to give them:

> It is only in a case of *extreme necessity* that a Lieutenant Governor should without such instructions exercise his discretion as a Dominion officer in reserving a Bill. In fact, with the facility of communication between the Dominion and provincial Governments *such a necessity can seldom if ever arise.*[40]

It is a wonder that modern students of the subject have not seen the importance of this statement, for at one stroke it undermined the traditional source of the lieutenant-governors' power—their discretion.[41] The analogy to the imperial power of reservation, which Macdonald had so often and misleadingly maintained, was by the principles of this 1882 report quite apposite. Henceforth, the lieutenant-governor would possess about as much discretionary authority to reserve bills of the provincial legislature as the governor general possessed to reserve bills of the federal Paliament; that is, almost none whatsoever. Technology and the lingering fear of political embarrassment combined to make the discretionary authority to reserve provincial legislation expendable.

Of course the 1882 report, while severely restricting the discretion which formerly had been associated with the office of lieutenant-governor, need not have eviscerated the power of reservation altogether. As Macdonald made clear, the federal government might still issue specific instructions to reserve a bill or a category of bills. In point of fact, however, the federal government made little use of such instructions, either before or after 1882. Indeed, on only one occasion in those early years, in 1874, was a bill reserved at the instruction of the federal government.[42]

Specific instructions were of little use for either of two reasons. In the first place, it was unlikely that the federal government would be sufficiently acquainted with every provincial legislature to recognize an offensive bill as it was making its way through the legislative process and to recommend reservation after third reading. The beauty of a discretionary reservation power was that it left the lieutenant-governors to winnow out the questionable bills passed by the provincial legislatures, thus making the federal minister's task of supervision a manageable one.

If, on the other hand, the federal government had actually gone to the effort of reviewing offensive legislation on the basis of which it would instruct its lieutenant-governor to reserve a bill, the power itself would soon become superfluous. The federal authorities could eliminate the instructions to reserve merely by disallowing the act themselves once it had received assent in the province. In other words, if the lieutenant-governors' independent judgment was unnecessary, their power was expendable as well. The power of reservation, then, could largely be read out of the BNA Act, and this is precisely what happened.

Blake and Macdonald, Liberal and Conservative, approached the question of reservation from different perspectives. Blake viewed it as a matter of legislative responsibility—which led him to the position that the lieutenant-governor "has no constitutional right as a rule to reserve bills." Macdonald viewed it more as a matter of indemnification from the intractable controversies of provincial politics—which led him to the position that the lieutenant-governor should reserve only when instructed by the federal government to do so. The one became Liberal, the other Conservative, orthodoxy. Both led to the gradual, but almost complete, disappearance of the power of reservation as a means of federal supervision over provincial legislation.[43] Intentionally or unintentionally, both served the cause of provincial autonomy.

III

The provincial autonomists' first goal was to neutralize the lieutenant-governor as a federal officer. To this end, as we have seen, they successfully discredited the reservation power as an affront to responsible self-government in the provinces. Having neutralized the lieutenant-governor as a federal officer, they then sought to conscript the position for the cause of provincial autonomy by showing that the lieutenant-governor was as much a representative of the queen for all purposes provincial as the governor general was for all purposes federal, and equally entitled, therefore, to exercise the "royal prerogative." Where, in the case of reservation, the provincial autonomists had wanted to counteract the activities of the lieutenant-governor as a federal officer, in the case of prerogative they wanted to dignify the office by verifying the lieutenant-governor's credentials as a representative of the Crown. But in both instances the autonomists' ultimate object was the same: to consolidate the power and independence of the provincial governments and to vindicate the principle of self-government.

The royal prerogative, the general term used to denote those discretionary powers that inhere in the Crown, is an unlikely enough subject for a protracted and bitter constitutional quarrel. Yet the arcane question of royal prerogative gave rise to a series of constitutional brushfires throughout John A. Macdonald's tenure as prime minister because various bodies, among them the Colonial Secretariat, the federal government and the Supreme Court of Canada, denied that the provincial lieutenant-governor was really a representative of the queen and hence could not exercise the Crown's prerogative. Some of the disputes, including the controversy over the provincial government's right to appoint queen's counsel, were of obvious political importance because they bore directly on the practice of patronage; others, like the row over escheats and forfeitures, had financial implications for the provinces. But most of the disputes that arose seem trivial and certainly incommensurate with the time, energy and invective devoted to them: whether lieutenant-governors could correspond directly with the imperial authorities; whether lieutenant-governors should be saluted; whether the national anthem should be played in their presence; whether they should be addressed "Your Excellency" or merely "Your Honor"; and whether a provincial legislature could call itself a parliament. There were surely no great political rewards riding on the resolution of these matters, no sources of patronage to be protected. For this reason a simply "political" explanation would hardly seem to account for the fuss to which they gave rise. These questions, rather, became important in the ongoing struggle for provincial rights because they challenged, indeed denied, one of the basic elements of the provincialist self-identity—the belief that in the provinces "our system is the English constitutional system, ... free but also monarchical."[44]

The appointment of provincial queen's counsel provides the best example of the way in which an "apparently unimportant"[45] matter was transformed into a constitutional question of the first order. The queen's counsel is a largely honorific, prerogative appointment which recognizes the achievements of those "learned in the law." It carries with it no great power or privilege, although it does confer certain rights of pre-audience or precedence in legal proceedings. Before Confederation, colonial governors had exercised the prerogative right to appoint such queen's counsel on behalf of the Crown. The first provincial governments understood that this power provided an efficient means of discharging political debts, and they too exercised it regularly for that purpose.

While there was no doubt that the governor general, who is appointed by and is the representative of the queen, would continue to exercise this and other prerogatives after Confederation, the status of the lieutenant-governor made the provincial claim in this regard more questionable after 1867. If the provincial governments were to be considered "subordinate" bodies akin to municipal councils, then there was reason to wonder if the lieutenant-governor was in any relevant sense a representative of the Crown. The text of the BNA Act itself seemed to confirm this view. According to the act, the governor general is clearly designated as the queen's representative, "carrying on the Government of Canada on behalf and in the Name of the Queen."[46] The lieutenant-governor, by contrast, is appointed by "the Governor General in Council";[47] that is, in effect, by the federal government, and would seem therefore to be the federal government's representative to each provincial government. Moreover, where section 91 refers explicitly to the queen and the federal Houses of Parliament, section 92 speaks instead of "an Officer, styled the Lieutenant Governor" and the provincial legislatures. The queen, in short, would appear to have little, if any, place in the provincial governments.

This understanding of the lieutenant-governor's status had been given the official imperial imprimatur even before the BNA Act existed to confirm it. Edward Cardwell, the colonial secretary responsible for the Confederation negotiations, had concluded upon reading the blueprint for Confederation that provincial lieutenant-governors would not represent the queen directly, and he had already teased out the implications of this federal-provincial difference for the exercise of prerogative:

> Her Majesty's Government are anxious to lose no time in conveying to you their general approval of the proceedings of the (Quebec) Conference. There are, however, two provisions of great importance which seem to require revision. The first of these is the provision contained in the 44th Resolution with respect to the exercise of prerogative of pardon. It appears to Her Majesty's Government that this duty belongs to the Representative of the Sovereign, and could not with propriety be devolved upon the Lieutenant-Governors, who will, under the present scheme, be appointed not directly by the Crown, but by the Central Government of the United Provinces.[48]

Cardwell was, of course, addressing a specific question, namely whether the lieutenant-governor should be allowed to exercise the prerogative of pardon. But he chose to couch his remarks in general terms, in a way that might be applied to all forms of prerogative power. Thus, when in 1872 the lieutenant-governor of Nova Scotia appointed several queen's counsel, John A. Macdonald quite rightly questioned the propriety of such appointments, and he quite properly sought clarification on the matter from the Earl of Kimberley, the new colonial secretary.

By the time Kimberley's reply arrived, the issue had been raised in Ontario as well. Throughout these years, the premier of Ontario, Oliver Mowat, "claimed for the Lieutenant-Governor the power *virtute officii* under the B.N.A. Act to issue such Commissions,"[49] on which basis queen's counsel had been appointed in Ontario in 1872. Macdonald immediately wrote to Mowat to explain that the matter had already been raised with the colonial secretary who, upon the advice of his law officers, had concluded that the provincial lieutenant-governors had no power to appoint queen's counsel simply by virtue of being lieutenant-governor. The colonial secretary did think it would be permissible, however, for the provincial legislature to confer such a power on the lieutenant-governor by statute if it so desired. Macdonald, seizing on the possibility of accommodation, told Mowat that he could see "no difficulty in a Provincial Legislature passing an Act of the kind referred to"[50] in Kimberley's letter. Mowat did not accept the principle that the lieutenant-governor has no inherent right to make prerogative appointments. But he did accept the suggested compromise, and in 1873 the Ontario legislature passed two bills that bore on the subject. As Paul Romney has observed, the bills "did not *confer* the power on the lieutenant-governor but *confirmed* that he possessed it already."[51] The difference was sufficient to satisfy Mowat and innocent enough not to bother Macdonald.

The matter might well have rested there had not the Supreme Court of Canada intervened in 1879 in the case of *Lenoir v. Ritchie*.[52] At issue were two acts of the Nova Scotia legislature, modeled after the Ontario acts of 1872, which allowed the lieutenant-governor to appoint QCs and regulate precedence before the bar. Ritchie, a federally-appointed QC, contested the validity of the acts when he discovered that several other QCs, appointed after he had been and pursuant to the provincial acts, were given precedence over him in Nova Scotia courts. The Supreme Court, in a 3–2 decision, ruled that the Nova Scotia legislation was *ultra vires* the provincial legislature because the lieutenant-governor had no right to exercise, and the legislature had no right to confer, this prerogative power. The court, in other words, both rejected Mowat's principle and invalidated the compromise accepted by the imperial authorities, Macdonald and several of the provincial governments alike.

As in so many other constitutional skirmishes of the period, the facts of the particular case are relatively unimportant. What is important is that the Supreme Court went well out of its way to develop and enunciate broad and basic constitutional principles that were offensive to the idea of provincial autonomy. For the provincial autonomists, the Court's reasoning in *Lenoir* became a crucial wedge in the larger struggle for provincial rights. That is why Oliver Mowat, David Mills, Edward Blake and others engaged the courts for nearly twenty years, until the *Lenoir* doctrine had been safely laid to rest.

The Supreme Court in *Lenoir* developed two broad lines of argument to demonstrate that the provincial exercise of prerogative violates both the letter and spirit of the BNA Act. The first, made most clearly by Justice Gwynne, denied the monarchical pretensions of the provincial governments. Like the colonial secretary, Gwynne expressly argued that the lieutentant-governor is not "in any manner" a personal representative of the queen or, indeed, that "the Queen forms (any) part of the Provincial Legislatures."[53] Rather, the lieutenant-governor should be understood as "an officer of the Dominion Government," the head of a provincial government that was "carved out of, and subordinated to, the Dominion."[54] This difference in status was crucial to the question of prerogative, Gwynne argued, because prerogative rights inhere in or flow from "the person of royalty."[55] Prerogative rights, in other words, are personal and discretionary and are tied to the Crown or to its representative. These prerogatives can be exercised by the Crown alone or, if Parliament expressly "divests" the Crown of these rights, by Parliament.[56] But under no circumstance can they be exercised by some body like a provincial legislature which has no direct relationship with the Crown. "Nothing can be plainer," Gwynne argued, "than that the several Provinces are subordinated to the Dominion Government, and that the Queen is no party to the laws made by these Local Legislatures, and that no act of any such Legislatures can in any manner impair or affect Her Majesty's right to the exclusive exercise of all her prerogative powers...."[57]

Gwynne's reference to the provincial governments as "subordinate" bodies was obviously offensive to the provincial autonomists. What was more offensive, and ultimately indefensible, was the further suggestion that as subordinate bodies, "the Queen forms no part of the Provincial Legislatures, as she does of the Dominion Parliament."[58] The advocates of provincial autonomy in Ontario were nothing if not loyal monarchists. One of their proudest boasts was that, unlike the

Americans, they had been able to gain almost complete colonial autonomy before Confederation without having to sever their connection to the Crown; this was what the triumph of responsible government in the colonies was all about. It was absolutely crucial to their self-conception to believe that Confederation had not altered this basic relationship to the Crown. Gwynne's argument squarely questioned this assertion. He wanted to argue that in joining together in a federation the former colonies, now provinces in the Dominion of Canada, had indeed been royally demoted; that within provincial jurisdiction, the Crown simply did not participate in the legislation or the governance of the provinces as it had in the former British North American colonies. Of course the federal government, through the office of governor general, maintained the connection to the Crown once associated with the separate colonies. Yet this was of small consolation to the provincial governments. For no matter how "subordinate" the provincial governments were and no matter how exiguously their powers were defined, no one could deny that within the bounds of section 92, the legislatures had "exclusive" jurisdiction. The upshot of Gwynne's argument, therefore, was that in those matters "exclusively" provincial in nature, legislation was enacted without the aid, support and symbolic presence of the Crown. All of which meant that Confederation, which had been formed in part to defend the distinctive identity of British North America against the rising tide of American democracy, had actually made the provincial governments less British than they had been, not more.

Such a conclusion was anomalous, to say the least, and when in 1892 the Judicial Committee of the Privy Council (JCPC) was asked to rule on the subject of provincial prerogative, it seized on the anomaly in order to refute Gwynne's argument. Those, like Gwynne, who wanted to deny the right of the provincial governments to exercise prerogative powers had to admit that "until the passing of the British North America Act, 1867, there was precisely the same relation between the Crown and the province which now subsists between the Crown and the Dominion."[59] They then had to maintain, Lord Watson understood, "that the effect of the statute has been to sever all connection between the Crown and the provinces; to make the government of the Dominion the only government of Her Majesty in North America; and to reduce the provinces to the rank of independent municipal institutions."[60] For the purposes of the JCPC, it was not necessary "to examine in minute detail, the provisions of the Act of 1867"[61] to conclude that this argument was unpersuasive. The notion that a federation created as a matter of imperial policy to strengthen the colonists' tie to Britain had in fact severed that connection with respect to provincial legislation was simply too bizarre to believe. "It would require very express language, such as is not to be found in the Act of 1867, to warrant the inference that the Imperial Legislature meant to vest in the provinces of Canada the right of exercising supreme legislative powers in which the British Sovereign was to have no share."[62] Absent that evidence, Lord Watson could only conclude that "a Lieutenant-Governor ... is as much the representative of Her Majesty for all purposes of provincial government as the Governor-General himself is for all purposes of Dominion government."[63]

The second argument against the provincial exercise of prerogative was developed most fully by Justice Taschereau and turned less on the provinces' connection to the Crown than on the nature of the prerogative power itself. Taschereau, like Gwynne, maintained that provincial lieutenant-governors "are officers of the Dominion Government," not "her Majesty's representatives."[64] Taschereau was more sensitive to the implications of this fact upon provincial legislation than Gwynne had been, however, and he therefore went out of his way to find some monarchical element in the provinces. True, "Her Majesty does not form a constituent part of the Provincial Legislatures, and the Lieutenant-Governors do not sanction their bills in Her Majesty's name."[65] But Taschereau was willing to admit the theory that the queen, by consenting to the BNA Act, had in effect "authorized" the provincial legislatures to act on those matters listed in section 92 of the Act; and he was willing to concede, at least for the purpose of the argument, that in this roundabout, indirect way "[p]rovincial laws must be held to be enacted in Her Majesty's name."[66] The queen was not directly represented in the provincial legislatures, but neither was she wholly unconnected to them. Taschereau's middle ground thus saved the provinces' connection, slender though it was, to the Crown.

This concession to the provincial position was costly, however, for Taschereau was willing to preserve the provinces' connection to the Crown only at the expense of denying them full legislative sovereignty; and this conclusion, in the autonomists' view, was actually more offensive even than Gwynne's. However the relation between the queen and the provinces was described, it was crucial to Taschereau to distinguish between the queen's formal executive authority and her prerogative powers. As a matter of law, the queen possesses "the executive authority of and over Canada" in which exercise she is aided and advised by a "Council" which is "chosen and summoned" by her or her representative, the governor general.[67] According to the law, then, executive authority is shared with a council and cannot be fully effective without the further co-operation of the legislative branch. Thus, formally, "in the Federal Parliament, the laws are enacted by the

Queen, by and with the advice and consent of the Senate and the House of Commons."[68] Prerogative powers, on the other hand, are not shared and do not depend on the legislature. They are, Taschereau said, exclusive to the monarch; "these prerogative rights are rights inherent in the person of the Sovereign himself, which he alone, and without advice or consent, may exercise how and when he pleases."[69] Being personal rights, it followed for Taschereau that prerogative rights could only be exercised by the sovereign personally or, in the Canadian case, by the sovereign's direct representative, the governor general. As the lieutenant-governor was a dominion officer rather than a direct representative of the Crown, the idea that a provincial legislature could regulate the conferring of QCs was impermissible.

The difficulty with Taschereau's attempt to save a place for royal prerogative was that it could not easily be reconciled with the triumphant story of the development of the British constitution. That story, popularized in England by the likes of Dicey, Maitland, Bagehot and Freeman, told of the progressive, incremental, but essentially complete triumph of the principle of parliamentary sovereignty over the very sort of prerogative powers that Taschereau defended.[70]

A. V. Dicey's account of the triumph of parliamentary sovereignty in *The Law of the Constitution* appears to have been especially influential. The Crown's authority had not been destroyed, Dicey insisted, but there had been over the centuries a "gradual transfer of power from the Crown to a body which has come more and more to represent the nation."[71] Thus, while "the king held in his hands all the prerogatives of the executive government," these prerogatives could now be exercised legally "only through Ministers who ... incurred responsibility for his acts."[72] Dicey saw in this transformation the conscious articulation of the central principle of the British constitution, parliamentary sovereignty. The gradual disappearance of the Crown's personal and unfettered discretion reflected not some accident of history, but the conscious assertion of self-government over the rule of kings, of law over arbitrary, personal government, and of the superiority of British constitutionalism over French *droit administratif.*[73]

Of course Taschereau would not have dissented from the general lines of this account. He recognized perfectly well that in the normal course of things parliament is sovereign and that the will of the Crown is, practically speaking, directed by the cabinet, as that body is ultimately dependent on the confidence of the legislature. The twist is that Taschereau was not willing to admit the complete triumph of parliamentary sovereignty. He wanted to preserve a residual category of actions, called prerogative, in which the Crown could act unfettered; in which, as in the conferral of honorary titles such as QC, the

Crown could act alone. Yet in the context of the "well known" story of British constitutional development, the preservation of this form of prerogative could be achieved only at the cost of limiting or qualifying the fundamental principle of parliamentary sovereignty, of self-government under law. To say that the sovereign possessed some measure of complete discretion contingent neither upon the advice of a council nor the consent of elected representatives, was in effect to say that the British constitution was not as perfect, the evolution of self-government under law not as complete, as the textbook writers like Dicey claimed.[74]

The provincial autonomists were not about to admit anything that robbed the British constitution of its perfection or their own system of its symmetry. The leading autonomists argued that time and the progressive unfolding of the principles of parliamentary sovereignty had conspired to conflate the terms—executive authority and prerogative—that Taschereau wanted to distinguish. Prerogative powers still existed no doubt, but they had been completely democratized. Oliver Mowat, who wrote a long, discursive dissertation on the subject of prerogative powers in response to the *Lenoir* decision, made this evolutionary transformation central to his attack on the court's position. It may have been, Mowat suggested, that prerogative was once exercised "for the personal advantage of the Sovereign." "At the present day," however, "the Sovereign exercises *no* prerogative right without the advice or consent of Ministers who have the confidence of the people's representatives"; it is "a trust for the people."[75] David Mills, who prepared a brief on Ontario's behalf when the question of QC appointments came before the Ontario Court of Appeals in 1896, came to the same conclusion. There is, he said, an "old doctrine of the prerogatives" which refers to those powers "as though they were mysterious, occult powers, which belong to the sovereign outside the domain of the law of the constitution...."[76] This "old doctrine" refused to disappear entirely, but it was nonetheless clearly mistaken:

> It is well known that all powers of Government are, under the constitutional law of England, reposed in the Crown. Yet the Crown can in no case, alone perform any of its functions. The Queen is sovereign, yet she is not possessed of sovereign power. The sovereign power of the state, is, on its legal side, in parliament.[77]

The sovereign "*never* acts, nor can she act, alone. She acts *always* through agents who make themselves responsible for what the sovereign does."[78] This was, Mills argued, in fact the way things worked in England, where QCs were appointed "upon the advice of a responsible

Minister of the Crown."[79] Moreover, this is the way it had to be in a constitutional system that was "free but also monarchical."[80] The Crown was crucial to the Canadians' self-identity because it provided ballast, a symbol of continuity and certainty in a rapidly-changing world. But the Crown, for all of its symbolic importance, could not be allowed to interfere with the legislative will or qualify its sovereignty without undermining the unqualified triumph of self-government through the forms of responsible, parliamentary government.[81]

In denying Taschereau's distinction between executive authority and prerogative, the provincial autonomists deliberately raised the political stakes. For if executive authority and prerogative were essentially indistinguishable, then virtually any ordinary executive act could be called an act of royal prerogative. If the appointment of QCs were considered a prerogative act, then the appointment of police magistrates, justices of the peace, coroners and virtually every other provincial office were "matters of prerogative"[82] because all of them were made in the name of the sovereign by a responsible ministry. For that matter, legislation was "in a sense" a prerogative act "for the Royal Assent is necessary to legislation."[83]

But if this view of prerogative raised the political stakes, it also returned the QC question to the familiar terrain of federal-provincial jurisdiction. The real constitutional question to the provincial autonomists was not whether the appointment of QCs was an executive or a prerogative act for, by their reckoning, those were identical terms within the meaning of the modern British constitution. The real question was whether the provincial legislatures had the jurisdictional right or authority to make these appointments. The position of QC was arguably a provincial office as intended by section 92:4; the appointment of QCs affected the "property and civil rights" of those so honored; it affected "the administration of justice"; and in any event, the appointment of QCs was really a "local matter" that did not interfere in any way with the federal government's own powers. For any or all of these reasons, the autonomists argued, the appointment of QCs fell squarely within provincial jurisdiction.[84] When the matter finally reached the JCPC in 1898, Lord Watson accepted the provincial understanding both of modern prerogative and its own jurisdictional competence under the BNA Act. "It is entirely within the discretion of the provincial legislature," Lord Watson concluded, "to determine by what officers the Crown, or in other words the executive government of the province, shall be represented in its courts of law or elsewhere ... and the rights and privileges which they are to enjoy."[85] There have been skirmishes since, but the principle of parliamentary sovereignty in matters of prerogative has never been successfully challenged.

IV

Despite their arcane nature, these controversies over the proper understanding of prerogative were absolutely pivotal episodes in the early attempts to realize provincial autonomy in Canada. Nor, indeed, is their importance simply a matter of historical curiosity. Over the last twenty-five years, numerous observers have pointed out that one of the truly distinctive qualities of modern Canadian federalism is its dependence at almost every level—from program operation to high level constitutional rearrangement—on negotiation between governments; on what Donald Smiley has called "executive federalism"[86] and Richard Simeon "federal-provincial diplomacy."[87] From an institutional perspective, this dynamic follows directly from the basic premises of modern parliamentary government in which parliament is sovereign, in which the executive leads, and in which, therefore, governments can speak with one voice. The dynamic of executive federalism in Canada follows, more specifically, from the fact that *both* federal and provincial governments come as genuine parliamentary governments, fully loaded as it were. This means they can negotiate as formal equals, as if distinct international actors.

It is here that the legacy of the provincial rights movement is especially clear and direct. For to the extent that the autonomists succeeded in transforming provincial legislatures from what Macdonald called "nominally" responsible governments[88] into fully self-governing and sovereign parliaments, they paved the way for the modern practice of executive federalism. It is no coincidence that long before Simeon popularized the diplomatic analogy to explain modern federal-provincial relations, the provincial autonomists were already referring to the federal government as a foreign government and to their negotiations with Ottawa as a form of international relations.[89] For them parliamentary sovereignty and provincial sovereignty were mutually reinforcing. This is precisely what they were aiming to achieve, and this is precisely the context in which the modern practice of executive federalism, whether cooperative or adversarial, must be understood.

Of course this institutional logic does not alone explain the prevalence of executive federalism in Canadian politics. To say nothing of other factors, the politics of summit diplomacy has been reinforced by the elitism of Canadian political culture. The connection between executive federalism and elitism seems particularly striking in the case of constitutional politics. As Reg Whitaker has noted, where the American Constitution begins with a clear affirmation of the sovereignty of the people, and where American political experience has been shot through with examples of direct democracy, "the constitution of Canada has been, from 1867 onward, an arrangement between elites, particularly between political elites."[90] Most of the original Fathers of Confederation were openly anti-democratic because they believed that democracy would threaten the sanctity of private property.[91] The challenges in the late nineteenth century to the bourgeois order reinforced this "deeply-ingrained anti-democratic strain among the political elites."[92] Even the Charter of Rights, which at first glance would seem to be quintessentially democratic in its regard for the equal rights of citizens before and against government, and in this sense "a major step forward,"[93] is deeply ambiguous, for these rights are variously qualified and compromised by the very constitutional charter that is meant to protect them.[94] Besides, when all is said and done the Charter of Rights remains hostage to the old elite-driven process of constitutional change. The procedure for amending the Constitution Act, which bypasses direct popular action, springs in part from the tradition "that politics is an affair for governments and politicians alone."[95] And the Supreme Court has reinforced the legitimacy of this view by defining sovereignty in terms of the division of powers between politically independent governments.[96]

While the provincial autonomists clearly helped to lay the institutional foundations for executive federalism, their contribution to the elitist style of constitutional politics that continues to plague Canadian politics is rather more difficult to assess. In one respect, the leading autonomists fit Whitaker's general description well. David Mills, like most of the Ontario autonomists, found the "Jeffersonian" doctrine of "pure democracy"[97] inferior to British parliamentary government, and he clearly was apprehensive about the extension of democratic rights to those groups, like native Canadians, who did not measure up to his standards of property-holding respectability.[98] Yet it would be misleading to lump the autonomists together with the more bluntly anti-democratic politicians of the late nineteenth century, Macdonald foremost among them. The provincial autonomists prided themselves on their commitment to democratic principles and popular government, and they considered the difference between their openness to broader democratic participation and the Tory defense of "privilege" to be one of the crucial political distinctions of their time.[99] Besides, whether they were completely comfortable with the implications of mass democracy, the fact is that the provincial autonomists were forced to adopt uncompromising democratic rhetoric by the need to create a clear alternative to Macdonald's politics. Macdonald's use of the reservation power and the Supreme Court's crabbed doctrine of prerogative jeopardized provincial autonomy.

The best way to blunt these centralizing impulses, they discovered, was to defend provincial government as a form of self-government and political liberty, to expose reservation and prerogative as forms of arbitrary executive power, and to argue that *real* self-government meant *complete* self-government. Under the stewardship of Blake, Mills and Mowat, the doctrine of provincial autonomy thus came not only to be tied to the cause of self-government, but to the view that only absolute legislative sovereignty was consistent with the idea of self-government or political liberty.

Yet the autonomists' use of democratic rhetoric sought to do more than establish the full sovereignty of provincial "parliaments." For all of their devotion to the conventional belief that parliament is sovereign, the autonomists had begun to understand that their defense of provincial autonomy actually required them to explore the rather-more-novel possibility that the electorate in a self-governing democracy is distinct from, superior to and can act as a check upon the legislature. While they did not typically go so far as to say that the people are sovereign in the constituent, American sense of the term,[100] the autonomists at least began to glimpse the possibility that the people, at least adult, white, male people, can and should consider themselves as "watchmen" whose task it is to ensure that the legislature does not overstep the boundaries of legitimate legislative power by violating individual rights. Having argued that provincial autonomy was necessary to ensure majority rule, the provincialists maintained that local self-government was the best protection for minority rights as well.

The autonomists pushed their reflections on democratic politics furthest in the course of decrying the Macdonald government's use of the veto power of disallowance. Disallowance is a veto power, modeled after the imperial power of the same name, which gives the federal government the unqualified right to strike down or nullify any act of the provincial legislature within one year of the act's passage. Disallowance, in other words, is a blunter form of the power of reservation in the sense that it is exercised directly by the federal cabinet rather than through the intermediary of the provincial lieutenant-governor.

The inclusion of the power of the disallowance in the BNA Act provoked considerable controversy at the time of Confederation. For critics like the brothers Dorion, the unqualified right to strike down provincial legislation fatally compromised the claim that the provinces would have complete freedom within their jurisdiction to legislate as they saw fit. To the leading defenders of Confederation, however, the inclusion of a federal veto power was a defensible qualification upon provincial sovereignty in that it provided a way to protect the

rights of individuals and minorities from punitive provincial legislation. Some such protection was of crucial importance to those groups,
notably English Protestants in Quebec, who formed the minority in
the province and who were anxious that the new Confederation
would render them vulnerable to unfriendly legislation. One such
delegate, John Rose, spoke openly of his constituents' fears that a legislature dominated by those of another "race and religion" might attempt to manipulate the electoral laws so as to reduce the influence of
the English Protestant minority in Quebec. Rose entertained no such
apprehensions, however. "If the Local Legislature exercised power in
any such unjust manner, it would be competent for the General Government to veto its action—even although the power be one which is
declared to be absolutely vested in the Local Government."[101] As if on
cue, and mindful of his English-Canadian support in the Montreal
financial community, George-Etienne Cartier rose immediately to reinforce the point. If ever the Quebec legislature should attempt to disenfranchise English Canadians in Quebec, "the General Government
will have the right to veto any law it might pass to this effect and set it
at nought."[102] By 1867, indeed, the view that the veto of disallowance
could and should be used to protect individual and minority rights
had been endorsed by all of the major players in the coalition, even the
Ontario Reformers. George Brown thought that "by giving a veto for
all local measures, we have secured that no injustice shall be done
without appeal in local legislation";[103] Oliver Mowat, who as premier
of Ontario became one of the fiercest opponents of disallowance,
actually moved its inclusion in the draft resolutions that led to Confederation.

We will have the opportunity to follow the course of the disallowance power in detail in chapter 5. For the moment, it is sufficient to
know that, despite the various predictions cited above, disallowance
has never routinely been used by the federal government to protect
the rights of individuals or minorities. The federal government was
indeed urged in several key cases to exercise its veto powers to redress
such grievances. In such cases Ottawa would typically explain to the
injured party that grievances of this sort were to be taken up with the
provincial government in question. In the relatively few cases in which
the federal government did consider the use of disallowance to vindicate an individual's rights, the supporters of provincial rights seized
the opportunity to read Macdonald a lesson in British constitutional
principles and practice.

The most controversial, as well as revealing, case in which the
Macdonald government did act involved the disallowance in 1881 of
an Ontario "Act for Protecting the Public Interests in Rivers, Streams

and Creeks."[104] The act provided that all persons have the right to float logs down Ontario waterways and further stipulated that those who had taken the trouble to improve previously unfloatable waterways should be compensated for their trouble by the users. While couched in general terms, the act had in fact been passed to resolve a dispute between one McLaren, who had widened and dredged a tributary of the Ottawa River, and one Caldwell, who wanted to benefit from McLaren's labor by sending logs down the newly floatable river. McLaren obtained an injunction to prevent Caldwell from floating logs down the stream which, in good Lockean fashion, he believed was his exclusive property. The Ontario legislature, seeing matters differently, passed the Rivers and Streams Act to allow Caldwell the passage he needed.

The Rivers and Streams episode was redolent of party politics from start to finish. McLaren was a Conservative; Caldwell was, or was said to be, a Liberal. The partisan character of the controversy may explain the federal government's desire to veto the law, but it does not justify it. Whatever part these political considerations may have played in the matter, the government was still obliged to make its case for disallowance in constitutional terms. This John A. Macdonald (conveniently substituting for the minister of justice), accomplished in the following terms: "I think the power of the local legislatures to take away the rights of one man and vest them in another, as is done by this Act, is exceedingly doubtful, but assuming that such right does, in strictness, exist, I think it devolves upon this government to see that such power is not exercised, in flagrant violation of private rights and natural justice...."[105] With this summary explanation, the Rivers and Streams Act was disallowed.

Needless to say, the Ontario administration did not react favorably to the federal government's action, and for the next three years Mowat and Macdonald played constitutional cat and mouse. Having seen its act disallowed by the federal government, the Ontario legislature reacted by re-passing the legislation, only to have it disallowed again. Passed and disallowed three times, the Rivers and Streams Act ultimately was allowed to stand only after the Judicial Committee of the Privy Council in 1884 ruled in Caldwell's favor in a private suit.[106] In the interval, the Rivers and Streams controversy became the focus of a larger controversy about the general "principle regulating the use by the Government of the power of disallowing Provincial legislation."[107] Parliament debated the question; editorialists discoursed endlessly about it; and the Liberal party attempted to transform it into an election issue by demonstrating that "of all the controversies between the Dominion and the Provinces," the quarrel over the

Streams Bill was "by far the most important from a constitutional point of view" because it involved a "vital question as affecting our local liberties."[108]

Of the many critics of disallowance none was more persistent than David Mills. For most of his career, Mills was associated in one capacity or another with one of the daily newspapers in London Ontario, the *Advertiser*. He wrote occasional editorials for the paper throughout the 1870s, became steadily more involved in writing for the paper in the early 1880s, and from 1883 to 1887 served as its chief editorial writer.[109] Under Mills's direction the *Advertiser* became, alongside the Toronto *Globe*, the chief popular exponent of the doctrine of provincial rights and John A. Macdonald's harshest critic.

For Mills, the disallowance of the Streams bill was doubly offensive because it both threatened "the integrity of the federal principle"[110] and declared war "upon responsible Government."[111] The federal constitution of Canada had entrusted to the provincial governments the exclusive power to deal with those "matters which are in their nature local," the regulation of property and civil rights among them, just as "the larger questions of general concern" had been assigned "to the Government and Parliament of the Dominion."[112] "But each within its own sphere is supreme," there being "under the constitution, no superiority of the one to the other."[113] No one, not even Macdonald, denied that the regulation of local rivers and streams was principally a matter affecting property and civil rights and, therefore, clearly a matter of provincial jurisdiction. The disallowance of the Ontario legislation was, then, simply an attempt on the part of the federal government to "meddle with what is none of its business."[114]

Such "meddlesome oversight" was a "theory" which "our constitution expressly denies to the Federal Ministry";[115] moreover, history discountenanced it. In an earlier era the Family Compact had acted as the agent of the Crown, exercising "a meddlesome and irresponsible oversight of public affairs on its behalf," until, their patience exhausted, ordinary citizens "took up arms" in protest.[116] Before that, King James had attempted to "exercise a meddlesome oversight over not only Great Britain but over Europe" in a vain attempt to establish himself as "an infallible and authoritative expounder of theological doctrines." Sir John A. Macdonald, the *Advertiser* concluded wittily, was "a modern edition of King James, and he does not appear to have any greater success than his royal type."[117]

Stated in this now-familiar form—as a choice between "popular rights" and arbitrary executive power—the provincial autonomists had an easy time of showing that disallowance of this sort was pernicious. To support the disallowance of the Streams bill was to support "political janizaries" and "back-stair advisers"[118] who would "retire into a room, lock the door, post a sentry without, to prevent the too near approach of the common herd."[119] The cabinet was a veritable "Star Chamber sitting in Ottawa"[120] who, emerging from their "secret" deliberations, would abuse and pervert the Crown's prerogatives, arbitrarily exercising their "autocratic and tyrannical"[121] power. To support provincial autonomy, on the other hand, was to sustain "the educating and glorious attributes which belong to self-government, to a government of the people, by the people, for the people."[122] It was to make the provincial community at large responsible for the "inspiring and ennobling task of self-government."[123] The autonomists simply would not let go of the Rivers and Streams issue, in part because it allowed them to deploy their most powerful cultural symbols and to summon up their deepest collective cultural memories. As the Glorious Revolution had been fought to win freedom from kings; as progressive Upper Canadians had struggled through the 1830s and 1840s to win freedom from a combination of oligarchical rule and imperial supervision; as the Reformers of the 1850s and 1860s had fought to be delivered from "French domination"; so now the autonomists took up the cause of freedom, of political liberty, of self-government, against Ottawa. So stated, the disallowance question was made to assume much broader cultural meaning than the squabble between McLaren and Caldwell might at first suggest. So stated, the choice between the federal and provincial positions was really no choice at all.

From the perspective of Macdonald and the Conservative press, the *Advertiser* misunderstood the power of disallowance in general as it mischaracterized the Streams bill in particular. Macdonald accepted the argument that, as a rule, the provincial governments should be left to legislate as they wanted on matters within their jurisdiction. He argued in his official report on the case that he had taken the somewhat extraordinary liberty of disallowing the Ontario bill not because he disagreed with the bill as a matter of policy, but because he believed the federal government had a duty to protect McLaren's individual property rights.

Far from placating the autonomists, this attempt to explain disallowance as a way of protecting rights actually angered them all the more; for conceived as a safeguard against the violation of individual rights, disallowance was "out of accord with the theory of popular government."[124] In the first place, it was not at all clear that McLaren had any inviolable rights in this instance or that this legislation was

anything more than an attempt to regulate the use of Ontario's waterways in a way that would secure the public interest. It was not, therefore, a matter of private rights, but of public policy. If the federal government could veto this act of the Ontario legislature on the pretext of
protecting McLaren's inviolable rights, then it could "override the
policy of the local ministers"[125] on virtually any matter within provincial jurisdiction. The possibility that the veto power would be politi-
cized in this way had been part of the colonists' complaint against the
imperial power of disallowance, but at least in those days "the colonies
were always protected against interference... by the ignorance, the
indifference, the preoccupation of the Imperial authorities."[126] In
post-Confederation Canada, the danger of politicization was much
greater, if only because the federal ministry was connected by partisan association to the provincial legislature. A Conservative ministry
in Ottawa could thus use disallowance to thwart a provincial policy
that the local Conservative opposition had been unable to stop:

> The minority who form the Opposition in the Provincial Legislature
> have only to appeal to their friends, the Federal Ministry, and the
> prerogative of disallowance is at once used to frustrate the policy of
> the Provincial Ministers.[127]

"Every one will see," the *Advertiser* concluded, "that if a war of this
sort is to be carried on, responsible government is at an end."[128] The
ultimate question was "who shall govern the province—the majority
or the minority?—the ministry to whom the electors have entrusted
the Government, or the minority whom they refused to trust?"[129]

Yet for all of Mills's denials that McLaren's rights had been
violated, it is clear that Macdonald's emphasis on the protection of
individual rights struck a raw nerve. McLaren did not have a strong
case, but that did not mean that in other cases the federal government
would not feel justified in intervening to protect individual rights
against the actions of a provincial legislature. Mills understood, therefore, that if he were to disarm the federal power of disallowance he
would have to show not only that it contradicted the spirit of responsible self-government, but that it was unnecessary for the protection
of individual rights as well. And it was this, more than anything, that
forced him to the limits of his democratic understanding, to view the
electorate not merely as the source of authority for a sovereign legislature, but the independent judge of its actions—a body which would
enforce legislative limitations necessary to protect its own rights.

Thus even if it were conceded that McLaren had been treated unjustly by the provincial legislature, it still did not follow, according to

Mills and the *Advertiser*, that the federal government was the appropriate body to judge and correct the action. Anyone who supported the right of the federal government to act as a censor upon the provincial governments had to assume that the "executive" branch of a "foreign" government is better equipped than the people to judge what is wise and unwise, expedient and inexpedient, just and unjust. Yet that could not be admitted without denying "the theory of popular government":[130]

> Our system of parliamentary self-government is based upon the theory that the people are fit to govern themselves; that they know what they want; that they are ultimate judges of what is best. We assume that Parliament may err; but that the public can do no wrong, and that in the last resort the electors must decide what the public policy shall be. If the Legislature make a mistake it was not intended that the strangers of other Provinces should correct it. They know much less of our local wants than the men who are on the ground—the men whom the people have trusted. They are much more likely to blunder. The corrective power is with the people, and to them the appeal lies.[131]

Several weeks later the *Advertiser* reiterated the point. "If any private right has been invaded, if any wrong has been done by the Legislature, there is a proper, a constitutional way of redressing that wrong, and it is not by violating the principles of Parliamentary Government."[132] Parliamentary sovereignty did not mean that the provincial legislatures could act in a way that was completely limitless. It merely meant that the "check" upon its actions was to be imposed by "public opinion"[133] and by a vigilant electorate rather than by another government or courts.

In sum, the provincial autonomists' appeal to the principles of self-government served to consolidate the constitutional claim of provincial sovereignty in two distinct ways. One appeal proceeded from the view that since "absolute power must reside somewhere,"[134] the provincial legislatures are sovereign on matters within their jurisdiction and cannot be held accountable by another government; the other appeal to self-government presumed that the sovereign legislature can and ought to be controlled, checked, and its actions redressed—by a vigilant public acting like "watchmen...to guard the citadels of freedom."[135] In the former sense responsible self-government meant to protect majority rule and political liberty; in the latter, it was understood to be the best defense for individuals and minorities against majority rule. In one case the object was to empower and unify government, in the other to limit government by dispersing power. In neither case, however, did the autonomists think that their commitment to the fundamental principle of self-government need force them to choose between governments and people; between liberty understood as responsible, representative government and liberty understood as individual freedom. Like the framers of the Charter of Rights, whom they perhaps prefigure, the autonomists were profoundly confident that they could have it both ways.

CHAPTER 4

Provincial Autonomy
and Imperialism

"The idea of progress was the major certitude of Victorian culture"[1] in general and "the most hallowed maxim"[2] of late-nineteenth-
century Canadian society in particular. To borrow Paul Rutherford's
term,[3] the idea of progress was one of the central myths of the Victorian age which provided a way of ordering and sustaining the world, of
making the world appear coherent. Coherent but not unsettled. For if
the idea of progress carried with it absolute certainty that the condition of the world was improving, it also rested on the observation that
"change ruled man's life" and that one of the symptoms of the progressive march to a better life was the sense that "society was being swept
off its moorings." If many Canadians were "imbued with the smug conviction that things must turn out right eventually," they nevertheless
found developments in science, medicine, social mores, politics and
economics bewildering, if not simply threatening. And their first reaction, as Rutherford shows, was to attempt to reconcile the new and
unfamiliar to the settled and familiar patterns of their social, cultural
and intellectual milieu.[4]

Federalism was no exception to this pattern. The principle of
Confederation was almost universally praised at the time as an
advance over the deadlock and pessimism that infected Canadian
politics in the 1850s and 1860s. Yet as we have seen, even the most
experienced, knowledgeable, and cosmopolitan members of the political elite were at the time of Confederation quite confused as to how
federalism would in fact work. The reaction of those who were assigned the responsibility of translating federal principle into practice
was to explain the unfamiliar by retreating to the familiar. In learning
to live with federalism, the experience of imperialism provided just

the model the provincial autonomists were seeking. The empire provided an essential link between the past and the future which, according to the provincial autonomists at least, gave their cause pride of place. The empire served throughout the period we are examining as an extremely powerful metaphor that both illuminated and justified the autonomists' understanding of Canadian federalism. Thus on the one hand, the successful imperial policy of "home rule" became the model for provincial autonomy; on the other, the English failure to solve the Irish problem confirmed the autonomists in their belief that the rights of minorities could be protected only through the sort of political protection offered by federalism.

The themes of empire and federalism were closely entwined from the moment Confederation was first discussed seriously. One of the stock arguments for some form of federal union of the British North American colonies centered on the Canadians' recognition that they ought to, or at least were in effect being forced to, shoulder a greater part of the burden of defending their corner of the empire, a view heartily endorsed by the imperial authorities themselves. Once the negotiations began in earnest, the support, and in some cases the direct intervention, of the imperial authorities proved critical.[5] Notwithstanding imperial support for Confederation, several of the plan's most vocal opponents argued that Confederation was in effect anti-imperial, a first, giant step down the slippery slope toward complete autonomy. John A. Macdonald, no doubt bearing such criticisms in mind, went out of his way to show not merely that he was a loyal imperialist, but that the Confederation scheme was meant precisely to create a form of empire in microcosm. The aim, he argued, was to reproduce the empire within Canada, with Ottawa taking the place of London and the provinces replacing the colonies. Thus the federal government in Canada, like the imperial government, was given the right to disallow any provincial law, and the federal government's representative to the provinces, like the colonial governor, was given the right to reserve assent from any provincial bill. That federal disallowance and reservation had to be exercised within one year of a bill's passage, rather than the two years allowed the imperial authorities, was simply a modification to scale.

Macdonald's dedication to the imperial analogy has often been taken to show that the "intentions" of the framers were, to use constitutional shorthand, British rather than American; that they thought of federalism as a species of imperialism in which one power is sovereign and others subordinate, rather than a form of limited constitutionalism in which each level of government is supreme within the jurisdictional sphere assigned to it. We saw in chapter 2, however, that this portrayal does not capture the variety and complexity, not to say confusion, of the visions of federalism that existed in 1867. The proponents of Confederation were simply not a homogeneous and monolithic lot.

What is still more troubling about this interpretation is that it fails to see that the organization of the empire, the ostensible basis of Macdonald's centralism, was itself complex and could with some little imagination be used to justify conclusions quite congenial to the autonomists' purpose. The provincial autonomists who led the assault against Macdonald's understanding of Canadian federalism in the 1870s and 1880s did not believe for a moment that their cause was compromised by the imperial analogy. On the contrary, they were enthusiastic imperialists who believed that the organization of the empire on the principle of "home rule" vindicated the very position they were struggling to assert within Canada. To the provincial autonomists, the problem with Macdonald's use of the British empire as the definitive model for Canadian federalism was less that it perpetuated a "colonial" relationship between the federal government and the provinces than that it misrepresented the nature of the colonial relationship that existed between London and its mature colonies. Far from providing the federal government with a legitimate basis for supervising the provinces, the provincial autonomists maintained that the imperial model actually supported broad claims of local self-government as a matter of constitutional right.

David Mills, who along with Edward Blake developed the imperial analogy in the greatest detail, argued that local self-government had evolved in the colonies to the point that "the Imperial Parliament does not venture to interfere," indeed that "it could no longer constitutionally interfere"[6] with matters that posed no threat to larger imperial interests. Mills of course had to acknowledge that the imperial Parliament "has ... always claimed for itself the right to legislate on behalf of the colonies upon every conceivable subject,"[7] and he had to admit that this was the view taken by the "courts of the United Kingdom."[8] As a "theoretical rule," it was true that even now "Parliament is not excluded from legislating for any section of the Empire, as it may deem, in its discretion, proper."[9] Mills was not particularly bothered by this concession, however. The imperial Parliament typically used its sovereign position to pass "constitutional legislation, at the request of the colonies," which then served as "the supreme law of the colony."[10] Moreover, the basic "conventions of the constitution"[11] supported colonial self-government even when the law, strictly speaking, did not.

The most basic rule, honored by constitutional practice, was to leave the mature colonial legislatures alone to govern themselves. From this perspective, Mills concluded, it is "well settled" that "in all matters of domestic concern, the electorate of each colony where the Parliamentary system is established is as much the political Sovereign of the colony as if the colony had declared itself independent and as if that independence were fully recognized."[12] To model Canadian federalism on the example of the empire, in sum, was not to question local autonomy, but to reinforce its legitimacy. Like mature colonial legislatures everywhere within the empire, local legislatures in Canada had a basic right to act on matters of a local nature without the slightest interference from any outside authority.

We have already encountered one example of this sort of constitutional argument in the controversy over the power of reservation. The autonomists argued that the imperial power of reservation, exercised by an agent of the Crown, was offensive to the basic principles of parliamentary government when used to thwart the passage of colonial legislation on matters clearly relating to local affairs. The imperial reservation of colonial bills was, like other prerogative actions, in effect a throwback to "the arbitrary doctrines of the Stuarts"[13] which treated the rule of Parliament as a matter of grace rather than right; and Edward Blake was successful in having the royal instructions amended to make the imperial reservation of Canadian legislation exceptional.[14] That accomplished, the same argument was used with the same effect to question the propriety of federal reservation of provincial legislation. As we have seen, by the mid-1880s no responsible federal official could deny that it would violate a basic convention of parliamentary government were the lieutenant-governor to withhold assent routinely from provincial legislation on instructions from the "metropolitan" government.

A similar strategy was adopted in the provincial attempt to circumscribe the federal veto of disallowance. It had once been common, Mills maintained, for "Downing Street, to interfere in Canadian affairs." But thanks to the efforts of "our fathers," the imperial authorities had finally conceded the "constitutional principle" that "in all matters of domestic concern, the authority of the provincial parliament should be as free from all outside interference, and from all meddlesome supervision, as if it had been the parliament of a sovereign and independent state."[15] If the empire was the model for Canadian federalism, then it followed that the same rule of non-interference should apply, *mutatis mutandis*, to the disallowance of provincial legislation. "If the Imperial Government could not, according to the settled practise of the constitution interfere," Mills concluded, "still less could the Federal Executive in this country."[16]

Most of the prominent provincial autonomists were lawyers whose first instinct was to demonstrate that the provinces had a constitutional right to local self-government. But they were also politicians who approached the question from the perspective of what they liked to call "policy." In their view, local self-government was desirable not simply because it was right, but because it was the basis of the most successful imperial policy the modern world had known. The genius of the British empire was that it was built on the premise that an empire could be maintained successfully only if its citizens were contented. It was sustained by the realization that colonists would be contented only if they were allowed a large measure of local autonomy. What the architects of Britain's modern imperial policy had discovered was that the bonds of empire could be strengthened only if they were loosened; that colonists would remain more loyal to the empire if the imperial authorities were less intrusive in local affairs. That was the general prescription for successful imperialism. It became, by extension, the provincial autonomists' prescription for successful federalism as well.

The autonomists were quick to infer a general "axiom" of political development from the British imperial experience. "Wherever the Anglo-Saxon race have gone," Mills maintained, "they have failed to establish a consolidated government over a large extent of country":

> The old thirteen colonies which afterwards became the United States, the several colonies of British North America, the several Colonies of South Africa, and the Australian group, were all historical protests against the suitability, if not against the possibility, of having a single Government ruling a people distributed over so vast an extent of country, and who, although they may in time have some common interests which may unite them for certain common purposes, must for ever have local interests peculiar to each section, about which every other section can know but little, and which must, if dealt with by a common assembly, be the constant source of discontent or corruption.[17]

When this prescription was denied or forgotten, difficulties invariably ensued. The most spectacular example was, of course, the United States, which had been forced to declare independence rather than suffer massive political interference from outside. India was "the great problem of the future"[18] because the rule of the East India Company had been "despotic,"[19] producing a "very discreditable" state of affairs in which the office-holding European population imposed "oppressive"[20] financial burdens on the local populations. Even in the 1880s, the Indian government was administered by a "privileged class" which refused to have faith in "the integrity of native judges."[21] On the other side of the world, the black majority of Jamaica had begun to grow restive under the yolk of "oligarchical rule."[22]

But no example spoke more eloquently to the importance of local self-government as an ingredient in successful imperialism than Canada itself. The Reformers of the 1830s and 1840s complained alternately that "the country was ruled from Downing Street"[23] and that it was run by a local clique, called the Family Compact, which was composed of the "most unscrupulous opponents of self government on the continent,"[24] that is Tory Loyalists, who took refuge in Upper Canada after the American Revolution. In fact, as Mills pointed out, these complaints were simply two sides of the same coin. In the darkest days of rule by the Family Compact, the imperial authorities were too ignorant, too indifferent and too preoccupied with other business to care whether Canada was being well governed or not. That, presumably, is why Downing Street simply "gave effect to (the Family Compact's) wishes, listened to their representations, (and) were guided by their advice,"[25] even though "this system led to oppression, political corruption and rebellion."[26]

The Canadian example was particularly instructive because it demonstrated not only that the imperial authorities had erred, but that they had learned from their mistakes. They had learned, specifically, that by allowing Canada to govern itself they could both pacify the Canadians and actually strengthen the imperial connection. And, indeed, Edward Blake concluded that "a fuller measure of Home Rule and responsible government" in Canada "at once secured, in large measure, the contentment and affection"[27] of the Canadians. The precedent, established in Canada in the 1840s, had been extended progressively throughout the empire. By the mid-1880s, the London *Advertiser* could report with considerable satisfaction that the colonial authorities in Egypt had sown "the germs of self-government ... in that country." "The village sheiks are now elected"; local administrative agencies had been established "which militate against corruption and intimidation"; and by making Arabic the language of the courts, the colonial authorities had rendered the Court of Appeal "above suspicion in the popular mind."[28] In India, Lord Ripon had taken great strides in reforming the political and judicial systems over the complaints of "the English residents of India."[29] Although India was not ready for complete self-government, Lord Ripon had at least made an honest effort "to extend the governmental authority of native officials." He had shown "more sympathy for the native population" and had "made greater efforts to improve their condition" than any governor general before him. As a result, he had left behind him in India "thousands of Hindoos who feel for him a friendly regard such as no other English Viceroy has ever evoked."[30] The principle, then, of successful imperialism was simply "to give the people of each section a guarantee that their local needs will be attended to by persons having a knowledge of them."[31] The principle of successful imperialism, in other words, was home rule.

The autonomists' account of the state of the empire in the 1880s was full of ethnocentric stereotypes, self-serving bromides and wishful thinking. Yet even if they had been able to overcome those prejudices, the autonomists would still have wanted to tailor their account of the empire to serve the broader rhetorical purpose of providing a model for Canadian federalism. The plain difficulty facing those attempting to administer an enormous empire on several continents was that the interests of the colonists were diverse. To legislate well, therefore, required a knowledge of local conditions, a sympathy for local customs, and a direct interest in the outcome. In the autonomists' view, the lesson to be drawn from the history of the British empire was that the empire flourished when the imperial authorities accepted the basic fact that local populations understood their own interests more clearly than London did; that the colonists had a greater incentive to legislate well because they had to live with the consequences of local legislation; and that the colonists had a greater attachment to and sympathy for their local institutions and customs than did the imperial Parliament.[32]

The problem facing the imperial authorities, in short, had always been to find a way to reconcile representative self-government with diversity; it did not take much imagination to view the problems of Canadian federalism in essentially the same way. The great difficulty with John A. Macdonald's desire to produce a legislative union that would subordinate the provinces to a predominant central government was its failure to profit from the monitory lessons of imperial history. According to the provincialists, Macdonald simply did not understand that the provinces valued their traditions of self-government as highly after Confederation as the British North American colonies had before. And he failed to see, therefore, that provincial autonomy would provide as happy a solution to the problem of diversity in Canada as home rule had in the empire.

"The Federal system is a perfectly rational one," Mills argued in introducing the subject of federalism to his law students at the University of Toronto,[33] and it was rational for the same reason that the British empire was great—it accommodated diversity:

We can all readily assign reasons against the abolition of colonial parliaments and the representation of the whole empire in the parliament at Westminster. We would say that many important interests
would be overlooked, that much needed legislation could not be had,
that blunders might readily be committed, but could not be readily
redressed, and that instead of a single legislature serving to create
unity it would only prove itself the author of divisions and discontent, and centralization instead of creating a strong government
would create a weak one.

"The very same reasons which operate to secure the establishment of
colonial governments," he continued, "also prevent the representation
of a widely scattered population in a single consolidated parliament":

> Over so vast a territory as B.N.A. it would be impossible . . . to establish
> representative government by a single parliament. There are no
> doubt large questions which possess universal interest where uni-
> form legislation is desirable, . . . but a large proportion of our social
> and political interests which must be regulated by law are not of this
> character, there are numerous questions that in their nature are
> local and which can only be adequately considered by the commun-
> ity immediately interested; there can never be successful legislation
> where the community do not sympathize with the work of the legis-
> lature.

The differences between, say, Prince Edward Island and British
Columbia were no doubt less dramatic than between England and one
of its African or Asian colonies. Still, to the late-nineteenth-century
Canadian the political and social differences between widely separated provinces must have seemed enormous. The completion of the
transcontinental railroad in 1885 reduced the physical distance between the provinces, but the psychological distance remained imperial in proportions and elicited the same set of arguments that had
been used to justify home rule:

> What possible interest can we have in the local improvements of
> British Columbia or Prince Edward Island? In their schools, their
> reformatories, in their courts of law? Place these matters under the
> control of a common legislature and how is responsibility to be
> secured? Mistakes are made, wrong is done, abuses spring up, how
> are they to be corrected? Nine tenths of the community at large feel
> no interest in them, they are in no way injuriously affected and so
> they never can be made living issues at the polls, except to the merest
> fraction of the population. If abuses are corrected, or a change of
> policy is had, it must be due to some other cause than public opinion;

the only way to secure the effective operation of a representative government is by calling into existence local representative bodies to deal with such questions, and so we find that the theory of a legislative union is only applicable to a very limited extent of territory and that with a wide area and diversified interests, a Federal system is a necessity if the government and legislature are to be truly representative.

Diversity was "a powerful element of progress"[34] and deserved, for that reason alone, to be protected politically by some form of home rule, be it imperial or federal. But to the provincial autonomists, as indeed to most nineteenth-century Canadians who wrote on the subject, diversity was also simply the inevitable consequence of differences of climate, geography, history and race.[35] Any attempt to obliterate these differences was therefore bound to be futile and disruptive. Home rule in the form of provincial autonomy was in this respect not only a matter of right; it was also the only policy consistent with the " 'peace, order and good government' of the country."[36]

In sum, diversity was the shared condition that rendered the British empire and Canada comparable. Indeed, the nature of the imperial and federal problems were to the autonomists so similar that they frequently used the language of one to describe the other. As the imperial Parliament could be described as "a federal legislature for the Empire,"[37] so the provincial autonomists routinely claimed that their cause was "home rule for Ontario."[38]

II

Of the several forms of diversity to be found in Canada, none was as important, or as elusive, as the diversity that followed from what the autonomists called "race." The term race was customarily used in late-nineteenth-century Canada to refer to the ethnic and cultural differences between, especially, French and English Canadians. To be sure, the boundary between this ethnological and cultural understanding of race, on the one hand, and a physical or physiological understanding of race on the other was often blurred. George Stocking has shown that among professional anthropologists in Britain and the United States the attempt in the late nineteenth century to separate the cultural attributes of race clearly from such things as skull size, pigmentation, blood and other physical characteristics was rather less successful than has often been supposed. The strict separation of physical race and culture came later.[39]

The leading members of the provincial rights movement, like most intellectuals of the time, thought quite rightly that the professional debate on evolution and race was of enormous importance for their social and political thought.[40] They followed the debate closely, derived what they could from it, and on occasion even contributed to it.[41] It is hardly surprising, then, that the discussions of race that occurred in such places as Parliament reproduced at a political level the essential ambiguity and confusion that plagued the professional discussion of race. That is, they finessed its precise definition. As Carl Berger has noted, "sometimes the phrase 'Anglo-Saxon race' was simply a synonym for a total culture which was itself understood to be the product of history and not only racial instincts; sometimes, race was quite explicitly associated with the biological analogies of Darwinian science."[42] Still, it seems fair to say that the meaning of race in late-nineteenth-century Canada was usually ethnological. It referred to the shared characteristics of language, history, religion, literature, political and legal principles that together constituted what David Mills once called a distinctive "mental vision" of a "section" or community of people.[43] The meaning of race in this context, indeed, is better captured by the word "nation," a word that the provincial autonomists and other politicians frequently used as a synonym for race.

The national or racial characteristics of groups were in this sense understood to form the basis of social analysis because they helped to explain the constitution, not merely of group, but of individual identity. For those who took nationality seriously, individuals do not exist, even in theory, as "atoms," as "unencumbered selves" whose identity consists in more or less rational, self-contained choices about "life plans." Rather, the individual's identity—what one prizes, what one values, what one can attain—depends on and in turn reflects the characteristics of the national community to which one belongs. The English Canadian, it was commonly observed, generally identifies with and takes inspiration from English and American literature; the French Canadian relies more heavily "upon French sources of culture, literature and information."[44] But in either case, the "nation," no less than the family, has a powerful constitutive influence on the make-up of each individual; we are, individually, the products of the "national" community to which we belong.[45]

Yet if the provincial autonomists accepted this basic premise of what has more recently been called communitarianism, they did so without thinking it necessary to abandon their liberalism. For if the individual's identity is constituted in an important way by the larger community, it is no less true that the individual's freedom to express that identity is paramount. For its part, the state is instrumental. It is a "means to an end" and exists to protect "life, liberty and intellectual freedom."[46] The state cannot, therefore, of right "undertake to destroy the mental vision of one section of a population"[47] because it cannot violate the rights that it exists to protect. Were the state to attempt to outlaw the use of a "national" language, for example, individuals would not only have every right to defend that crucial element of their identity, they almost certainly would defend themselves because "there are claims on men stronger than the claims of the state. There are rights which the state has no right to invade, and which, if it attempts to invade, it is a man's right to defend."[48] If the provincial autonomists accepted the basic premise of communitarianism, they nevertheless chose to express that communitarianism in the classic liberal language of individual rights against the state. They were what one nowadays might call "liberal communitarians."

The provincial autonomists developed this liberal vision of national or racial communities most thoroughly in the context of the debate in 1890 over the official use of the French language in the North-West Territories, a debate that Lewis Herbert Thomas has called "one of the most notable... in Canadian parliamentary history,"[49] and one which has really not been resolved to this day.[50] When the North-West Territories were acquired from the Hudson's Bay Company in 1869, the federal government immediately took administrative control of the region, corresponding roughly to the present provinces of Alberta and Saskatchewan, establishing a structure of local government which the federal authorities expected would grow into a fully responsible, provincial government once settlement grew. In the course of its haphazard concession of self-government in the North-West, the federal government, in 1877, accepted a formal amendment to the North-West Territories Act permitting the use of French in the records and proceedings of the legislative council and in the courts.

D'Alton McCarthy, who by the late 1880s had become a renegade member of the Conservative party, served notice that he would ask Parliament to prohibit the use of French as an official language in the North-West. McCarthy argued that it was in "the best interests of this country"[51] to "create and build up... in this country one race with one national life, and with a language common to us all."[52] McCarthy assumed that "nation" and "state" are co-extensive terms. He assumed that the state must inevitably take on the characteristics of the "races" that comprise it, and he concluded from this that for the state to be united the population had therefore to be ethnically and culturally homogeneous. The state, in McCarthy's view, was in effect the political manifestation of race. The state was the vehicle through which one race imprinted its vision of what is good and bad on the world and gave force of law to the things it valued. As there was room for only one sovereign politically, there was room for only one nation sociologically. Otherwise the national differences and jealousies that divided national or racial communities sociologically would reproduce themselves politically, leaving the state as disunited as the races comprising it were numerous. Since a majority of Canada's population spoke English and belonged to the "Anglo Saxon race," McCarthy had no difficulty in concluding that the Canadian state, in the interests of political unity, should take every necessary step to ensure the predominance of English. The proscription of the official use of French in the North-West Territories was, from his perspective, a perfectly reasonable attempt to nip disunity in the bud.

The debate on McCarthy's motion was joined by all of the most prominent provincial autonomists in Parliament—Mills, Blake, and the new Liberal leader Wilfrid Laurier chief among them. The provincial autonomists realized perfectly clearly that McCarthy's motion was only "the thin edge of the wedge"[53] which, if allowed to succeed, would lend momentum to a more ambitious campaign to blunt French and Catholic influence throughout Canada. They therefore took the occasion to develop a broad critique not only of McCarthy's policy towards the North-West, but of the general principles for which he stood.

The great error in McCarthy's prescription, Mills argued, was that he "confound(ed) nation with state."[54] The identification of nation and state was contradicted in the first place by "the condition of things existing in almost every country in Europe."[55] If the relation between nation and state were as symbiotic as McCarthy supposed, one would expect to find a simple correspondence between ethnic groups and political authority, a perfect match between society and state. In fact, no such simple relationship existed. "The Gypsies are a nation; the Jews are a nation; the Poles are a nation, but neither Gypsies, Jews nor Poles are a state."[56]

What was still more serious, according to the autonomists, was that McCarthy misunderstood the very purposes for which the state existed. In McCarthy's view, apparently, the state existed to give expression to a national or racial vision. For the provincial autonomists, on the other hand, the state existed first and foremost to protect rights, to create the conditions under which "we may ... accomplish something for ourselves."[57] Thus language was not meant to be "a badge of either sovereignty or humiliation,"[58] the means by which racial winners dominate losers. Language was, rather, "a mere instrument of the state,"[59] indeed a "vehicle of thought, ... an instrument for conveying intelligence"[60] by which individuals both participate in a cultural tradition and improve themselves.

Because McCarthy did not "recoginze the individual as having rights distinct, and separate, from the state,"[61] he misunderstood equally the political consequences of denying these rights. Individual rights are God-given. That is what makes individuals value them so highly, and that is what makes them cling so stubbornly to them:

> There are upon the Royal Arms certain mottoes, and it happens that they are all in French. One of them means in English "God and my right." That traces the rights of men to their original source. That source, high above every human authority to the contrary, is the one to which every free man traces his right to resist wrong and oppression. It is from that source that the French Canadian derives his right to speak the language of his fathers, and any law which attempts to deprive him of those rights which belong to him, in the manner in which the hon. gentleman proposes to wipe out and obliterate the use of the French language, would be a law doing violence to those very objects for the maintenance of which a Government exists.[62]

"Ancient governments were united; ancient governments counted men as nothing; the individual had no rights against the state." By contrast, modern, that is liberal, governments recognize individual rights. Moreover, they recognize the individual's "right, when those rights are encroached upon to stand up in their defence."[63] McCarthy's policy, if allowed to pass, would thus not only be unjust, it would be counterproductive, for it would mobilize those who were disenfranchised to protect something they believed to be "dearer than life itself."[64] The compulsory policy of linguistic and cultural homogeneity would almost certainly produce the very resentment, bitterness and conflict it was meant to overcome. The current policy that recognized linguistic rights was therefore both just and sensible.

Here again the empire proved a useful model, for it demonstrated precisely what McCarthy denied—that it was possible to combine different nationalities into one, united political community. If McCarthy were right that political unity requires "racial" homogeneity, then it would be necessary "not simply to undertake to establish English at the foot of the Rockies, but a common language at the foot of the Himalayas as well."[65]

This was not, however, how the imperial authorities had proceeded. The imperial authorities had organized the empire on the principle of direct but incomplete rule. They understood that it was possible, and actually preferable, to export the external manifestations of Anglo-Saxon "civilization"—its political principles, its legal system, its system of commerce—without forcing local populations to abandon what was distinctive about their "culture," especially their language and literature. Such a "magnanimous" policy of "toleration" had preserved French Canada's loyalty to England at the time of the American Revolution.[66] It had worked in England itself, where the Scots, Welsh and Irish were allowed to keep their national traits even while forming part of a larger United Kingdom politically. Indeed, cultural toleration had in effect become British policy throughout the empire:

> A man may be a British subject put on trial for treason and convicted without knowing a word of English. He may talk Italian in Malta, French in the Province of Quebec, Dutch at the Cape, Hindoo at Calcutta, and Chinese at Hong Kong, without in any degree sacrificing his rights or lessening his obligations as a British subject.[67]

The example of the British empire, in short, demonstrated that "differences of language are not incompatible with the Union of the State."[68] Wilfrid Laurier discerned the nice irony in McCarthy's position. The policy to require the use of English in the North-West, he concluded, was not only anti-French, it was "anti-British" and "at variance with all the traditions of British Government in this country."[69]

III

The autonomists were uncompromising in their opposition to McCarthy's assumption that national unity requires a community of language. Yet when it came to give institutional expression to the protection of minority language rights in the North-West, they were much more equivocal. Despite their principled defense of linguistic rights, the autonomists ultimately supported a compromise motion that, while preserving the use of French before the courts and in government ordinances, allowed the local territorial assembly to determine how its proceedings were to be recorded;[70] even though, in light of the growing anti-French sentiment in the North-West, this was "for all practical purposes, an acceptance of abolition."[71] Nor, of course, was this the only occasion on which local legislatures were ultimately allowed to abridge minority rights. When the Manitoba government acted in 1890 to dismantle the separate school system in the province, the Laurier government professed its dismay, but it refused to enact "remedial" legislation to force Manitoba's hand. In the end, as Laurier himself put it, it seemed better to seek the "sunny ways" of compromise and to exhort Manitoba to act generously rather than force it to protect the educational rights of its Catholic minority; to persuade the Manitoba government to recognize minority educational rights, even though this allowed Manitoba, once the sun had set, to dismantle the separate school system yet again. As Ramsay Cook has observed: "Laurier himself was certainly never wholly committed to the view that provincial rights took precedence over minority rights, but in practice this is what his victory in 1896 and the subsequent Laurier-Greenway settlement represented."[72]

What accounts for the gap between the provincial autonomists' uncompromising rhetorical defense of minority rights on the one hand and their ready acceptance of political compromise on the other? In part, the equivocation, first in the North-West then in Manitoba, can be explained by electoral considerations. The provincial autonomists were, after all, the descendants of George Brown, whose advocacy of constitutional reform in the 1850s and 1860s stemmed from his distaste for what he called the "French-Canadian domination" of Ontario politics. Most of the Liberals who followed Brown were considerably more tolerant of and sympathetic to linguistic and cultural diversity than was Brown himself. But by all accounts, Laurier, Mills, Blake and other prominent federal Liberals were still concerned that the advocacy of French-Canadian rights would cost them support in Ontario where many traditionally Liberal voters cleaved to the old Reform position. At the same time, the Liberals understood very well that their status as a truly national party, and with that their electoral fortunes, depended on their ability to attract support in Quebec, where the Macdonald government was highly vulnerable for its handling of the Riel affair. The strategy adopted during the debate on the North-West language question thus allowed the Liberals to have it both ways. The stout defense of French language rights in speech would win favor in Quebec; cautious compromise that did not trench on provincial autonomy would prevent the erosion of support in Ontario.[73]

Electorial considerations aside, deference to the principle of provincial sovereignty suited the autonomists' understanding of Canadian history. The autonomists believed that provincial autonomy was ultimately the only responsible organizing principle in such cases of "racial discord" because they were convinced that the historical record demonstrated that when one "race" was given the authority to rule, or for that matter even to supervise, the acts of another, discord and hostility invariably ensued. The Canadian experience taught that harmony could be achieved only by separating the "races" politically so that each could govern its own affairs. That is why the idea of provincial autonomy was sacrosanct.

The progress from the old days of hostility and intolerance to the modern solution of federalism formed the basic plot line of every autonomist's story of Canada. As Edward Blake put the case to a partisan English audience, the problem in Canada had always been to deal "with various races of different creeds, possessing the strongest national and religious feelings, with minorities and majorities in different provinces."[74] At first, Blake said, there had been numerous missteps. Following the lead of Lord Durham, the British authorities at first "hoped to fuse the French and English populations in one harmonious English whole" by creating "a legislative union of the English Province of Upper Canada with the Province (mainly French) of Lower Canada." This attempt "to extinguish French national feeling" was "doomed to failure," however, and provoked "only more determined and gallant efforts to maintain its strength":

> This failing, we tried for years, under the form of a Legislative Union, to work on some, at any rate, of the principles of Home Rule for each division of the Province, but without success. The relations between the two divisions became more and more strained and hostile. The West, overpassing its elder sister, demanded representation according to population. The East resisted. Friction and deadlock, faction and antagonism, instability and inefficiency in government ensued; almost all things to be deprecated ensued. Your system of Legislative Union broke down.[75]

David Mills, who rehearsed the same story in 1889 in the course of his speech on the Jesuit Estates bill, struck with uncommon terseness to the nub of the problem with the old arrangement: "Once Ontario and Quebec were represented in one parliament, for all purposes. Then each could meddle in the affairs of the other."[76]

The only solution to the unrelenting problems of "sectional discord," therefore, had been to separate the two "races" by giving to each "absolute" control over its own affairs within a larger federation;[77] "to allow each province to pursue that course, on these old questions, most satisfactory to the *majority* of its own people."[78] The autonomists realized that legislating in a way that satisfied the majority was not necessarily best for the minority, and they exhorted the majority to recognize its "moral obligation"[79] to grant justice to minorities. Yet autonomists like Blake and Mills were clearly most impressed by the fact that "the relations of hostility and suspicion, jealousy and opposition, which were most conspicuous as between the two Provinces...

have now largely disappeared."[80] And they drew from this insight the same moral that George Brown had drawn at the time Confederation was first suggested: "We have said from the beginning that government and legislatures must abstain from meddling with each others affairs. It is (the) only possible course open to us compatible with the peace, order and good government of the country."[81]

Canada's turbulent constitutional history thus furnished an unambiguous lesson: the only way to do justice to minorities and prevent the sort of instability produced when minorities are pushed too far was to ensure that each province is free to act without the fear of external interference. If, therefore, Canadian politics was troubled by this all-too-familiar form of "racial" agitation, it was only because the Macdonald administration refused to heed the lessons of history by attempting systematically to undermine provincial autonomy. If only each province were allowed to go about legislating for itself without the fear of federal intervention, the argument went, minority rights and the "racial" peace that followed from the acknowledgment of their rights would be restored. "In so far as there has been conflict," the editorialist for the London *Advertiser* concluded in October 1883, "it was due solely to Federal interference, and it only goes to show that our constitutional system does not go sufficiently far in the direction of complete severance."[82]

In fact, of course, this was a highly questionable conclusion that depended upon a highly selective interpretation of Canadian constitutional history. Moreover, it essentially finessed the basic ambiguity in the meaning of the term "minority" that has always existed in Canada. In arguing that federalism was necessary to protect minorities from the meddlesome interference of others, the Liberals were thinking of those populations, culturally and geographically defined, which formed minorities within the country as a whole. In this sense, French Canadians, centered in Quebec, were a minority. In this sense as well, a good many Ontarians, while not a minority, feared the sort of external interference and "domination" that typically characterizes minority-majority relations. Thus federalism, by insulating provincial populations from a national one, was intended to be a form of minority protection, and it was to this understanding that the Liberal autonomists returned again and again in their historical disquisitions.

Yet almost everyone understood that the territorial and cultural boundaries were not identical. There existed minorities within the provinces—Franco-Manitobans, Anglo-Quebeckers and others—for whom federalism was arguably less a solution than a threat. The attempt to protect these provincial minorities also formed an important chapter in Canada's constitutional history, and the problems that arose when provincial minorities protested against their treatment continued to pose serious political problems—witness the New Brunswick and Manitoba schools question and the Riel affair, among others. Yet on the questions of these minority rights, the autonomists were much less vocal and much less ready to offer a quick solution. Hence, what is interesting about the autonomists' historical account is less what it said than what it ignored. And the historical question left unanswered, therefore, is this: why did the autonomists insist on viewing the question of the protection of minority rights through the lens of provincial autonomy?

IV

One answer to the question is that by the 1880s, leading Canadian Liberals had begun to tailor the story of Canadian federalism to suit the needs of their co-partisans in England who were struggling to defend the policy of Irish home rule.[83] Faced with the objection that Irish home rule would lead to disunity and the breakup of the empire, the example of Canadian federalism was held up time and again by British and Canadian Liberals alike to demonstrate that home rule provided the solution to the sort of "national" agitation that plagued Britain. Yet as the Canadians rehearsed their story for British audiences, the image of Canadian federalism was itself refracted in a way that affected their own understanding of Canada. In their enthusiasm at demonstrating that Britons had something to learn from Canadians, the concept of provincial autonomy came to assume mythic proportions in a way that simplified and reinforced the autonomists' understanding of their own problems.

We have seen that the provincial autonomists identified themselves as liberal imperialists who were committed to the view that the protection of diversity through home rule paradoxically contributed to the unity of the empire; imperial bonds, they argued, were as strong as they were loose. And we have seen that this vision of the British empire became the standard by which home rule in Canada, that is provincial autonomy, was justified and against which it was judged. The extension of home rule had pacified Canada's relations with England; the recognition of full and fair provincial autonomy would, by analogy, smooth relations between Ottawa and the provinces.

In fact, however, the provincial autonomists considered the few imperial failures to be as instructive for constitution-makers as the many successes. For as impressed as the autonomists were by the apparently relentless progress of even the most distant colonies toward greater home rule, by the early 1880s they were no less struck by the "agitated, alienated and lawless"[84] state into which Ireland had fallen. To the autonomist mind the difference between imperial success abroad and trouble at home could be explained by the simple fact that where home rule had been extended throughout the empire, it had been denied Ireland. In the North-West language debate, Wilfrid Laurier compared the attempts of those like D'Alton McCarthy to anglicize the North-West to British policy in Ireland:

> They want to make this country British in the same manner they have tried to make Ireland British. For the past seven hundred years, English statesmen have attempted to make Ireland British, not by justice, not by generosity, not by appealing to the better instincts of the generous hearts of that people, but by every form of violence and cruelty. They have proscribed her religion, they have killed her agriculture, they have destroyed her commerce, they have done everything to degrade the land and the people.[85]

The result of this policy, Laurier concluded, had been to make "Ireland a thorn in the side of England" and to fill "the heart of the people of Ireland with bitterness against England."[86] The Irish problem thus confirmed what the imperial triumphs had already shown—that some form of home rule had to be the foundation of any successful political system in which significant "racial" or "national" diversity existed.

The support of Irish home rule fit nicely both with the autonomists' partisan sympathies and with their view of the world. The autonomists revered Gladstone, whom they considered the greatest exponent of liberalism in the English-speaking world,[87] and quite naturally followed his example in putting the Irish question first. Many of the prominent Canadian autonomists, Blake and Mills among them, were of Irish extraction and took a natural interest in Irish affairs. And here again electoral considerations also presumably played a part, although it is not exactly clear how the advocacy of Irish home rule played in traditionally Liberal strongholds in southwestern Ontario.[88]

Even so, electoral considerations alone cannot explain the autonomists' obsession with the Irish question. For one thing, the Irish question was useful because it paid handsome psychological dividends to colonial politicians who wanted to impress their metropolitan mentors. The great advantage of understanding the agitation in Ireland as a function of ethnic domination was that it allowed the autonomists to read British audiences a lesson in how to run an empire, using their own Canadian experience as a guide. There was, indeed, considerable room for free historical association. The Irish situation reminded the editorialist for the London *Advertiser* alternately of the 1840s, when a "minority in the country"[89] resisted the establishment of responsible government, and the 1850s, when Canada was effectively governed as a unitary state:

> It was just such a union as that existing at the present time between Great Britain and Ireland, a kind of union that has always produced dissatisfaction wherever it has been tried. A legislative union here gave to the people of Lower Canada an opportunity of uniting with the minority of this Province, and carrying on its local affairs, in a manner contrary to its wishes.[90]

The reluctance to grant responsible government to the British North American colonies in the 1840s, on the "belief that the majority in race and creed would use their power to oppress the so-called loyal minority, which posed as the English party," led to discontent, agitation and ultimately rebellion.[91] "The experiment of a Legislative Union" that attempted to "extinguish French national feeling" was doomed to "a deserved failure." The further attempt to give French and English their due while retaining a common legislature led to "friction and deadlock, faction and antagonism, instability and inefficiency in government."[92] The Canadian and Irish situations, in short, were full of ominous parallels.

As agitation stemming from "racial" tension was the common problem, so the granting of home rule was the common solution:

> If Ireland had a legislature of its own, dealing with local questions in the same way that they are dealt with here by the provincial legislatures and governments, we believe that life and property would be immeasurably more secure; that order would soon be restored; that there would be more progress made in a decade than has been under the existing system, made in a century.[93]

If only Ireland were given what "the Reform party are now struggling to uphold here,"[94] namely "the right of local self-government,"[95] they would stand a chance of securing their rights and vindicating them through law. And that would be beneficial, as Canadian experience demonstrated, both for Ireland and Great Britain:

> We, in Canada, know well the advantages of local self-government, and can feel with our Irish fellow subjects in their desire to legislate

for themselves in all matters not of Imperial concern. The strength of the federal system, both here and in the United States, has, in its bearing to each component part of the Union, unrestricted control of its local affairs, and relieving the general government from interference in matters of little or no moment to the nation at large. The application of the federal system to the United Kingdom would, in our estimation, not only remove Irish discontent but bring about a Union between Great Britain and Ireland based on loyalty, mutual goodwill and identification of interests.[96]

As Blake put it succinctly: "I am arguing from Canada, once discontented and rebellious—but which Home Rule has made peaceful, contented and law-abiding—to Ireland, which has been for want of Home Rule agitated, alienated, and lawless, but which from my soul I believe will, under Home Rule, become peaceful, contented and law-abiding."[97]

Having struck on the notion that Canadian federalism could be used as the model for solving Britain's problems, the autonomists extended the insight with their usual enthusiasm. If home rule made sense for Ireland as a whole, then it made sense within Ireland as well. "If there is a great diversity of race between North and South; if the north and south are separated in opinion and feeling, as Quebec and Ontario are, that may be a reason for giving a separate local Government to each Province...."[98] While the autonomists recognized that Scotland had over the years been treated more generously than Ireland, there was still an argument to be made for home rule in Scotland. "We are very sure that the work of legislation would be much more promptly and much more satisfactorily done" in Scotland if there were "another legislature having jurisdiction over the local affairs of Scotland, elected by the Scottish people, and pursuing a policy in accordance with national wishes."[99] And if federalism were useful in Ireland and Scotland, it might "possibly" work in England and Wales as well.[100]

These suggestions for the full federalization of Britain were, of course, not taken particularly seriously; nor, apparently, did the Canadian analogy tip the rhetorical balance in favor of Irish home rule. But that is rather beside the point. The important thing is that Britain's mishandling of the Irish question in the 1880s reinforced the autonomists' conviction that peace, stability and the rights of minorities themselves could only be sustained in Canada by allowing French and English to control local affairs free from outside interference. Some form of political autonomy was the non-negotiable and fundamental condition of liberal political stability. That was the premise from which the Canadian Fathers of Confederation had worked; that was the lesson to be drawn from the Irish difficulties; and that was the policy the autonomists were dedicated to uphold against John A. Macdonald. Blake put it to his English audience in terms sufficiently general that they could be applied with equal ease to Canada, Britain and beyond: "(Home rule), after all, is the great solvent. Without this all schemes will fail; while, with it, even an imperfect scheme will accomplish a good and blessed work."[101] Provincial autonomy thus became a model for imperial reform, and the empire's problems confirmed the sanctity of provincial autonomy as a basic constitutional principle in Canada.[102]

The difficulty with seeing the Irish question in Canadian terms, however, is that it forced the Canadians to portray the principle of provincial autonomy as a constitutional remedy which, like some miracle drug, would cure the disease without producing its own harmful side effects. Such claims were clearly unrealistic, but having invested the Canadian-Irish analogy with such importance they became rhetorically necessary. Having promoted home rule as a constitutional panacea, the provincial autonomists were not about to admit that the laboratory tests were anything but unequivocal. The result was that the Irish question forced the Canadians to tell their story in a way that idealized the federal structure and suppressed its imperfections, that lionized provincial autonomy and veiled its difficulties.

The way in which exigencies imposed by the Irish analogy colored the autonomists' understanding of Canada is especially clear in Edward Blake's treatment of minority rights. One of the many objections brought against Gladstone's proposal for Irish home rule was that it would endanger the rights of the largely Protestant population in Ulster which, under the home rule scheme, would be vulnerable to the southern, Catholic majority. One particularly revealing version of this argument was put in the British House of Commons by the Liberal-Unionist T. W. Russell in the course of the debate held in 1893 on Gladstone's second Home Rule bill. Russell's speech was based on a fairly conventional anti-Catholicism, which purported to explain that Ulster's Protestant population would neither prosper nor be safe under Catholic control. Searching for historical support, Russell seized on the example of Quebec. "If (the Home Rulers) wanted a real analogy to Irish Home Rule, they had to find it in the Province of Quebec at the present day":

> What were the conditions there? The conditions were practically the same as they would be in Ireland under this Bill. They had got, in the first place, two races inhabiting the Province. They had a large French population—mainly Roman Catholic and argicultural; they had also got a small English population—mainly Protestant and

commercial. So far as that went, that was Ireland. They had got in Quebec Home Rule, and all the blessings that it could convey.[103]

And what had been the result of home rule in Quebec, Russell asked?

They had got, in the first place, corruption in the Government of the country.... They had got a Debt rolling up, Quebec being the only Province in the Dominion which had a Debt. They had got an empty exchequer, a poor population, and a Church rich beyond the dreams of avarice. They had got education in the hands of the Church, and it was a farce. They had got the English minority paying five-sixths of the whole taxation of the Province, with no more power over the Government than they had over the Government in England.[104]

In short, Russell concluded: "When they were asked what the people of Ulster were afraid of his reply was that one Quebec was enough for the 19th Century, and another ought not to be set up in Ireland."[105]

Edward Blake, who by this time had assumed a seat in the British House of Commons, was not about to let the Canadian analogy be used to weaken the case for Irish home rule, and he quickly seized the opportunity to answer Russell's claims. Indeed, faced with Russell's extravagant claim that home rule in Quebec had been a complete disaster for the English minority, Blake felt compelled to respond equally extravagantly. Where Russell had claimed that the English minority in Quebec had been effectively disenfranchised, Blake replied that they were generally given "more than a proportionate share, in the government of that country."[106] Where Russell asserted that the educational system in Quebec was controlled by priests, Blake maintained that the French-speaking majority had not only been generous in its treatment of English education, in fact they had given "more amply than they were constrained to give by a faithful observation of the Constitutional and fundamental obligations."[107] And where Russell concluded that the English minority had had to endure corruption, mismanagement and injustice, Blake told a fundamentally different story, a story that was, "upon the whole," one of "tolerance, liberality, and recognition of the rights of minorities, of the rights of those of a different creed, and of the obligations of common citizenship...."[108] It was undoubtedly true, Blake admitted, that there had been those among the English minority in Quebec who at first did not want to give up their "predominant"[109] position in Quebec society; and it was true as well that Quebec politics since 1867 had not been entirely free of corruption. Still, Blake concluded that, "considering all its conditions and circumstances," Canada was "wonderfully contented"[110] with its system of home rule.

Nor was this conclusion drawn only from the evidence presented in Quebec or in response to Russell. As Russell himself noted, Blake had traveled extensively throughout Ireland trying, among other things, to convince the Ulster minority they "had nothing to fear"[111] from home rule. Speaking to a partisan English audience in 1892, Blake explained that on his tour through Ulster he had been able to press the Canadian analogy vigorously:

> We have in Canada a powerful Orange party; we have doubtless bigoted men in the Roman Catholic and in the Protestant denominations; we have good men with nerves. But the sober and settled thought of the great majority of our people, of each creed and race, has shown itself superior to the efforts of bigots, the cries of alarmists, the aims of extremists of whatever creed or race, and has satisfactorily proved our general adhesion to the principles of civil and religious liberty, and of equal rights.[112]

Home rule would not threaten minority rights, in other words, as long as local majorities adopted certain basic principles:

> first, the sacred observance of statutory organic covenants or restrictions; next, the recognition of the high and God-given claim of justice and equal rights; lastly, the moral obligation of a majority to grant, as it can afford to grant, to a minority not merely a literal grudingly-measured quantum of strict justice, but full measure heaped up and running over.[113]

These were the principles that Blake believed were "held by the masses of the Canadian people." These were, equally, the principles that he had attempted to expound in the course of "addressing Irish meetings."[114]

Blake's account of the protection of minority rights in Canada is striking for its buoyant optimism and its faith in the power of moral exhortation to effect progress. What is still more striking is how much more optimistic Blake sounded in England than in Canada. In the course of the parliamentary debate on the North-West in 1890, Blake had strained to find a silver lining in the cloud produced by D'Alton McCarthy's resolution to prohibit the official use of French in the territorial government. Blake put the best possible face on the situation and maintained that, after all, "the (r)ight will triumph in the end,"[115] but it is clear from the speech as a whole that he had some difficulty in convincing himself that the story would have a happy ending. Where in England he wrote off the problem of religious bigotry by consigning it to a minority of fanatics, his tune in Canada was quite different.

While he was consoled by the faith that "we were moving on ... to a higher plane"[116] in the treatment of minorities, the McCarthy resolution clearly made him question that faith:

> But although I did so believe, as I shall still venture to entertain that hope, I knew well that all this time there were great masses of prejudice and suspicion, of ancient hates and misconceptions, and bitter memories of former conflicts, lying ready to the hand of the incendiary, easy to be kindled, difficult to be extinguished; and that the proportions of the conflagration which they might excite were impossible to be calculated in advance.[117]

Far from being "wonderfully contented," in other words, Canada was actually at "a turning point."[118] Blake's conclusion betrayed his unease: "I may not see aright; but if I at all discern the signs of the times, until Canadians on such lines agree, there will be for Canada neither progress, prosperity, nor peace."[119]

That by 1892-93 Blake's gloomy assessment had given way to almost unbridled optimism surely has little to do with the progress made in the interval toward the actual protection of minority rights in Canada. If anything, the gathering storm over Manitoba must have made the situation appear worse, the controversy more intractable, than two years before. The more plausible explanation for Blake's rather abrupt change of tone is that the rhetorical exigencies of the Irish situation forced him to adopt a more upbeat account of his country's history. For having made Canada the model for Irish home rule, and having been challenged to show that home rule would not lead to the persecution of minorities, Blake really had no choice but to wax lyrical about the fine protection of minority rights within a federal Canada. Thus, the Irish question profoundly influenced autonomists like Blake not merely because it reinforced their conclusion that home rule or provincial autonomy was the solution to the problem of "racial" diversity, but because it encouraged them to discount the extent to which provincial autonomy created its own problems of diversity. In short, the autonomists' tendency to reduce the problem of minority rights to the terms of provincial autonomy had much to do with their obsession with Ireland and the problems of the empire.

V

For those autonomists who did not have the luxury of viewing the problem of minority rights from the safety of the British House of Commons, there was another reason for giving provincial autonomy weight in such critical political calculations. As the autonomists were encouraged by the Irish example to gloss over the complication posed by provincial minorities, so they believed that there existed an irresoluble tension between maintaining the integrity of provincial self-government and protecting provincial minorities. Leading autonomists were keenly aware that the provincial governments could not always be trusted to treat their minorities with the sort of generosity of spirit that liberal principles required. But they were inclined to make provincial autonomy the foundation of their minorities' policy because they trusted the federal government even less, and they simply could not conceive any way of making direct federal supervision of minority rights both effective and limited. Haunted by the possibility that the federal government would use the protection of minority rights as a versatile and open-ended pretext to interfere routinely and constitutionally in provincial affairs, the leading autonomists retreated behind the wall of provincial autonomy. In so doing, they adopted a strategy of minority protection that depended less on constitutional supervision than on moral exhortation and negotiated political compromise; a strategy, in short, that was meant to achieve a reasonable balance between the rights of minorities and the basic principles of a federal constitution.

The classic exposition of this view is to be found in Wilfrid Laurier's great speech to the House of Commons in March 1896 on the Manitoba schools question. Laurier rose on that occasion to explain why his party could not accept the government's remedial legislation to restore Manitoba's separate school system. Laurier began by setting out the tension I have just described. While "it is always a great and noble thing" to do "justice to a minority," he said, it was equally clear that the means of achieving justice had to be carefully constructed so as not to produce "a most violent wrench of the principles upon which our constitution is based."[120] Now, to frame the question of remedial legislation as if it posed a threat to the integrity of the constitution was provocative and, at least at first blush, strikingly curious. After all, Laurier could not deny that the constitution itself permitted the federal government to supervise the provinces, either through the blanket veto power of disallowance or by means of the remedial provisions of section 93; and the Conservative government's argument throughout the affair was that it was acting in strict accordance with the positive terms of the BNA Act.[121] But Laurier had chosen his words carefully. He did not say that federal supervision of minority rights ought to be considered in light of the positive text of the constitution. He said, rather, that in considering whether to act, the federal government had to be careful not to wrench the "*principles* upon which our constitution is based." That the underlying principles might be useful in understanding and qualifying the constitution's positive provisions was, from Laurier's perspective, the premise that informed his inquiry into the permissible use of federal supervisory powers. That, indeed, is why the greater and more interesting part of the speech was devoted not to a detailed analysis of the situation in Manitoba, but to a general discussion of the constitutional rules governing the federal protection of minority rights in the provinces.

From this larger perspective, federal supervision was problematic because it could not be reconciled easily either with the basic principles of federalism or, still more deeply, with the rule of law. Federalism, as Laurier liked to point out, was itself conceived as a solution to the problem of protecting minorities. Because Canada's population was composed of "different communities," separated by "long distances" and divided by "creed and race," it had been "imperative" that the power to legislate on local matters be entrusted to local legislatures; this "division of powers" was "absolutely essential to the federal form of government."[122] Moreover, and this was the crucial corollary, it was "also essential that all the legislatures should be *absolutely* free of each other, and free of supervision,"[123] for once the legitimacy of supervision had been granted it would be impossible to confine.

Laurier was led to view the alternatives—provincial sovereignty and federal supervision—so starkly in part because he feared the political consequences of federal action so greatly. He believed that federal supervision would inevitably nationalize contentious questions, importing them to the Parliament of Canada where they would "rage not only with equal violence but, perhaps, with increased fury."[124] Federal supervision, therefore, would almost surely produce the very "friction, disturbance and discontent"[125] that it was meant to control —not occasionally, but frequently. As long as the federal government possessed the constitutional power to disallow "*all* Acts passed by the local legislatures"[126] it would be under constant pressure to intervene in provincial affairs on behalf of virtually every aggrieved minority, pressure that even the most restrained of governments would have difficulty ignoring. Lacking any clear standards, the protection of minority rights would be utterly discretionary. The federal government would act "when it suits them" and "when they think it is convenient to apply the doctrine"[127] rather than according to strict constitutional standards or even with a view to doing justice. In short, federal supervision seemed to Laurier to combine the worst of all possible worlds. On the one hand, the constitutional open-endedness of the supervisory powers invited the federal government to intervene so routinely and arbitrarily in provincial affairs as to call into question the basic integrity of the federal principle, limited constitutional government and the commitment to minority protection that federalism represented. On the other hand, the absence of clear standards made the use of these powers unsuitable for the few instances in which they really were necessary. The cause of justice was not likely to be served by devices so easily sacrificed to considerations of expedience.

Nor, from Laurier's perspective, was this merely a hypothetical problem. "Is it not a fact," he asked rhetorically:

> that, almost from the first moment of its existence until now, confederation has been torn, not once, not twice, but repeatedly, by agitations which more than once have shaken it to the very roots, and threatened its very existence?[128]

The use of disallowance in the name of minority rights had indeed produced "frequent recurrences of agitation and commotion":[129]

> That, Sir, has been our experience within the last twenty-five, yes, almost thirty years. Recall the fierceness of the agitation over the New Brunswick school Act; think of the feeling aroused by the Jesuit estates question. In these cases the whole country was convulsed. In one, disallowance was demanded in the name of Roman Catholicism, while in the other disallowance was demanded in the name of Protestantism, and the old feuds which divided our ancestors threatened to invade our country, and here work the mischief which they had worked in other lands.[130]

The fact was, Laurier concluded, that "there was only one cause" for all this commotion, "and that was the feature of our constitution which abridges the independence, the sovereignty of the provincial legislatures."[131] As Laurier saw it, in other words, there was an irreconcilable, zero-sum tension between discretionary supervision of the provinces and the constitutional principle of provincial autonomy, between one minority policy and another. One could not protect provincial minorities through disallowance or remedial legislation without threatening the other form of minority protection embodied in the federal principle.[132] Given that premise, the only workable solution to the problem of overlapping minorities was to combine negotiation, local agitation, and compromise with the frank recognition of provincial autonomy as a fundamental constitutional principle. Once he became prime minister, that is precisely the spirit in which Laurier undertook to resolve the Manitoba question. For Laurier, the "sunny ways" of enlightened negotiation was the only way to address the provincial treatment of minorities that was consistent with the federal principle and the rule of law.

The Manitoba schools question divided the country deeply; so too it divided the Liberal party.[133] Yet even those, like David Mills, who were more inclined to support the idea of remedial legislation in the Manitoba case did not disagree with the main thrust of Laurier's argument. For Mills, as for Laurier, the crucial problem in protecting minorities was to find clear, precise and limited standards that would permit the federal government to protect provincial minorities without at the same time threatening the integrity of provincial jurisdiction. The difference is that Mills was far more optimistic about finding and defining such standards and hence of confining the use of the supervisory powers. The provincial power over education was not, in fact, one of those areas of exclusive jurisdiction in which the categorical logic of absolute provincial sovereignty applied. It was limited by the remedial power, but as Mills insisted over and over again, this remedial power was quite specific, leaving Parliament with an "extremely limited"[134] range of powers and a "narrow field of jurisdiction"[135] that could be used only in the "last resort."[136] Stated more generally, Mills was simply more optimistic than Laurier about the ability of politicians and judges to establish clear boundaries between legitimate and illegitimate action, between provincial sovereignty and federal usurpation, and between discretion and principle. In the draft version of his speech in the Manitoba schools debate, Mills explained his optimism in the following terms:

> It must be borne in mind that the Acts and pacts which make up our Federal Constitution are not a Code. They assume that the meaning of the words employed are known. They assume that the province of legislation, which each enumeration covers, is known. This may be a very broad assumption, looking at the controversies which have arisen on almost every one of them; but it is the only one consistent with English Parliamentary Government, and with the popular basis on which it rests. So far the Courts have found nothing which offers an insuperable barrier to the ascertainment of the boundary which separates Dominion from Provincial jurisdiction. Sometimes the line has been dimly drawn by a faltering hand; and is, therefore, difficult to find; but in almost every instance this can be traced to an imperfect acquaintance with the surrounding circumstances, and, perhaps, in no case is the importance of such knowledge made more clearly to appear, than in the arguments and decisions relating to the

93rd. Section of the British North America Act, and the 22nd. Section of the Manitoba Act....[137]

As difficult as the task of defining such "boundaries" was, Mills had enormous faith in the ability of lawyers to bring the protection of minorities under the rule of law, rather than leaving it to the convenience and expedience of politicians. For Mills, the rule of law was not only the ideal in light of which minority protection should be viewed, it actually resolved the dilemma of how to act in the Manitoba case. What he appreciated less keenly is that the devotion to the rule of law led to an even more difficult dilemma for the supporter of provincial autonomy. This dilemma, how to reconcile provincial and individual rights under the rule of law, is the subject of the next chapter.

CHAPTER 5

Provincial Autonomy
and the Rule of Law

The imperial analogy provided the autonomists with a powerful metaphor by which to explain and justify "home rule" in the provinces. Yet even they were compelled to admit that the comparison between the empire and the federation was in one crucial respect imperfect. For if by the time of Confederation it was generally agreed that Downing Street had no right to interfere in those matters that were "local" in nature, it was also recognized that the colonial right of self-government was a "conventional" rather than a "legal" right. The imperial authorities did not interfere routinely in colonial affairs because to have done so would have violated the basic, if unwritten, principle of parliamentary self-government. Yet as a matter of law there was "no limit to the legislative authority of the Imperial Parliament."[1] Parliament could commit any of the colonies to a certain course of action, as it could change the basic rules of political life in the colonies. Parliament had "absolute authority"[2] over the colonies as a matter of legal right; it was constrained as a matter of constitutional convention.

The relation between the Parliament of Canada and any of the provinces was "wholly different,"[3] for in Canada the central government was limited not merely by constitutional principle or convention but by the "barrier of a superior law:"[4] the division of jurisdiction set out in the BNA Act that conferred on the federal and provincial governments respectively "exclusive jurisdiction" over a set of legislative subjects. To the extent that the imperial and federal cases were different, the flaw in the analogy invited, indeed forced, the advocates of provincial rights to think of provincial autonomy as something more than the domestication of imperial home rule. It invited them, specifically, to expound on the meaning of the "federal principle" as a strict division of powers set down in law and policed by courts. Having defined federalism as a set of legal categories and relationships, the autonomists were then able to fit their cause into the mainstream of late-nineteenth-century Anglo-American legal thought. To defend provincial autonomy was thus not merely to safeguard parliamentary self-government or to preserve and extend the empire; it was to embrace the ideal of the rule of law. The federal principle and the rule of law thus served the same large purpose that the argument for parliamentary self-government and imperial home rule had served; they provided a larger and richer set of ideas and symbols with which to explain, justify and ground their defense of provincial rights. At almost every turn—in legal briefs, in parliamentary debates, in political picnic speeches—the provincial autonomists went to considerable lengths to show that beneath the Macdonald administration's policy of hostility to the provinces lay a fundamental and inexcusable disregard for the rule of law. Such, at least, was the leitmotif of the debate over Macdonald's use of the power of disallowance, the focus of this chapter.

II

Disallowance is a sweeping veto power which gives the federal government the unqualified right to strike down or nullify any act of a provincial legislature within one year of its passage.[5] As one might expect, it is difficult, if not impossible, to discern with absolute clarity the "original intentions" of the "framers" with regards to disallowance. As we saw in chapter 2, "the Fathers" simply were not a monolithic group. For that reason alone, generalizations about their intentions are dangerous and probably misleading. It is clear, however, that at least some of the leading Confederationists supported the veto power for the same reason that James Madison originally supported a national veto over state legislation in the U.S.: simply put, they believed that disallowance would be a useful tool in protecting individuals and minorities from unjust, tyrannical or discriminatory provincial legislation.

As we saw briefly in chapter 3, the argument that disallowance could be used to protect minorities against tyrannical provincial majorities was made with special vigor by the likes of John Rose—representatives from the English-speaking, Protestant community in Quebec.[6] It should be underscored, however, that this view was not confined to Anglo-Quebeckers. Alexander Mackenzie, one of the leading Upper Canadian Reformers and Canada's second prime minister, thought the inclusion of disallowance "necessary in order that the

General Government may have control over the proceedings of the local legislatures to a certain extent."[7] George Brown suggested that the power of disallowance would provide aggrieved individuals or groups with an "appeal" against "injustice" that had been perpetrated by a local legislature.[8] And John A. Macdonald seems to have understood that disallowance would act as the linchpin between centralism and the protection of individuals and minorities. "Under the Confederation scheme," he is reported to have said at Quebec in 1864, "we shall...be able to protect the minority by having a powerful central government."[9] Of course it is easy to make too much of this evidence, for the fact remains that most of the settlement's supporters in the Canadian assembly apparently had no clear idea as to how the veto power would be exercised. Still, it is not insignificant that the leaders of the Great Coalition seem to have agreed that the disallowance power would or could be used as an instrument to protect individual and minority rights.

It is ironic, therefore, that when the federal government came to exercise the power of disallowance in the first years after 1867, it was guided neither by the bare and unqualified words of the constitution nor by the suggestion that the veto should be used to check provincial abridgement of individual or minority rights. And it is doubly ironic that the person primarily responsible for limiting the scope of the veto power and directing it away from rights questions was John A. Macdonald.

As minister of justice in his own first cabinet, Macdonald took it upon himself to circulate a report among the provincial governments that explained under what circumstances his government would feel compelled to veto provincial laws. Macdonald's report was repetitive and sometimes ambiguous, but the fundamental point—that the practice of disallowance would be more limited than the unvarnished words of the BNA Act allowed—was clear. Basically, Macdonald indicated that the federal government would consider it appropriate to exercise the veto only in the following cases: 1) if provincial acts were "altogether illegal or unconstitutional"; 2) if they were "illegal or unconstitutional in part"; 3) "in cases of concurrent jurisdiction, as clashing with the legislation of the general parliament"; or 4) in cases "affecting the interests of the Dominion generally."[10] Nor was disallowance to be used in every case falling under these headings. It was "of importance," Macdonald said, that provincial legislation "should be interfered with as little as possible," and he therefore promised that disallowance would be exercised "with great caution" and "only in cases where the law and the general interests of the Dominion imperatively demand it."[11]

Why did Macdonald emphasize the limitations upon disallowance and what precisely did these categories entail? One answer to the question is surely that Macdonald was simply adapting imperial rules for domestic use. By the time of Confederation, as we have already seen, the use of the imperial supervisory powers was quite strictly limited. It was generally recognized by the time this report was written and circulated in 1868 that the imperial authorities would not interfere with Canadian legislation unless it manifestly affected imperial interests. This basic rule had allowed the Canadians to legislate quite freely on internal Canadian matters. Since the federal power of disallowance was explicitly modeled after the imperial power of the same name, it made some sense to restrict the federal power of disallowance in an analogous way.

Yet Macdonald's reference to the imperative of "the law and the general interests of the Dominion" suggests another answer to that question that has little to do with the now-familiar imperial model. For what Macdonald seems to have realized is that the BNA Act gave the provincial governments a legal claim to legislate "exclusively" on those matters enumerated under section 92, as it gave the federal government the "exclusive" right to legislate on matters listed in section 91.[12] And he seems to have concluded from this that the legal right to disallow provincial legislation simply could not be exercised in an unqualified way without undermining the provincial legislatures' right to legislate exclusively on those matters entrusted to them by the constitution. His report of 1868 was thus an attempt to formulate rules for the exercise of disallowance that would balance the veto power as a tool of national consolidation against the provinces' legal claim to exclusive power; it was an attempt to reconcile a tension or conflict in the terms of the BNA Act itself and to vindicate his claim that the Confederation settlement was indeed "a happy medium"[13] between two extremes.

Macdonald seems to have believed that a workable balance could be achieved if disallowance were used exclusively as a jurisdictional veto. Within the confines of section 92, the provincial legislatures enjoyed the exclusive right to legislate, and Macdonald strongly implied that on such matters clearly within provincial jurisdiction the federal government had no business interfering. There were two corollaries and one exception to this basic rule. First, Macdonald clearly understood that the provincial legislatures might attempt to legislate on matters not covered by the list of subjects in section 92. In this case they would be guilty of overstepping the boundaries of their jurisdiction or encroaching on the subjects reserved to the federal government. In such cases they would be legislating "illegally" or "unconstitutionally," and Macdonald was quick to say that if this occurred the federal government had every right, consistent with the idea of provincial autonomy itself, to veto provincial legislation that was in this sense *ultra vires*. Second, Macdonald seems to have realized that even if the provincial legislatures were acting within their jurisdiction, their legislation might collide with a legitimate federal law. Macdonald was almost certainly thinking here of the areas of agriculture and immigration, which section 95 of the BNA Act itself designated as matters of "concurrent" jurisdiction. On these subjects the federal and provincial governments would share legislative responsibility, and Macdonald seems to have realized that their policies could well be inconsistent. Thus the veto power here would simply serve the purpose performed by the supremacy clause of Article 6 of the U. S. Constitution. In the case of conflict between federal and provincial legislation on the subject of immigration or agriculture, federal legislation could be made to prevail.

These specified areas of concurrent jurisdiction did not exhaust the possibility of policy collision, however. Macdonald seems to have realized that provincial acts might still impinge on national policy without actually exceeding provincial jurisdiction. Macdonald's language was vague on this point, but one can easily enough understand his fears. He perhaps foresaw the possibility, already anticipated by the official categories of concurrent jurisdiction, that federal and provincial jurisdiction would to some extent overlap. And he perhaps concluded that in such cases federal policy had to be protected from provincial acts that were perfectly "legal," that is within provincial jurisdiction, but which nevertheless conflicted with federal policy. He perhaps realized as well that legitimate provincial legislation might occasionally have to yield to what Parliament considered to be some greater national purpose—even if that purpose could not easily be fit under any of the enumerated headings of section 91. In any case, he seems to have thought it necessary to provide the federal government with a third line of defense against provincial legislation: the disallowance of provincial legislation which "affects the interest of the whole Dominion."

The obvious difficulty with this third category was its vagueness; for, after all, in what did the "interests of the Dominion generally" consist? If the national interest were used routinely as a pretext for disallowing provincial legislation which was perfectly legitimate save for its incompatibility with the national interest, the power of disallowance would destroy the very balance that Macdonald claimed to want to maintain. As we will see in due course, this is precisely one of the reasons that the power of disallowance became especially controversial in the 1880s.

Yet at the time Macdonald circulated his report in 1868, these fears were little mentioned. The rules laid down by Macdonald in the year after Confederation received broad bi-partisan support, and the report served as the standard for the use of disallowance for some twenty years thereafter precisely because Conservatives and Liberals alike accepted what they understood to be Macdonald's basic premise: that the federal government could by right disallow provincial acts, but only for jurisdictional reasons. What precisely was included in the term jurisdiction was of course open to question; what was excluded by it was not. For if Macdonald's working assumption was that the provincial governments must generally be allowed to act freely within their jurisdiction, it followed that disallowance could not be used routinely to protect individual or minority rights as long as the provincial governments stayed within provincial jurisdiction. Nor, by the same reasoning, could the federal cabinet act to strike down provincial legislation that it found imprudent, unwise, unappealing or downright obnoxious as long as the legislation fell within the provincial sphere. From Macdonald's perspective, it was crucial that the federal government have the capacity to act quickly to prevent provincial governments from thwarting the task of nation-building. If the cost of wielding the veto power in this way was to allow the provincial governments to act freely within the limited ambit granted to them by the BNA Act, it was a price Macdonald was quite willing to pay. That was Macdonald's way of reconciling centralization with the federal principle.[14]

At the very least, this interpretation of the guidelines is consistent with the way in which Macdonald in fact exercised the power of disallowance in the first government. As minister of justice from 1867 to 1872, Macdonald recommended to the governor general, the disallowance of five acts, all of them on jurisdictional grounds. Thus, when the Ontario and Quebec legislatures attempted to confer parliamentary privileges and immunities on themselves, Macdonald argued, as we saw in chapter 2, that provincial legislatures lacked the "competence" under sections 92–95 of the BNA Act to enact such legislation.[15] One portion of the supply bill passed by the Ontario legislature in 1869 was disallowed because, in Macdonald's words, it was not "within the competence" of the provincial legislature to pay judges' salaries; this was a federal responsibility.[16] An act of the Nova Scotia legislature empowering the Halifax city police court to sentence juvenile offenders was held to be *ultra vires* on the grounds that it was a matter of the criminal law, on which the federal government has exclusive power to legislate.[17] And another act of the Nova Scotia legislature, this one regulating pilotage, was also disallowed for encroaching on federal jurisdiction.[18]

In fact, Macdonald's inaction is arguably even more revealing than his action in this regard. On several occasions in those first years Macdonald received petitions from citizens who claimed some grievance against a provincial legislature, and who appealed to Ottawa in the hopes that the federal government would disallow the offending act. The most notable of these petitions centered on the will of a certain Mr. Goodhue, the terms of which had been changed by an act of the Ontario legislature after the man's death. The original will favored the man's grandchildren, the revised will his children. The executor of the estate, presumably acting on behalf of the grandchildren, asked the federal government to disallow the act on the grounds that it was "unconstitutional, in depriving persons of rights and property without their consent, and without any compensation whatever."[19] Macdonald's reply was succinct and blunt: "Petitions have been received for the disallowance of this Act, but as it is within the competence of the provincial legislature, the undersigned recommends that it be left to its operation."[20] Disallowance, in short, was meant and used in the first years after Confederation to reach jurisdictional questions only.

If there were any doubts as to the meaning or foundation of the guidelines respecting disallowance, these were erased during the most divisive episode in the immediate post-Confederation period, the New Brunswick schools question. In 1871 the New Brunswick legislature undertook to massively reform the public education system in the province through a Common Schools Act. Inasmuch as the Common Schools Act attempted to provide a more secure financial foundation for New Brunswick schools, it was both unobjectionable and sorely needed. But the new law also effectively instituted secular in place of religious schooling. Under the previous regime, Catholics had been granted what in practice amounted to separate schools; this was publicly-funded education organized by parish and controlled along denominational lines. Under the new law no accommodation was possible, for which reason the sizeable, but minority, population of Catholics in the province opposed it.[21]

It must be stressed that the arrangement that had been worked out in the old system was an accommodation in practice, not law. The Parish Schools Act of 1858 provided for broadly religious education, and within these parameters Catholic education had developed a certain autonomy. But the legislation did not provide for a dual system of education. Such, at least, was Macdonald's interpretation of the statute when a group of Catholics from New Brunswick petitioned for remedial action under section 93 of the BNA Act. That section provides that if sectarian educational rights recognized "in law" at the time of union are abridged by a provincial legislature, the federal government may enact remedial legislation to restore them. As the educational rights enjoyed by New Brunswick Catholics were established as a matter of practice or convention, not law, Macdonald believed that it would be inappropriate for the federal government to act.[22]

When the matter came before the House of Commons in 1872, one of the English-speaking Catholic members from New Brunswick, Timothy Anglin, criticized the federal government for its refusal to entertain the request for federal remedial legislation. If remedial action were impossible, he argued, surely the law could have been disallowed:

> There could be no doubt of the soundness of the policy of not interfering with the Local Legislature where it could be avoided, but this was a case in which the greatest excitement and dissatisfaction had been occasioned throughout the whole Province, and he could imagine no good or sound reason why the Act was not declared void. The greatest hatred and excitement prevailed at this moment throughout the Province, and he appealed to the Roman Catholics of Quebec and throughout the whole Dominion, not to sit down tamely and see their brethren in New Brunswick outraged, insulted, and deprived of their just rights and privileges.[23]

Yet despite such appeals, Anglin was forced to admit that the federal government had been unreceptive to his petitions. The difficulty he encountered in bringing his case to the federal government was that Ottawa insisted on viewing the question narrowly, even legalistically. It had approached the problem, Anglin complained, as "a legal question only" rather than one of "policy and justice."[24] As a result, the Macdonald administration had failed to protect the very things Confederation had been created to protect—"the rights of all classes."[25]

In his reply, Macdonald defended the very distinction that Anglin had said was at the root of the federal government's refusal to act. "The individual members of the House might have their individual views," Macdonald argued, as to whether the New Brunswick law was "good or bad, . . . fair or unfair";[26] he was himself "very much at one with the hon. gentleman (Anglin) who had just spoken"[27] in his support for minority educational rights. But the fairness or unfairness of the legislation, he continued, was not at issue here. The only question that the government need decide "was whether according to 'the British North

America Act, 1867', the Legislature of New Brunswick had exceeded its powers."[28] Macdonald then summarized the guidelines he had developed in the disallowance report of 1868:

> As the officer primarily responsible (for the exercise of disallowance), he could only say that he had taken uniform care to interfere in no way whatever with any Act passed by any of the Provincial Legislatures if they were within the scope of their jurisdiction. There were only two cases in his opinion in which the Government of the Dominion was justified in advising the disallowance of a Local Act—first, if the Act was unconstitutional, and there had been an excess of jurisdiction—and second, if it was injurious to the interests of the whole Dominion. In the case of measures not coming within either of those categories, the Government would be unwarranted in interfering with local legislation.[29]

It was perfectly clear that in this case "the New Brunswick Legislature had acted within its jurisdiction and that the Act was constitutionally legal and could not be impugned on that ground."[30] And since it applied only to New Brunswick schools, it could hardly be argued that "the Act in any way prejudicially affected the whole Dominion."[31] Macdonald reiterated his sympathy for those who thought that the law was both bad and unjust. But he maintained that if redress was to be won, the cause had to be "pressed at the polls"[32] and in the legislature of New Brunswick, not Ottawa. The federal government, in short, could only be concerned with the legality of provincial law, not with its wisdom, fairness or justice. If it were otherwise, parliamentarians would "set up their own judgment against the solemn decision of a Province in a matter entirely within the control of that Province"; and that would make them guilty of a "violent wrench of the Constitution."[33]

Macdonald explained the rationale for using disallowance strictly as a jurisdictional veto in still greater and more revealing detail the following year (1873), this time in response to a request that enabling legislation passed pursuant to the Common Schools Act be disallowed. Macdonald's speech on this occasion was a curious combination of autobiography and legal discourse which began with his own account of the process that led to the Confederation settlement. Macdonald portrayed himself as a late, but complete, convert to the "federal principle."[34] He confessed that:

> he had been from the first in favour of a legislative union, and had believed that the best interests of the country might have been

promoted by a legislative union of all the Provinces, aided by a subordinate system of municipal institutions with large powers. However, he had been overruled in that respect by large majorities in the
old Parliament of Canada.[35]

Not surprisingly, Macdonald emphasized the leading part played by
Quebec in shaping the compromise that ultimately was reached. "The
Lower Canadians," he said:

> drew themselves up, and said, if the constitution were not so drawn
> up as to give them the power to protect beyond a doubt their institu-
> tions, their religion, their language and their laws, in which they had
> so great a pride, they would never consent to a union; and if that had
> not been agreed to, we should not now have the Dominion of
> Canada.[36]

But Macdonald was quick to point out that local autonomy was the
non-negotiable demand of the other conferees as well. "The feeling
had been unmistakable," he continued, "not only in Canada but also in
the other provinces, that we could have only reunion on the federal
principle." He therefore, "yielded his opinions and went in with the
Government of which he was a member for the establishment of one
great Dominion and the principle of a federal union, and he had
loyally and to the best of his judgment, power and ability endeavoured
to carry out that principle faithfully."[37]

As Macdonald understood it, his duty in carrying out the federal
principle consisted first and foremost in ensuring that the provincial
legislatures were free to act as they wished within the bounds of their
jurisdiction:

> (The provinces) had their rights, and the question was not whether
> this House thought a Local Legislature was right or wrong. But the
> whole question for this House to consider, whenever such a question
> as this was brought up, was that they should say at once that they
> had no right to interfere so long as the different Provincial Legisla-
> tures acted within the bounds of the authority which the constitu-
> tion gave them. There was this fixed principle, that every Provincial
> Legislature should feel that when it was legislating, it was legislating
> in the reality and not in the sham.[38]

Again Macdonald was quick to sympathize with the Catholic minority
in New Brunswick. He believed, he said, that the New Brunswick legislature "had made a great mistake." But he emphasized that his opinion
was spoken "*sub judice*, because those who passed the law had a right

to maintain its wisdom." The question before him was not "a matter of sympathy" but of "constitutional principle."[39] If the principle of non-interference were not respected, if Parliament "undertook the great responsibility of interfering with local laws," then it would inevitably become a "court of appeal to try whether the Provincial Legislatures were right or wrong in the conclusions that they came to." And that, Macdonald believed, "would destroy the independence of the Provincial Legislatures."[40] Indeed, it would ultimately create the very sort of legislative union that he had once hoped would be established, but which he had been persuaded was inappropriate in a country like Canada.

There surely was an element of political opportunism in Macdonald's stout defense of provincial autonomy in the New Brunswick schools debate. Macdonald's concern with the integrity of provincial legislation seems difficult to reconcile with his public promise, just before Confederation, that the provincial legislatures would remain at best "subordinate" to the federal government and his private prediction that they would soon disappear altogether.[41] One might well argue that Macdonald changed his tune quickly, decisively, but temporarily during the debate over New Brunswick schools because it was in his interest to do so. Sir John wanted at all costs to avoid entangling his government in an issue as volatile and uncontrollable as minority religious education. An appeal to "provincial independence" allowed him to express his solidarity with the supporters of Catholic education, both in New Brunswick and elsewhere, while it prevented him from doing anything about it, thereby reducing the political damage all round. It surely occurred to him as well that by posing as the champion of provincial rights he could embarrass those traditionally associated with that cause—men like A. A. Dorion, David Mills and Luther Holton—who swallowed their principles and voted for the disallowance of the New Brunswick acts.[42]

Macdonald's position was by no means wholly self-serving, however. For one thing, his defense of New Brunswick's right to legislate as it pleased exacted a much higher political price than he expected or than is consistent with an explanation that would reduce his position to simple opportunism. His government's handling of the New Brunswick affair became an important issue in the general election of 1873, especially in Quebec, and it has been argued forcefully that the failure to protect Catholic education in New Brunswick played an important part in the defeat of several members of Macdonald's government—George-Etienne Cartier first among them.[43]

More importantly, it is easy to exaggerate the contrast between Macdonald's statements during the Confederation Debates and his defense of provincial autonomy in 1872-73. In fact, his understanding of the scope and limitations of disallowance square quite well with his conception of Confederation as a "happy medium" between a legislative and a federal union. On the one hand, the veto power was necessary, in Macdonald's view, to protect the dominant position of the federal government. Macdonald was nothing if not a centralist, and disallowance seemed useful, indeed crucial, in protecting the federal government's expansive authority from the depredations of the provinces. On the other hand, Macdonald understood that freedom from national interference, that is provincial autonomy, had been the nonnegotiable condition imposed by the various sub-groupings for their participation in the Confederation settlement and remained vital thereafter. Thus for Macdonald, a strictly jurisdictional veto occupied the "happy medium" between two unpalatable alternatives: provincial intrusions in the great business of running the nation and federal interference in merely local affairs. As long as the veto could be used by the federal government to protect its expansive jurisdiction, the political predominance of the federal government would be preserved. As long as disallowance was used only to reach jurisdictional questions and not to second guess the wisdom of provincial legislation, it would respect the formal legal equality of the provinces.

Nor was the understanding of the use of disallowance peculiar to Macdonald or Conservative administrations. The question of provincial rights in Canada is often treated as a partisan dispute in which Liberals defended provincial autonomy as uncompromisingly as Conservatives supported central domination. Yet there was really precious little dispute about the principles that should guide the exercise of disallowance, at least through the 1870s. The Liberal government of Alexander Mackenzie, which held office from 1873 to 1878, accepted disallowance as a perfectly legitimate constitutional instrument for vetting provincial legislation and was untroubled by the possibility that it could be used to undermine provincial autonomy. Indeed, the Mackenzie government used the power rather more freely than Macdonald had. All told, the Mackenzie government disallowed some eighteen provincial laws in its five year tenure (as opposed to just five over a comparable period by the first Macdonald administration).[44]

The Mackenzie government also followed Macdonald's lead in maintaining that the exercise of disallowance should be restricted to jurisdictional questions. In this regard the four men who served as ministers of justice in the Mackenzie cabinet—A. A. Dorion, Fournier,

Blake and Laflamme—were as firm as Macdonald had been in refusing to disallow laws which had been impugned solely on non-jurisdictional grounds. Two cases, both of which came before Edward Blake, stand out. In the first, a complicated Quebec law involving the claim by a provincial officeholder that the government had deprived him of property by abolishing his office, Blake replied that even if the Quebec law had violated his property rights, such a violation "in matters purely local, would not, by itself furnish grounds for disallowance."[45] In the other, an Ontario statute which legalized the union of several Presbyterian churches against the wishes of some of the parishioners, Blake said simply that he need not "express an opinion upon the allegations of the petition as to the injustices alleged to be affected by the Act." That, he said, was "a matter for the local legislature."[46] On one or two occasions Blake did allow considerations of this kind to creep into his reports, but only if the act were objectionable, and hence disallowable, on jurisdictional grounds as well. The apparent injustice of an act did not provide sufficient grounds for disallowance, and no provincial act was disallowed solely for such reasons during the Mackenzie years.[47]

In 1879, Wilfrid Laurier summarized the Liberal understanding of disallowance to the House of Commons in the following terms:

> The doctrine is now well settled that, if Provincial Legislatures keep within the jurisdiction which is allotted to them by the Constitution, however odious their laws may be, however despotic and tyrannical, however desirous both the Executive and the Government might be of affording relief against such laws, yet this House will not interfere....[48]

Any other conception of disallowance "would be a violation of the Federal principle";[49] by which he meant, of course, that a jurisdictional veto was not.

III

During the first decade of Confederation there was no serious partisan disagreement about the general rules governing the exercise of disallowance. The opposition, whether Liberal or Conservative, sometimes quibbled with the government's use of the power in particular cases, but there was no disagreement about the general principle that the disallowance of provincial legislation was legitimate as long as, but only as long as, it was confined to jurisdictional questions. That consensus was shattered in the 1880s. As the nation-building pretensions of the Macdonald government grew, so did its use of disallowance. And as disallowance came to be used more broadly, so its legitimacy became more questionable and the debate surrounding it more partisan.

The growing controversy over the use of disallowance came to a head in 1881 when the Macdonald government struck down Ontario's Rivers and Streams Act, an episode to which I have already referred in the context of the autonomists' defense of parliamentary self-government in the provinces. To recall, the dispute centered on an act of the Ontario legislature which declared that all persons have the right to float logs down Ontario waterways. In addition, it stipulated how those who had invested time and money in improving these waterways were to be compensated for their efforts by those who made use of the improvements. The law had been passed in part to resolve a dispute between Peter McLaren, who had widened a tributary of the Ottawa River, and Boyd Caldwell, a logger whose attempts to use the widened river had been thwarted by McLaren. McLaren complained that the Ontario law deprived him of his property rights. Having at considerable expense transformed a stream that was unnavigable "in a state of nature"[50] into a small river, McLaren maintained that he had certain proprietary rights, among them the absolute right to decide who could use the river and at what price. He therefore petitioned the federal government to have the law disallowed.

As Caldwell, whose political connections were to the Liberal party, was able to get the ear of the Liberal government in Ontario, so McLaren, a Conservative, was successful in persuading the Macdonald government to strike down the Ontario law. It is a sign both of the depth of partisan feeling and constitutional moment that when it came time to explain the reasons for the disallowance, John A. Macdonald himself took responsibility for writing the official report. Macdonald concentrated in his report, as McLaren had in his petition, on the effect of the Rivers and Streams Act on property rights. "The effect of the Act," Macdonald asserted, "seems to be to take away the use of his property from one person and give it to another, forcing the owner, practically, to become a toll-keeper against his will, if he wishes to get any compensation for being deprived of his rights."[51] He continued:

> I think the power of the local legislatures to take away the rights of one man and vest them in another, as is done by this Act, is exceedingly doubtful, but assuming that such right does, in strictness, exist,

> I think it devolves upon this government to see that such power is not
> exercised, in flagrant violation of private rights and natural justice,
> especially when, as in this case, in addition to interfering with private
> rights in the way alluded to, the Act overrides a decision of a court of
> competent jurisdiction.

"On the whole," he concluded, "I think the Act should be disallowed."[52]

Macdonald's defense of his disallowance of the Rivers and
Streams Act was a turning point in the development of the provincial
rights movement in Ontario in that it provoked the first concerted
attack on the veto power itself. The disallowance of the Ontario act,
first exercised in 1881 but repeated each time the Ontario legislature
repassed it, became an essential element of the struggle for provincial
autonomy for several reasons. For one thing, this was the first occasion in which disallowance had been used against Ontario to strike
down an act that appeared clearly to be within provincial jurisdiction.
That is, it was the first time Macdonald had strayed from the
guidelines he had set down for the use of disallowance. Adam Crooks,
the attorney general for Ontario, made the most of Macdonald's apparent inconsistency when, in his reply to Macdonald's report, he pointed
out that the disallowance of legislation on the grounds of injustice
flew in the face both of the rules of 1868 and subsequent practice. In
light of Macdonald's own actions, in the Goodhue will case for instance, the disallowance of the Rivers and Streams Act was "singular,"
"exceptional," and incompatible with the view that the federal and
provincial governments are "alike sovereign in their nature, within the
limits of the subjects assigned to each respectively."[53] The federal
government had done precisely what Macdonald himself had said it
must not do. It had assumed the responsibility of reviewing "the
provisions of a provincial Act within (the province's) competency." In
so doing, the Macdonald government had failed to respect "the
responsibility and sovereign authority of the provincial legislature in
considering, making and framing all such laws respecting property
and civil rights within the province, and the other subjects exclusively
assigned to it by the Confederation Act...."[54]

The Mowat government's protest was joined by Liberal Members
of Parliament and the Liberal press. Edward Blake reminded Macdonald of the 1868 guidelines, pointed out the evident inconsistency
of his action in the Rivers and Streams case, and returned to the general principle on which the original guidelines had been based. "It
would impair the Federal principle, and injuriously affect the autonomy of the institutions of our several Provinces," Blake argued, "were
this power to be exercised on subjects which are within the exclusive

competence of the Local Legislatures, on the ground that in the opinion of His Excellency's advisers, or of the Parliament, any such legislation is wrong."[55] The Toronto *Globe* put it more pithily:

> Never once for fifteen years has the Dominion interfered, never at all has there been any cause for interference. And now, for the first time in the history of the Confederation, the Dominion has asserted a right to interfere in matters within our own concern under the Constitution, within our own province. An Act dealing with our rivers and streams has been flung back in our face, and the whole force of the Union used to prevent its becoming law.[56]

Still enraged, the *Globe* devoted another editorial to the question two days later, in the course of which it summarized succinctly the Liberal position: "The interference was in fact a violent invasion of Provincial rights perpetrated by the Dominion Premier."[57]

Macdonald was unpersuaded by these criticisms of course, but his parliamentary rejoinder differed in one crucial respect from the explanation contained in the official disallowance report which had been sent to the Ontario government. That difference, offered in the spirit of conciliation, had the unexpected effect of deepening his opponents' distrust. The principle that guided the exercise of disallowance, Macdonald maintained before Parliament, was simply that the "independence of every legislature should be protected unless there is a constitutional reason against it."[58] Sir John was compelled to admit that the Rivers and Streams Act, as a matter respecting property and civil rights, was probably within the competence of the Ontario provincial legislature. It was neither "illegal" nor "unconstitutional" in the precise sense in which he used the terms in the 1868 guidelines, and he as much as admitted that he could not defend the federal government's decision to strike down the act on these conventional grounds. But according to Macdonald, the act was still objectionable—if not in the narrow then in the broad sense of the term jurisdiction. The principle of provincial autonomy was not dispositive in this case because the Rivers and Streams Act "violated distinctly the most important"[59] of the conditions set out in the 1868 report; that is, it affected "the general interests" of the Dominion. Where Macdonald at first argued that the federal government had acted to protect private rights and the *public* interest, he now shifted ground to argue that the federal government had acted to protect private rights and the *national* interest. The difference was meant to save his action from the Mowat government's trenchant criticism by making the grounds for the act's disallowance consistent with the guidelines of 1868.

In 1873 Macdonald had rejected out-of-hand the suggestion that the New Brunswick schools question affected "the general interests" of the country. He now strained to show how an act passed to resolve a dispute between two lumbermen, and which applied only to Ontario, could be called a matter of national importance that required nullifying legislation that everyone, even Macdonald, admitted fell within provincial jurisdiction:

> We were protecting a man from great wrong, from a great loss and injury, from a course which, if pursued, would destroy the confidence of the whole world in the law of the land. What property would be safe? What man would make an investment in this country? Would capitalists come to Canada if the rights of property were taken away, as was attempted under this Bill? This was one of the grounds on which in that paper of mine, of 1867 (sic), I declared that, in my opinion, all Bills should be disallowed if they affected general interests. Sir, we are not half a dozen Provinces. We are one great Dominion. If we commit an offence against the laws of property, or any other atrocity in legislation, it will be widely known....[60]

The dispute between McLaren and Caldwell, according to Macdonald, was a matter of no mean significance. The protection of property rights and their uniform enjoyment had become a sort of national necessity. At stake were the reputation, the prosperity, perhaps even the whole future of Canada.

What is significant here is not the tortuousness of the argument—that is obvious enough. What is significant is that in attempting to defend the Rivers and Streams disallowance on the broadest grounds of national interest, Macdonald's almost desperate attempt to show that this was in some sense a jurisdictional question backfired. Instead of propitiating the autonomists by showing that this veto was exercised according to the well-understood rules of 1868, Macdonald's defense of the Rivers and Streams veto almost inadvertently led the autonomists to question the rules themselves. And once the subject had been opened, they were quick to conclude that *any* use of disallowance—even for jurisdictional reasons—threatened the integrity of provincial legislation and the federal principle in a way that could not be tolerated.

The Rivers and Streams case thus fundamentally recast the debate over disallowance. As we have seen, the provincial autonomists had argued for the first fifteen years of Confederation that the disallowance power, when used as a jurisdictional veto "to guard (the federal government) against encroachments by the Provinces,"[61] was consistent with the federal principle and the fundamental conventions of responsible, parliamentary self-government. Macdonald's tortured defense of the Rivers and Streams veto forced the autonomists to reconsider this compromise. It demonstrated that as long as disallowance could be used legitimately and routinely to strike down provincial legislation on the pretext that a provincial act offended "the general interests of the Dominion," it could be used against provincial legislation that clearly was *intra vires* the provincial government. The autonomists began to understand, in other words, that the great flaw in the power of disallowance was that it granted discretion to the federal government to determine whether legislation was jurisdictionally sound and consistent with the national interest. And they began to realize, equally, that as long as disallowance were controlled by someone like Macdonald, the definition of what was in the national interest was almost infinitely expandable. If a question as parochial as the one at issue in the Rivers and Streams case could be construed as a matter of national importance, almost anything could; and as Macdonald came in the 1880s to disallow provincial laws more frequently on the shadowy grounds that they were inconsistent with the "national interest," the autonomists tumbled to the conclusion that the power of disallowance had become a dangerous weapon in the prime minister's larger plan of centralization.[62]

The Rivers and Streams case stood out larger than life to the provincial autonomists, in other words, because it made them see that as long as the federal government felt free to use the veto, it could fabricate dubious, indeed phony, jurisdictional claims to extend its own jurisdiction at the expense of legitimate provincial goals. Seen in this new light, Macdonald's disallowance of the Rivers and Streams Act was not an isolated and discrete violation of his own guidelines, it was part of a larger attempt to create a centralized state. The federal government had been given the power of disallowance, according to the London *Advertiser*, in order "to protect itself against encroachments, by the numerous Provincial Legislatures:

> but it never was intended that the Federal Government should use this defensive power for aggressive purposes. It never was intended that a power conferred for the purpose of upholding its own jurisdiction should be employed to destroy the more ancient fabrics of the Provinces. But this is what is being done, and political partizans in the press and in the Legislature are crying out against centralization at the very time they are defending by gross misrepresentation these unwarrantable encroachments upon self-government in the Provinces. No centralization![63]

What was at stake in the Rivers and Streams case, the *Advertiser* argued, "was not simply a matter of rivers and streams" nor even "a matter of private rights or the compensation to be given therefor." What was at issue, rather, was "something above and beyond both," namely "the right of the Province to enjoy the inestimable privilege of local self-government" on matters "within (its) own sphere."[64] The autonomists had believed that their sphere of jurisdiction was protected by "a barrier of a superior law."[65] The Rivers and Streams episode demonstrated, to the contrary, that the federal government was prepared to "trample under foot the barriers which the principles of the Constitution impose."[66] The charge, in short, was not simply that Macdonald had applied his rules inconsistently, but that the rules were themselves flawed. Macdonald's policy of disallowance was "a death blow" aimed "at the Federal system, and the responsibility of the Provincial Ministry to the Local Legislature and electorate."[67] That is why the Rivers and Streams case elicited such a fierce response.

IV

The autonomists insisted on making the Rivers and Streams disallowance a major constitutional issue because it illustrated rather graphically that, however defined, a federal veto threatened provincial power and the larger idea of federalism on which provincial power rested. But this summary still fails to capture the deepest strain of the autonomists' objection to Macdonald's use of disallowance. For if the Rivers and Streams episode was a turning point in the understanding and practice of disallowance in Canada, it is still more significant for the light it sheds on the broader intellectual context in which the provincial autonomists positioned themselves. As the foregoing passages suggest, the autonomists took issue with the Macdonald government's use of disallowance not merely because it deviated from the established rules that were meant to govern and limit the use of the veto power, nor simply because they came to believe that the veto power could not be reconciled with the federal principle under any circumstances. The more general and ultimately more serious claim, rather, was that disallowance was incompatible with the ideal of the rule of law and with the larger "transatlantic project" of liberal reform being carried on in the name of the rule of law.

In one respect, of course, there is nothing surprising about the autonomists' emphasis on the rule of law. Most of them, after all, were lawyers turned politicians who, if nothing else, had a solid professional

interest in asserting the importance of law. Most were committed to
the view that politics was best studied and understood through the
lens of constitutional politics and legal forms. Moreover, the ideology
of the rule of law was a crucial component of their imperialism. One of
the basic claims for the superiority of the empire and, indeed, British
civilization more generally, was its ancient and honorable tradition
that arbitrary power must be curbed and that the rule of law is especially important in protecting liberty against tyranny. By the mid-
nineteenth century this view had been reduced to a common political
slogan and had become a test of conventional legitimacy. Certainly in
Canada no mainstream politician would have dissented from it.

In the late-nineteenth century, however, the ideal of the rule of
law came to be associated more precisely with a powerful intellectual
movement of Anglo-American legal reform which attempted to show
how a scientific understanding of the law could be put in the service of
liberal ends. The spiritual home of this "legal liberalism" (as it has been
called) was in the universities, and while it "began to appear as early
as 1850" it "became most conspicuously abundant in Anglo-American
academic circles during the 1870s and 1880s,"[68] that is, at precisely
the moment the provincial rights movement was hitting its stride. In
England the movement was centered at Oxford where it came to be
associated with the likes of Dicey, Pollock, Anson, Holland and Bryce;
in the United States, it was most closely associated with Harvard and
the efforts of Langdell, Holmes, Ames and Williston. In either case, it
profited from an extraordinary transatlantic collaboration among
legal scholars who were also friends. There were, of course, many
important differences among such scholars, some of which reflected
different national styles and problems, others of which are more idio-
syncratic and difficult to categorize. Still, it is possible to describe
relatively easily, at least at the level of intellectual caricature, what
united these various minds and what forms the core of legal liberalism.[69]

The movement of legal liberalism was concerned to place the law,
and more specifically courts guided by scientific principles, in the
service of individual liberty. As David Sugarman has pointed out,[70]
legal scholars like Dicey were much taken with John Stuart Mill's
celebration of creative individualism, and they took no less seriously
than did Mill the problem of protecting individual autonomy either
from other individuals or from the state, or both. Given the apparently
natural predilection for individuals and political bodies to want to
expand their power at the expense of others, the crucial political
problem for late-nineteenth-century liberalism was to set clear limits
or boundaries within which each actor is sovereign, that is free to will

without interference from others. The task for liberalism was to distinguish public from private, state from society, other-regarding from self-regarding behavior. In short, the irreducible liberal aim was to maximize liberty by keeping each actor within appropriate and assigned limits.

The distinctive contribution of legal scholarship in the late-nineteenth century was to suggest that the law contained objective principles that could be used to enforce the boundaries or limits of individual or state behavior. Rather than entrusting the protection of liberty to the discretion of political officials whose judgment could be distorted by self-interest in one of its many forms; rather than making the protection of rights a matter of statesmanlike balancing of individual and public considerations, the view of legal liberalism was that the boundaries should be settled, inferred scientifically from a number of general principles, and applied objectively by the courts.

Perhaps the greatest champion of this vision of the rule of law was A. V. Dicey, whose *Law of the Constitution*[71] furnished an extraordinarily influential interpretation of the systematic, purposeful development of the rule of law in England. Dicey's story of the triumph of the rule of law in England was unapologetically nationalistic; the British story thus stood in stark contrast to the baleful decline of the rule of law in France. Yet for all his anglophilia, even Dicey seems to have been willing to admit that the rule of law (and from that, the rule of courts) was most deeply entrenched not in Britian, but in the United States, where the common law was supplemented by judicial review and by a legalistic conception of federalism.[72] The European "americomania" that Dicey described as a correspondent for *The Nation*, and which he seems to have shared, was an entirely apt manifestation of legal liberalism.[73]

To the legal liberal, the beauty of the American conception of the rule of law was its versatility in describing and explaining a whole universe of legal and political relationships between individuals and the state. The premise of legal liberalism, as Duncan Kennedy has noted,[74] "was that the legal system consisted of a set of institutions, each of which had the traits of a legal actor" and each of which was comparable or even convertible one to the other. "Each institution had been delegated by the sovereign people a power to carry out its will, which was absolute within but void outside its sphere." "The physical boundaries between citizens" were in this sense "like those between states," and "the non-physical division of jurisdiction over a given object between legislature and citizen was like that between state and federal governments." Moreover, each legal actor had to worry that this sphere of sovereignty would be challenged, violated or compromised by another actor. Precisely "(b)ecause all the actors held formally identical powers of absolute dominion, one could speak equally of trespass by neighbor against neighbor, by state against citizen, and by citizen against state." And precisely because the problem of setting and maintaining boundaries was the same throughout the system, the task of the judge was "identical whether the occasion of its exercise was a quarrel between neighbors, between sovereigns, or between citizen and legislature." The task of the law—be it the common law, the law of federalism or judicial review under the Bill of Rights—was to prevent usurpation and preserve rights.

This understanding of the purpose and function of the law was developed largely in the universities, but it cannot be overstressed that it was at base a project to reform the way in which the law was actually applied by lawyers and courts. The historical importance of this conception of legal liberalism consists in its influence in shaping political and legal practice in the 1880s, 1890s and beyond. In England, for example, Dicey's understanding of the rule of law was a crucial element in the political debate over the legitimacy of administrative tribunals and the regulatory state. In the United States, this conception clearly had great appeal to the Supreme Court in what has been called the *laissez-faire* era, that is roughly 1880 to 1930. In Canada, the least studied or known of the three, this vision of the rule of law was adapted for practice in a rather pure, albeit inchoate, form by the provincial rights movement.

The Canadian legal community contributed little to the general or theoretical elaboration of legal liberalism in England and the United States, but it followed developments in both places closely. In a few important cases the external influence in shaping the Canadian legal mind was quite direct and explicit. As I noted in chapter 2, David Mills, whose elaborate defense of provincial autonomy is arguably unparalleled in English Canada, learned his law at the University of Michigan under one of the great mid-century systematizers of American law, Thomas Cooley. Through Cooley and others, Mills was introduced quite directly to a vision of law that anticipated many of the core concepts of legal liberalism, and he kept abreast of American legal developments thereafter.[75] In most of the other cases, the foreign influence was less direct but scarcely less important. American cases were frequently cited in Ontario courts well before Confederation,[76] and the names of Story, Kent and others cropped up not infrequently in the provincialists' defense of provincial autonomy.[77] More typically, however, especially from the 1880s on,[78] Canadians looked to English law for guidance and to English lawyers for authority. The autonomists had read Dicey,[79] admired Bryce[80] and generally attempted to keep astride of developments in English law.

The provincial autonomists were quick to realize that the doctrine of legal liberalism provided a congenial framework for understanding their own experiences with and hopes for federalism. The BNA Act was a "superior law," a "constitution" which divided legislative jurisdiction into two independent "spheres" of power which "are mutually exclusive."[81] Within each sphere, therefore, each government was "sovereign" or "supreme," subject only to the will of its electorate. If the federal government attempted to act on a matter within provincial jurisdiction, it was in effect "trespassing" on another government's property. "So far as the Provinces continue their autonomy as Provinces," the *Advertiser* concluded, "the Federal Government has no more authority than it has over the affairs of the state of New York."[82] "The Provinces for Provincial purposes are not in the Union. For all these exclusive purposes, they are as much out of the Union as if no Union existed."[83]

The object of federalism was thus to preserve the "freedom," "autonomy," "independence," indeed the "rights" of the individual provinces from other governments in much the same way as the object of the liberal state was to protect the rights of individuals from overbearing governmental power. The autonomists were quite aware of the rhetorical possibilities of describing provincial autonomy as a form of liberalism, and they therefore drew out the analogy between provincial and individual rights enthusiastically. Thus Mills, in a particularly expressive editorial written for the *Advertiser* in March 1883, explained to his readers that, within the sphere of their jurisdiction, the provinces had the right to do what they pleased so long as it did not encroach "upon the rights of others."[84] That qualification understood (and it is an exception that again reflects Mills's liberalism), the provincial legislatures were free to act as they pleased. They were as free, that is, as any rights-bearing individual in a liberal state.

Mills drew out the implications of the analogy explicitly. The federal government, he argued, had no more right to second-guess the wisdom of an act that was within provincial jurisdiction than the state had a right to tell citizens what religious beliefs they must hold, what foods they should eat, what color clothes they should wear, or what crops they must plant:

> We go to the farmer, and we find him cultivating his fields in a way which we think a system of scientific agriculture does not warrant. We tell him that the prosperity of the country depends upon the prosperity of each individual, and that the wrongheadedness of himself and hundreds of others are interfering with the general well-being of the country. We call in some one else of our own way of

thinking who expresses similar opinions. He replies, "I am cultivating my own lands; upon them I am master of my own actions; in their cultivation my judgment and not yours must prevail, because I, and not you, have exclusive jurisdiction here. It is possible I may err, but I don't think you are infallible, and since the judgment of somebody must prevail, the law which gives me exclusive control here says that it is my judgment and not yours which shall be preferred. It is your privilege to give me advice, but it is not your right to give me commands."[85]

The idea that the state had a right to tell individuals how to act or behave within that sphere of individual autonomy was, from this perspective, simply indefensible. "The most absolute Government that the world has ever known never ventured to carry out in minute detail any such political theory,"[86] and nothing could justify it if it tried. "It may be wrong to invest money in a steamboat instead of a farm," he argued in another version, "but these are wrongs based upon the rights of a man to do what he pleases with his own—the right of preferring his own discretion to the discretion of his neighbor."[87] These illustrations all occurred in the context of Mills's attempts to explain why Macdonald's use of the disallowance power was wrong. As individuals have rights to do as they please consistent with the rights of others, so too the "Local Legislature has the power to do as it chooses, so long as it does not interfere with the corresponding rights of others."[88] And just as the state has no right to tell the farmer how to plant his crops, so "(n)either Sir John Macdonald nor any other outside party has any right to substitute their judgment for the judgment of those to whom the constitution has entrusted the matter."[89]

The analogy between federalism and liberalism was useful, in other words, in explaining the autonomists' growing discontent with the Macdonald administration. The protection of rights turned on the strict maintenance of the boundaries that separated individual from individual, state from individual and, in federalism, state from state. For the provinces to enjoy their rights, each government, federal and provincial, had to "keep within the boundaries drawn by the constitution"[90] just as the state had to recognize the boundaries of legitimate public power if individual rights were to be maintained. The difficulty in federal Canada, according to the autonomists, was that the Macdonald government had shown scant regard for these jurisdictional boundaries and for the provincial rights they protected. Nowhere was this clearer to the autonomists than in the controversy over disallowance, and that is why it became a rallying point. The Rivers and Streams case was interpreted as a grave threat to provincial rights because it signalled the federal government's intention to "interfere" with, "violate," "trespass" upon, "invade," "plunder" and "usurp" provincial rights. As long as the exercise of disallowance was considered acceptable, it was subject to the "treachery," "vindictiveness" and "intrigue" of a prime minister trying to "impose his will upon"[91] unwilling provinces.

As the autonomists viewed the problem of disallowance within the context of the rule of law, so they looked to it to provide a solution. If the federal government had taken to using the veto power to impose its political will upon the provinces, then the remedy was to have "a clear, explicit amendment to our Constitution, which (would) put an end to the vetoing power of the Dominion Administration,"[92] and which would leave the resolution of jurisdictional disputes "as in the neighboring republic, entirely to the courts."[93] Only this would "relieve the Local Legislature from all possible intrigue between the leader of the (provincial) Opposition and his confederates in the Dominion Administration."[94]

Of course this was not the first time an amendment to do away with disallowance had been suggested; Mills had objected to the veto power as early as 1869.[95] But it was only in the 1880s, with the theory of the rule of law and the practice of the Macdonald administration fresh in their minds, that it became fashionable to advocate the abolition of disallowance. David Mills used the editorial columns of the London *Advertiser* to advance the idea of abolishing disallowance formally;[96] the Toronto *Globe* supported the idea of a constitutional amendment to jettison the veto;[97] and Oliver Mowat made it the first item on the agenda of the first Interprovincial Conference of provincial premiers in 1887.[98] The federal government was obviously opposed to any change, but this did not deter the autonomists from trying to convince the Imperial Parliament that the disallowance power should be expunged from the BNA Act—even if that had to be done without the federal government's consent. Even here the convertible categories of constitutional law and private law, federalism and contracts, proved a useful guide. The BNA Act, the autonomists urged, should be understood as a "contract" among the several provinces which collectively had agreed to delegate a specified set of legislative powers upon a federal government that, by the terms of the contract, they had created. As the federal government was a creation of the contract, not one of the contractees, it was perfectly legitimate to alter the terms of the contract without its consent.[99]

In the end, the autonomists' demands fell on deaf ears. Neither the federal government nor the imperial authorities took the provincial "compact theory" particularly seriously. Indeed the imperial authorities did not even pay the provincial premiers the courtesy of

replying officially to the request.[100] This failure, however, only served
to redouble the autonomists' efforts. If they could not read disallowance out of the BNA Act altogether, they could at least render it
expendable. To that end, Edward Blake proposed an amendment to
the Supreme Court Act, the object of which was to make judicial
review a more attractive alternative to disallowance than it previously
had been.[101]

Blake's argument followed directly from the premise of legal liberalism. The idea of the federal principle, he argued, was to create two
mutually exclusive compartments of legislative power in which "the
sphere of the jurisdiction of the one is limited by the sphere of the
jurisdiction of the other."[102] To allow the federal government to strike
down provincial legislation was in effect to allow "one of these two
limited Governments . . . (to) decide the extent of the limits, of what in
a sense, is its rival government."[103] Disallowance thus permitted a
"political executive" to discharge "a legal and a judicial function."[104]
Understood as such, it violated one of the fundamental principles of
Anglo-Saxon law, for it allowed the federal government to judge cases
in whose outcome it had an interest. There was a sense, Blake argued,
in which the act of disallowance therefore "is the decision of a party in
his own cause."[105] It would be far better to enlist "neutral, dignified and
judicial aid"[106] in the enforcement of jurisdictional boundaries. It
would be far preferable to leave the interpretation of the constitutional division of powers to those who are trained to see federal and
provincial jurisdiction, in Mills's memorable phrase, "as if they were
separated by land marks visible to the eye."[107]

On the surface, this concerted attack on disallowance triumphed
impressively. The view that policing the boundaries between federal
and provincial jurisdiction is a "legal and judicial function" became
dogma, and as dogma changed so practice was gradually altered. To
be sure, the practice of disallowing provincial legislation did not disappear overnight, but by the early decades of this century the disallowance power had almost completely been replaced by judicial
review.[108] In light of the historical record, it seems plausible to suppose
that the power of disallowance became unusable by the early decades
of this century because the crucial audiences—provincial premiers,
federal cabinet ministers and certain portions of the electorate—
came to view the veto power as the autonomists wanted them to view
it: as a violation of constitutional principle to which political costs
were attached and for which there was a principled, that is judicial,
alternative. This certainly seems to have been the attitude of Ernest
Lapointe, Mackenzie King's veteran minister of justice, who rose

before the House of Commons in 1937 to explain that as long as "the provincial legislatures feel that they are still supreme and sovereign within the sphere of their jurisdiction"[109] it would be difficult for Ottawa to veto provincial acts. The very fact that disallowance has essentially passed into desuetude suggests that the autonomists' view of disallowance has carried the day.[110]

V

Yet at a deeper level, the Millsian attack upon disallowance did not end the debate over disallowance so much as it brought it back full circle to its point of origin; and in doing so, it paradoxically brought to the surface the problem of protecting individual and minority rights that had been largely submerged in the 1880s and 1890s. To recall, a number of the leading Confederationists had assumed that disallowance would and should be used to protect individuals and minorities from tyrannical provincial legislation. As we have seen in detail, this view of disallowance was quickly repudiated both by Conservative and Liberal administrations, who preferred to use disallowance as a jurisdictional veto when they used it at all. As we have also seen, the debate over disallowance therefore quite quickly resolved itself into a debate about federalism and the integrity of provincial communities and their legislatures.

Mills's original contribution to this debate in the 1880s and early 1890s inadvertently challenged the terms of the debate, for his contention that disallowance violated the rule of law, and his analogy between individual and provincial rights, re-introduced the theme of individual rights and the problem for which disallowance had once been seen as the solution. Mills had meant to use the analogy between individual and provincial rights to strengthen the case for the complete and utter autonomy of local decision-making. But the analogy was only as strong as the object of the comparison was deep. In Mills's view, the rights of the provinces were worthy of protection in the same way or to the extent that the rights of individuals were worthy of protection. To Mills the idea of rights protected by law was not simply a neat linguistic analogy which helped him to illustrate the dangers of federal disallowance; it was, more fundamentally, a valuable and intrinsically worthwhile model of political organization. Mills found the rights analogy persuasive, in other words, because he believed not merely that provincial rights could be compared to individual rights, but because, as a liberal, he believed that individuals have rights.

The difficulty with the analogy between provincial and individual rights, therefore, is that it cut both ways. On the one hand, it reinforced the argument for provincial autonomy by providing a well-nigh unassailable foundation for the integrity of provincial legislation. But the same association that strengthened the claim for provincial autonomy could be used just as easily to undercut it. For if the basis of the claim for provincial autonomy was its likeness or comparability to individual autonomy, could the consistent provincialist really sit idly by as a provincial legislature violated the rights of its citizens? If the provincial autonomists were really committed to the rule of law as the bulwark of liberty, could they simply ignore it when a provincial legislature abridged the liberty of some of its citizens? And if they couldn't, did not disallowance provide one means by which to thwart vicious provincial legislation, even (or perhaps especially) that provincial legislation that was clearly within provincial jurisdiction?

One answer to these questions was supplied by Mills himself when, as minister of justice in the Laurier cabinet between 1897 and 1902, he discharged the responsibility of vetting provincial legislation with a view to its disallowance. Considering Mills's firmly held and frequently expressed view that disallowance ought to be abolished, it is curious that as minister of justice he considered the use of disallowance at all. Yet use it he did. In all, Mills was responsible for recommending the disallowance of thirteen provincial and territorial acts in his tenure as minister of justice, which is to say that he disallowed as many acts in his five years as minister of justice as his predecessors in the post had vetoed in the previous ten.[111]

The way in which Mills used the veto power is still more remarkable than the sheer number of laws disallowed, however. Mills's patience was tested most sorely by the government of British Columbia, which passed a series of bills at the turn of the century that attempted to prohibit Asians from either immigrating to or working in British Columbia. In most cases, Mills seems to have proceeded on the traditional assumption that the federal government could legitimately invalidate only those laws that were *ultra vires* the British Columbia legislature or were inconsistent with some more general federal policy. Thus when Mills was called upon to judge a British Columbia law that effectively prohibited the immigration into the province of any person who could not write out an application "in the characters of some European language,"[112] he did not hesitate to exercise the veto. Such educational requirements, he wrote, were simply "inconsistent with the general policy of the law"[113] of the federal government. When, on the other hand, the B. C. legislature acted in a way that was clearly within its exclusive jurisdiction, Mills usually stayed his hand. Having explained that the aforementioned immigration bill was repugnant to the federal government's policy, Mills turned around in the same memorandum to explain that he could do nothing to blunt the effect of a similarly discriminatory law that disenfranchised Chinese, Japanese and Indian voters in Vancouver municipal elections. "Such enactments," he explained dryly, "are entirely local and domestic in their nature, and sufficiently justified, so far as the powers to be exercised by the government of Canada are concerned, by the fact that the local legislature has considered their provisions expedient or desirable."[114]

In fact, however, Mills was neither able, nor it seems was he disposed, to contrive such a neat, jurisdictional rationale for every one of the B. C. acts that came to his attention. Mills's duty as minister of justice in these cases was complicated by the fact that B. C.'s legislation had elicited a formal diplomatic protest from the Japanese government. Mills was clearly under significant pressure from the Foreign Office to prevent these provincial acts from jeopardizing Britain's relations with Japan. In the course of disallowing two acts that sought to disqualify those of Japanese and Chinese extraction from being employed by provincial corporations, he essentially suggested to the government of B. C. that the disallowance of these acts was a small price to pay for "a friendly sentiment on the part of Japan in matters of commerce and otherwise."[115] The B. C. laws might well have been *ultra vires* anyway as legislation the pith and substance of which dealt with matters—immigration and the rights of aliens—on which the federal government has paramount authority. From Mills's point of view, however, the existence of clear imperial interests obviated any need for a detailed jurisdictional analysis along these lines. For the purposes of disallowance, it was sufficient that the B. C. legislation conflicted with larger, imperial interests.

Yet by shifting the discussion over the B. C. laws from jurisdiction strictly speaking to the larger, political interests at stake, Mills also made it easier to inject into the review of these laws the very considerations of justice that he had earlier argued were incompatible with the exercise of disallowance. For at the root of the Foreign Office's fears that the B. C. legislation could poison British-Japanese relations, was the serious, and from Mills's perspective legitimate, complaint that the B. C. laws discriminated gratuitously and unjustly against the rights of Japanese workers in the province. In his explanatory report to the B. C. government, Mills could easily have confined himself to a description of the *realpolitik* of the situation, concluded that the B. C. legislation had to be sacrificed for the larger good of the empire, and left it at that. He did not. He considered the premier of B. C. to be an "unscrupulous and dangerous"[116] character; he seems personally to have disliked the B. C. policy; and as a result he apparently could not resist the temptation to read the B. C. government a lesson in liberalism. The problem with the legislation, he argued, was not merely that it threatened to become an irritant in British-Japanese relations; the problem was that the legislation was *"justly* regarded as offensive by a friendly power."[117] In the end, Mills's decision to disallow some but not all of the acts on jurisdictional grounds clearly reflected the dilemma that he faced in attempting to find a balance between provincial sovereignty, the larger interests of the empire, and what he called quite explicitly "the justice of the case."[118]

Admittedly, it is easy to overstate the importance of such considerations of justice, of the rights of a minority subjected to systematic discrimination, in Mills's calculations. These considerations were probably no more than an undercurrent in his discussion of the B. C. legislation, and Mills was himself ambivalent on the question of equal rights for Asian immigrants. Still, given the very powerful pressure to exclude such considerations altogether from the discussion of disallowance, even such an undercurrent is noteworthy. Moreover, when the issue was one which Mills considered to be morally unambiguous —protecting the rights of property for instance—the question of rights came to the fore.

The most striking example in this latter category concerns Mills's threat to strike down an Ontario law that required companies not incorporated in Ontario to apply and pay for a license to do business in the province. Again, Mills could well have disposed of the Ontario law simply on jurisdictional grounds. As he put it in his official report to the attorney general of Ontario, the Licensing Act arguably trenched both on the federal government's authority to legislate for the "peace, order and good government of the country" and on its exclusive power to regulate trade and commerce; it flew in the face of several judicial precedents; and the Ontario act was similar to several others that had already been disallowed.[119]

What is curious, then, is that when the premier of Ontario, George Ross, responded to Mills's report with a promise to amend the sections that were jurisdictionally questionable, Mills rejoined by saying in effect that Mr. Ross had misunderstood the federal government's objections. "The question is not," Mills wrote, "whether you have the power to tax Dominion corporations more than you do those of the local legislature, created for a similar purpose, but whether we ought to permit the policy of the Dominion to be frustrated by such unjust provincial legislation."[120] The real objection to the Ontario law, therefore, was not that it exceeded provincial jurisdiction—although Mills was certainly suspicious of it on those grounds. The more basic problem, rather, was that it imposed a burden on companies incorporated under federal law that it did not impose on Ontario companies; it discriminated against federal corporations as if these were somehow "foreign corporations."[121] Were the shoe on the other foot, were Ottawa to pass a similar licensing law that disadvantaged Ontario corporations, Mills was quite sure that Ontario "would at once cry out against our legislation, not because it was *ultra vires*, but because it would be unjust."[122] All the federal government was asking was that Ontario "recognize the principle of equality."[123] He concluded: "I think you see what my position is. The question of *ultra vires* in this matter is quite subordinate to the general question of public policy."[124]

These opinions cannot easily be reconciled with the purely jurisdictional use of disallowance that was current in the 1870s, much less with Mills's unconditional denunciation of disallowance that he made quite routinely in the 1880s. But it would be a mistake to conclude that Mills's position was, on this evidence, either inexplicably contradictory or expediently self-serving. Mills did not abandon his principles in these cases so much as he began to face up to the enormous, if frequently hidden, tension within them—the tension, that is, between his devotion to provincial autonomy on the one hand and the liberal protection of rights on the other. The tension did not manifest itself as long as Mills could assume that provincial autonomy and liberal rights were mutually reinforcing, in effect, as long as Liberals controlled most provincial legislatures and Tories the federal Parliament. The possibility, post-1896, that provincial legislatures would act unjustly and that he would be in a position to stop injustice in its tracks before and in preference to a legal challenge, forced him to consider violating the rule of law (in the form of provincial autonomy) in order to protect the rule of law (in the form of equal individual rights). That is the deep tension, not to say incoherence, in Mills's Canadian application of the late-nineteenth-century understanding of the rule of law.

VI

The tension in Mills's thought between federalism and liberalism helps to explain the curious evolution of the power of disallowance; it also sheds light on the contemporary debate over the implications of the Charter of Rights for the preservation of community and liberty. One of the most subtle and provocative analyses of the Charter's meaning in this regard is Charles Taylor's recent contribution to the series of research reports published in conjunction with the McDonald Commission, an essay entitled "Alternative Futures: Legitimacy, Identity and Alienation in Late Twentieth Century Canada."[125]

Taylor is concerned to understand, in the Canadian context, the "malaise of modernity" which in one form or another and to one degree or another seems to afflict all modern societies. By modern, Taylor means societies centrally dedicated to the maximization of freedom as understood in two distinct, and not perfectly compatible, ways. The first meaning of freedom, associated especially with the classical liberalism expounded by philosophers like John Locke, focuses on individuals as rational, independent agents "who discover their purposes in themselves" rather than seeing themselves as "part of some cosmic order, where their nature was to be understood by their relation to that order."[126] What follows from this definition of freedom as self-definition is that "as a free subject, one is owed respect for one's rights and has certain guaranteed freedoms." The condition of freedom thus understood is that one "must be able to choose and act, within limits, free from arbitrary interference of others." The "modern subject," in short, "is an equal bearer of rights. This status is part of what sustains his identity."[127]

But if freedom has often been defined as bearing rights and has centered on the individual, there is another sense of modern freedom which is better defined as self-governance and which has historically focused on the community. "The fact that we govern ourselves is an important part of our dignity as free subjects." But this definition of freedom as self-governance leads in quite a different direction than the first definition, for it suggests that "the modern subject . . . is far from being an independent, atomic agent." On the contrary, "an individual is sustained . . . by the culture which elaborates and maintains the vocabulary of his or her self-understanding."[128] The full realization of freedom so understood can only be achieved through identification with the community and by participation as a citizen.

These two definitions of freedom—as individual rights and citizen participation—have co-existed in some form of dynamic balance since they were first expounded during the Enlightenment; there is nothing new in this. What is distinctive about the situation that we face in the late twentieth century, according to Taylor, is that the individualistic, atomistic, rights-based dimension of modern liberalism has begun to crowd out or threaten the "community" dimension.[129] This threat can be illustrated in a number of ways. The demand for greater individual freedom, defined especially in terms of material well-being, requires, among other things: a population that is mobile; a government that can provide a wide range of services efficiently and operate a welfare system to mitigate the effects of economic dislocation and historical patterns of discrimination; the concentration of public and private energies to distribute goods and opportunities efficiently; and a system of courts which will protect rights "even against the process of collective decision-making of the society, against the majority will, or the prevailing consensus."[130] Yet as Taylor points out, these conditions of individual freedom serve to undermine community. Mobility destroys the fabric of stable, traditional communities; the need to provide services creates bureaucratized, largely unaccountable, government; the "culture of rights" effectively "circumvent(s) majority decision making through court judgments" and so "further entrenches taking a distance from community decision-making";[131] and concentration creates the sort of centralization that makes citizenship remote and participation difficult and unrewarding. The result— perhaps most plainly evident in the United States—is governmental overload, ungovernability, litigiousness and a decline in even the most routine forms of citizen participation. "Looked at in the light of the full demands of the modern identity," Taylor concludes, "the atrophy of citizen power negates an important dimension of our dignity as free agents, and hence poses a potential long-term threat to the legitimacy of a modern society."[132]

The alternative to these modern strains and tensions, Taylor argues, is not to abandon modernity (which is probably impossible anyway), but to revitalize the other side of the modern project—what he calls the "participatory model"—which stresses decentralization, political participation, attachment to community and the democratic protection of liberty. Taylor clearly endorses the participatory model as a matter of principle. More importantly, he argues that it is particularly well suited to Canada where, he says, "the sense of citizen dignity" has tended historically "to take the participatory rather than the rights forms"[133] and where there is a long history of regional resistance to centralization.

It is here that Taylor allies himself most closely with what Richard Simeon and others have called the provincialist understanding of Canada. For like the provincialists who opposed the entrenchment of a Charter of Rights on the grounds that it would undermine the integrity of local decision-making, Taylor is careful to tie the preference for greater decentralization to democratic or participatory aspirations. Decentralization is desirable because it offers the best opportunity to counter "the malaise of modernity." "The fate of the participatory model in Canada," he argues, "of the continued health of our practices of self-rule, depends on our continuing resistance to centralization . . .":

> If our aim is to combat, rather than adjust to, the trends to growth, concentration and mobility, and the attendant bureaucratic opacity and rigidity of representative democracy, then some measures of

decentralization are indispensable, with the consequent strengthening of more localized, smaller-scale units of self-rule.[134]

In the end, Taylor sketches this choice for Canada:

> In a sense, to oversimplify and dramatize, we can see two package solutions emerging out of the mists to the problem of sustaining a viable modern polity in the late twentieth century. One is the route of political centralization, at the cost of some citizen alienation but compensated for by an increasing incorporation of the American model in which dignity finds political expression in the defense of rights. The other is the route of continued decentralization, and a continued attempt to maintain and extend our historic participatory model, at the cost of putting a greater and greater strain on political vision and inventiveness through mechanisms of political coordination.[135]

Taylor's preference is clear. "If we look at Canada's future ... in terms of the way this country can best face the strains of modernity and the dangers of political breakdown implicit in them—then there seems no doubt that the centralizing solution would be an immensely regressive step."[136] Apart from everything else, the decentralizing, participatory model "is more in line with our traditional political culture."[137] Indeed, "the strength of our historic regional societies makes it virtually mandatory for us to practise a more decentralized style of government than other comparable federations."[138]

Taylor's defense of the participatory model of politics is extremely attractive, but it succeeds, I believe, only at the cost of distorting the historical tradition that is meant to sustain it. Taylor would have us believe that one of the reasons that a participatory form of politics is accessible to Canadians in a way that it may not be to Americans is that our political tradition, rooted in regional self-government, has historically "been more identified with the participatory model," while "the habit of litigation, and the elements of atomist consciousness that go along with it, are deeply rooted in American history."[139]

Yet even with the necessary qualifications, this characterization of provincialism in Canada, much less the Canadian-American contrast, is overdrawn. For one thing, it is by no means clear that the "continuing resistance to centralization"[140] in Canada has in fact been undertaken with a view to preserving and promoting greater citizen participation or that it serves as an historical precedent for the "participatory model" on which Taylor would have us build. For the fact is that the intellectual strategy of the provincial rights movement, the earliest and most successful example of resistance to centralization in

English Canada, entailed a basic ambivalence, if not hostility, to the ideal of full democratic participation of the sort Taylor thinks desirable. The core idea that informed the legal understanding of provincial autonomy, after all, was to put jurisdiction first. What mattered was not whether the provincial or federal governments acted well or wisely, but merely whether they acted permissibly or legally, within the boundaries of their jurisdiction. This was the crucial condition of autonomy and everything, including a broader form of political discussion, fell to it. In the autonomists' legal mind the defense of autonomy depended on treating the discussion of the most controversial issues as if they raised only jurisdictional questions that could be discussed and resolved in terms of legislative rights. The integrity of provincial communities depended, more specifically, on separating law and politics as far as possible; on separating the question of whether a measure was "wise or unwise, expedient or inexpedient," from the legal question of whether a given legislature had the jurisdictional right or capacity to act.[141]

What followed was a system of constitutional rules in which the federal government was meant to be barred not only from acting in areas of provincial jurisdiction, but in which political discussion was reduced to and centered on the determination of jurisdiction. It was a system in which jurisdictional claims themselves were not really to be discussed so much as derived from the black letter text of the constitution—and this by courts, not representative bodies. And to the extent that jurisdiction was unclear and a matter for debate, it was a system in which both levels of government soon learned that jurisdictional uncertainty provided a good pretext for refusing to address issues that divided the electorate.[142] Despite their liberal "creed that a wise decision can only be arrived at through the discussion of it from every point of view,"[143] the autonomists' scrupulous attention to the defense of provincial autonomy made them limit and narrow discussion in precisely the way that Taylor says discussion is narrowed when political questions are discussed in terms of rights. The provincial autonomists in Ontario, in sum, insisted on defending their claims in the very language that Taylor associates with the "rights model," and to that extent their conception of politics suffered from some of the very symptoms that a participatory form of decentralized power is meant to cure.[144]

Put slightly differently, it is not entirely clear that the principles on which provincialism has rested historically are as hostile to the "rights model" as Taylor's depiction of these "two packages" would imply. I have wanted to argue, rather, that beneath the important superficial differences there is actually a deep affinity between the claim for provincial autonomy mediated by the rule of law and Taylor's "rights model." At the level of political rhetoric, for instance, it is useful to remember that provincial governments still couch their claims to power in terms of rights, and they still reinforce these claims by comparing provincial rights to individual rights.[145] Indeed, it is at least arguable that one of the reasons that Canadians accepted the idea of an entrenched Charter of Rights so readily is that the longstanding debate over provincial rights had long since inured them to the usefulness and attractiveness of the language of rights, of legal boundaries, and of courts as impartial arbiters.

Yet there is a still deeper, substantive affinity here between the historical pursuit of provincial autonomy and the "rights model" that Taylor slights. For if the provincial autonomists were successful in protecting the integrity and sovereignty of local self-government, the record suggests that they neither could nor wanted to disentangle themselves completely from the liberal regard for the protection of individual freedom that informed the vision of the rule of law. To the extent that the provincial autonomists were liberals, therefore, it is arguable that, in legitimizing a rights model of federalism, they both protected provincial power and actually laid the conceptual groundwork for the Charter of Rights that places substantive limits on provincial power. In this sense the Charter represents the fulfillment of the liberal premises that informed the movement for provincial autonomy, in a way, however, that is not necessarily congenial to provincial autonomy. In sum, the Charter follows in the tradition of, and is the better alternative to, the power of disallowance as a way of protecting individual rights.

Taylor is surely right to say that the problem of community remains the crucial, unresolved question facing Canadians. And he is probably right, as well, that as long as it remains unresolved, there is bound to be a decentralizing impulse in Canadian politics that will always distinguish it from American politics. But it is too simple, even if attractive, to picture the alternative futures of Canada as resting on a choice between "two packages"—one decentralized and participatory, the other centralist and rights-oriented. The truth is that these visions cannot be so easily "packaged" or disentangled from a history in which each is implicated in the other. Like it or not, the Charter of Rights, and more recently the Meech Lake Accord, are in all of their awkwardness a fair representation of the various traditions from which they have grown. The attempt to preserve rights while allowing legislatures to override them under certain circumstances; the attempt to protect minority linguistic rights across the country while acknowledging that Quebec is a distinct society; the attempt to protect mobility while allowing provinces to prefer their own citizens if need be; the declaration that rights are fundamental but also, and explicitly, subject to reasonable limitation—all of this reflects not merely a compromise between two visions of Canada, but the extent to which each vision entails or is parasitic upon the other. What we are then left with is not a choice between our history and our future, between our more participatory tradition and the modern malaise, or between 1867 and 1776. We are left, rather, with two visions of Canada produced, bound inextricably together and held in tension by our history.

CHAPTER 6

Provincial Autonomy
and the Division of Powers

The first goal of the provincial rights movement in Ontario was to win recognition of the principle that each provincial government is autonomous, sovereign within its sphere of jurisdiction, and independent of the federal government. This basic objective informed the attempts following Confederation to abolish the practice of dual representation, to establish the provincial legislatures as fully clothed parliaments, to force the abandonment of reservation and to tame the power of disallowance. The provincial autonomists were not content, however, to define autonomy simply in terms of legal independence or supremacy within the sphere designated by the constitution. Rather, they were committed to the further view that real autonomy involved a claim to political power; that provincial autonomy meant both independence from the federal government and a fair sharing of power with it. Thus, while their strategy was on the one hand to render the sphere of provincial jurisdiction resistant to federal encroachments, it was, on the other, to make this exclusive sphere of jurisdiction as capacious as the words of the constitution would allow. While the two goals were connected and intertwined, it remains important for the purpose of analytical clarity not to conflate them.

This chapter will focus on the second strand of the provincialists' definition of autonomy, the constitutional division of powers set out in sections 91 and 92 of the BNA Act, but the story's outline will be familiar. I have argued throughout this study that the provincial autonomists in Ontario insisted that their provincialist understanding of federalism was the only one that could be reconciled with the basic political beliefs that most self-respecting Canadian politicians honored. Their vision of federalism was as powerful as it was because it drew upon the heavy symbolism associated in late-nineteenth-century English Canada with the values of responsible democratic government, imperialism and the rule of law. At the same time, however, I have wanted to suggest that the intellectual legacy of the Ontario provincial rights movement is rather more ambiguous than many assume. As successful as the provincial rights movement was in achieving its immediate goals, I have suggested that there was a deep tension, in its defense of provincial power, between the need to protect the sanctity of provincial communities and the desire to protect individual liberty. The provincialists strongly defended the autonomy and integrity of community, but they were also the carriers of a genuinely liberal strain in Canadian political culture that those like Charles Taylor would say threatens community.

A similar pattern of ambiguous triumph emerges from the early skirmishes over the division of powers. The conventional wisdom holds that the provincial rights movement was fortunate that in a series of key legal cases the Judicial Committee of the Privy Council (JCPC) interpreted the terms of the BNA Act in a way that betrayed its "provincialist bias."[1] There is, to be sure, considerable truth in this statement. But I will argue that the autonomists' vigorous, and apparently successful, defense of provincial power was rather more contingent and fragile than most commentators have been willing to admit. And I will argue that the principles that underlay this constitutional defense of provincial power could be manipulated to support federal power almost as easily as provincial power—a possibility, indeed, which the provincialists themselves acknowledged and from which they ultimately profited.

II

The leadership of the movement for greater provincial power fell to the same cast of characters that had spearheaded the campaigns against dual representation, an intrusive lieutenant-governor and the disallowance power—namely the lawyers who led the Liberal party. Edward Blake, whose defense of responsible government and provincial "home rule" were important elements of the case against federal interference in provincial affairs, played an equally important part in the formative jurisdiction debates, first as premier, then as leader of the federal opposition and, finally, as counsel hired to argue several key cases before the JCPC. Oliver Mowat, the Liberal premier of Ontario from 1872 until 1896, is widely regarded as the leading constitutional strategist among the autonomists, having successfully challenged the federal government's broad reading of the BNA Act in several crucial cases during his tenure as premier.[2] In my view, however, neither Blake nor Mowat expounded the provincialist reading of the constitution as comprehensively or exposed its difficulties as clearly as David Mills, the "philosopher from Bothwell." It is, therefore, on Mills that I will concentrate in the ensuing discussion of provincial rights and the division of powers.

Mills's approach to the division of powers rested on three fundamental principles. He began from the premise, first, that the BNA Act had effectively divided sovereignty between two levels of government, federal and provincial, such that each was supreme within its constitutionally defined sphere; each had "exclusive" jurisdiction over the subjects allotted to it by sections 91 and 92 respectively of the BNA Act. If the federal and provincial governments had exclusive jurisdiction over a set of legislative subjects, it followed that each government had absolute dominion within the sphere defined or comprised by those subjects and, conversely, no right whatsoever to act in the other's sphere. This was classic legal liberalism applied to federalism; each government "was absolute within the limits assigned to it, but when it went outside it was nothing."[3]

This logic, as we have seen in some detail, was crucial to Mills's critique of the power of disallowance; it was no less fundamental to his understanding of the constitutional division of powers. Mills explained the connection between provincial independence and provincial power most systematically in 1877 in response to a suggestion made by Sir John A. Macdonald and others to deal with the problem of administering temperance legislation. The various attempts to regulate, control and ultimately prohibit the sale of liquor in late-nineteenth-century Canada form one of the central chapters in the larger story of federal-provincial relations. Several of the legal decisions which attempted to define the jurisdictional boundaries separating federal and provincial competence in the area were absolutely pivotal at the time and continue to guide legal argument even today; we will return to them later in this chapter. In 1877, however, few decisions had been rendered, and of those that had none was understood to be authoritative. Most active politicians seemed to accept that both levels of government had some interest in wanting to legislate on temperance, and most seemed to realize that both levels of government could make a plausible jurisdictional argument to support their legislation.

Such at least was the position of the Conservative MP, J. B. Robinson, who proposed that, since both levels of government had legitimate claims in the area, some form of "joint action"[4] on the question of liquor regulation was appropriate. More specifically, Robinson proposed to revivify a pre-Confederation scheme of prohibition which gave local communities the power to decide for themselves whether or not to go "dry." Robinson seems to have assumed both that the federal government could claim some power over the regulation of liquor and that Parliament probably did not want to exercise that power in any detail. Hence, his apparently inoffensive solution to the jurisdictional/political problem was to have the federal government define the general outlines of the law, leaving it to the various provincial legislatures to determine precisely how this local option was to be exercised. That would give provincial governments the freedom they needed to administer local options; to the extent that the federal government did have jurisdiction in the matter, this explicit delegation of power would also foreclose further jurisdictional challenges.

When Edward Blake challenged the idea that the federal government had the right to delegate such power to a province or municipality, John A. Macdonald sprung to his colleague Robinson's defense:

> It was clear to him that if the question of a Prohibitory Liquor Law was within the jurisdiction of Parliament, it had the power to delegate its authority to a subordinate body, and could even distinctly limit the Legislature of Ontario or Quebec to dealing with the subject in a certain way; and so in the case of municipalities. So long as Parliament had jurisdiction over the subject of legislation, as a matter of administration it could employ the medium of any subordinate body.[5]

Macdonald simply could not accept Blake's position that Parliament "could not delegate to any power the execution of its legislative rights."[6] From Macdonald's perspective, if Parliament had jurisdiction it also had the right to determine the rules by which its laws were administered. Should it desire, Parliament could use the provinces and municipalities as instruments to carry out the clearly expressed will of Parliament quite mechanically, but Macdonald's theory certainly did not require that these "subordinate bodies" be treated merely as "machines." If it chose, "Parliament could call on them to exercise their judgment as *quasi*-legislators"[7] within the broad guidelines established by the national government.

The reference to provinces as "subordinate bodies" roused Mills, who immediately rose to denounce Macdonald's understanding of federalism. According to Mills, Macdonald had to assume for the purpose of his scheme that the federal government had the right to act. Indeed, he had to assume that the federal government "possessed paramount power"[8] in the area, for in the absence of paramount power it was unclear how Parliament could delegate power to provincial legislatures here, withhold it from municipal legislatures there, or keep it for itself—all of which Macdonald had implied were possible in the name of administrative flexibility. Yet a national legislature exercising paramount power was incompatible with federalism. From Mills's perspective, the problem was that Macdonald still had not come to terms with the fact that, by the BNA Act, "the functions of Parliament and the Provincial Legislatures were separate and distinct."[9] What Macdonald stubbornly refused to accept was that under the BNA Act, indeed in any properly federal system, provinces did not hold power at the sufferance of the central government. The truth of the matter was that the provincial legislatures:

> had their own legitimate sphere and were as independent of Parliament as if they were separate and distinct sovereignties. There could be no question about that point, and the idea of paramount power was one wholly inconsistent with the federal system of Government which, under the constitution, had been established in this country.[10]

"Parliament had all power and authority so long as it attended to its own business and kept within the limits of the Constitution."[11] If it did not keep within the limits assigned to it, there "would not be a Federal system under which Provincial Legislatures had an independent existence within their own sphere, distinct from the power of the Dominion Parliament."[12]

Actually, Mills exaggerated, indeed distorted, Macdonald's jurisdictional claims. Macdonald and his colleague Robinson did indeed make certain assumptions about federal jurisdiction over liquor regulation, and they were willing to act in the absence of definitive judicial rulings. But Macdonald did not assume that the federal government had paramount power in the matter of liquor legislation. On the contrary, the resolution had been moved precisely because some, like Robinson, assumed that both federal and provincial governments had jurisdiction. What informed the delegation resolution, therefore, was not a belief in federal paramountcy, but the recognition of shared responsibility. Mills may have had good reason to think that Macdonald generally believed that the federal government had "paramount" authority over "subordinate" provincial legislatures, but in this case he missed the target.

Yet in a way Mills's distortion of Macdonald's position is not decisive because it is clear that he would not have accepted Macdonald's delegation doctrine anyway—even on Macdonald's own terms and even if, as here, it worked to provincial advantage. Mills's position was as simple as it was uncompromising. Just as the federal government had no right to interfere in those matters beyond its jurisdiction, so it had no right to delegate or in any way deprive itself of its own power to

legislate on those matters which the BNA Act had confided exclusively
to it. If Macdonald's views on delegation were accepted, "there was not
a power possessed by Parliament under the British North America
Act" that might not be "handed over to and vested in Provincial
Legislatures."[13] Macdonald's delegation proposal might benefit the
provinces in the short run, but Mills was clearly worried that such a
practice would degenerate into precisely the sort of system that some
maintain was ultimately realized in the 1970s—a system in which the
boundaries dividing federal and provincial jurisdiction had become
"imaginary"[14] and in which federal and provincial politicians in effect
traded jurisdiction to gain some sort of competitive advantage.[15] If
ever that were to occur, Mills warned, it would ultimately work to the
disadvantage of the provinces. At least there would no longer be "a
federal system under which Provincial Legislatures had an independent existence within their own sphere, distinct from the power of the
Dominion Parliament."[16]

Mills's criticism of Macdonald's approach to the prohibition question was very similar to his criticism of Sir John's understanding of disallowance. From Mills's perspective, Macdonald behaved as if the
highest act of federal statesmanship was to assess the national interest case by case and act accordingly. If that required striking down
provincial legislation, so be it; if, as here, it required taking into account provincial diversity by delegating authority to the provincial
legislatures, that was fine too. The crucial condition of this "political
federalism"[17] was that the federal government have sufficient maneuverability to construct the right policy mix to achieve its ends.

Mills began from the quite different premise that the success of
federalism depended not on Macdonaldian statesmanship, but the
strict adherence to law and the constitutional boundary that divides
federal from provincial authority; and he was led, therefore, to take
jurisdiction rather more seriously. If the maintenance of federalism
really depended on the strict separation of federal and provincial
spheres, then it followed that the first and most important question in
a federation was, in Patrick Monahan's words, "to identify and to
police the boundaries separating the various zones of absolute entitlement from each other."[18] To embrace the principle of divided sovereignty was to put jurisdiction—and the rule of law—first. The highest
act of federal statesmanship was, thus, not to act in the national interest, to find the best balance between uniformity and diversity, or to
choose among a number of overlapping and conflicting claims and
interests. For a legal liberal like Mills, the highest act of federal statesmanship consisted, rather, in understanding and respecting the division of authority set down in the constitution, the fundamental law.

This respect for the legal boundaries separating federal and pro-vincial jurisdiction leads directly to the second pillar of Mills's ap-proach to the division of powers. For if Mills believed that political power in a federation is constitutionally divided between two inde-pendent and distinct governments, he was also committed to the position that the provincial share of that power under the terms of the BNA Act was equal to, if not greater than, the federal government's; and even in the very first years of Confederation he frequently rose in the House of Commons to question the propriety of national legisla-tion that allegedly violated provincial jurisdiction. Mills's targets in the first years of Confederation were varied, but in most cases they con-cerned legislation that he believed fell to the provincial legislatures by virtue of their exclusive power over "property and civil rights." He took strong exception to Macdonald's unilateral attempt in 1869 to unify the law relating to property and civil rights in the common law prov-inces. Such a reform, he argued, could only be carried out with the consent of the provinces themselves.[19] He opposed one bill that would have given the federal government the authority to carry out compul-sory vaccination campaigns and another that would have given fed-eral inspectors the authority to halt the spread of contagious disease among animals, again on the argument that these were matters that affected the property and civil rights of citizens.[20] Together with Blake, Mills opposed workplace safety legislation designed to protect miners in B. C. because "the Local Legislature had clearly control over matters relating to the protection of life and property, and could make all reg-ulations with a view to maintaining order and preventing disasters."[21] He even opposed the appropriation of funds to conduct a national geological survey because he "thought the matter was entirely one with which the Local Government should deal."[22]

These specific examples reflect a stark difference in the way Mac-donald and Mills approached the division of powers in general. To recall, Macdonald introduced the terms of the Confederation settle-ment to the Canadian assembly in 1865 by arguing that centralization provided security against the sort of political unraveling that had occurred in the United States. By giving the central government "all the great subjects of legislation," the conferees had "avoided that great source of weakness" which had "been the cause of the disruption of the United States."[23] Mills disagreed not only with Macdonald's ac-count of the causes of the Civil War[24] but also with the prime minister's underlying assumption that strength at the center was simply better than the alternative. As if responding to Macdonald's view, Mills told Parliament in 1869 that if ever it were "a question whether Federal or Local Legislatures should be destroyed" his view was that "the country would suffer far less by the destruction of the Federal power."[25] It would be hard to imagine a clearer statement than this of Mills's jurisdictional decentralism.

Third, Mills's approach to the division of powers was court-centered. If federal and provincial legislatures had absolute dominion within their respective spheres, it was obviously crucial to know where one sphere began and the other ended. Since the distinctive thing about those boundaries was that they were established by law, it fell to the courts, quite naturally in Mills's view, to determine in any given case whether legislation was legitimate, that is whether it was *intra vires* the legislature that had passed it. To employ a familiar image, the courts were the "umpires" of the federal system whose task it was to resolve jurisdictional disputes according to the rules established by the constitution. And the final court of appeal—in the Canadian case the JCPC—enjoyed a position of special prominence.

The notion that the courts should serve as authoritative jurisdictional umpires was hardly unique to Mills. All of the major participants in post-Confederation politics accepted the role of the courts in this regard (although for a time there was considerable controversy about which courts ought to be entrusted with the task),[26] and judicial analysis has become a mainstay of federalism scholarship ever since. Alan Cairns has warned that it is all too easy to exaggerate the influence of judicial decisions on the evolution of Canadian federalism; it is, as he puts it, simply implausible to believe that a few judges deciding two or three cases a year could singlehandedly have changed the course of Canadian federalism.[27] Yet it is no less misleading to suggest that the power of the courts in general and the JCPC in particular can be understood simply in terms of the discrete cases that came before it. For the confirmed legal liberal like Mills, the courts were much more than umpires in the narrow sense that they "settled" or "resolved" disputes that the political system itself had been unable to resolve. The courts did that to be sure, but Mills also treated the decisions of the courts as authoritative cues about how *political* institutions should address constitutional questions. "The question of jurisdiction," he once told Parliament, "is a difficult question, on which the House is liable to err. But we have now the decisions of legal tribunals which enable us to interpret the Constitution...."[28]

As the final arbiter in jurisdictional disputes involving the federal and provincial governments, the influence of the JCPC thus extended far beyond the legal results themselves. The JCPC was so influential in the formative years of Canadian Confederation because it helped to shape the structure of the political debate over federalism that raged throughout the period in Parliament, in the provincial legislatures, in the newspapers and on the political hustings. The JCPC both defined an approach or method of constitutional interpretation and rendered substantive judgments concerning the precise scope of federal and provincial jurisdiction. The difficulty, however, is that its judgments were almost always terse, frequently elliptical, and sometimes simply contradictory. All of this posed an enormous challenge to someone like Mills, who had to adapt the Judicial Committee's technical decisions and legal reasoning to the real world of party politics and intergovernmental relations. His attempts in the 1880s and 1890s to grapple with and apply the JCPC's doctrine to political practice provide an enormously revealing perspective on the development of the provincial rights movement and on the larger attempt to sustain a principled legal liberalism.

III

Among the first judgments rendered on the Canadian division of powers by the JCPC, the 1881 case of *Citizens Insurance Company of Canada* v. *Parsons*[29] stands out. *Parsons* was by no means the first judicial attempt to make sense of the division of powers set out in sections 91 and 92 of the BNA Act. A considerable number of jurisdictional cases had been decided by the provincial courts in the first decade of Confederation. From its establishment in 1875, the Supreme Court of Canada had been hearing cases that involved the division of powers. For that matter, the JCPC itself had already rendered judgment in a handful of Canadian cases that raised jurisdictional questions. *Parsons*, however, merits special attention because it marked the Privy Council's first sustained attempt to develop a principled methodology with which to approach the interpretation the BNA Act; and it was the first serious attempt to define clearly the key categories of federal and provincial power. It was, as Mills himself put it, a "most important case."[30]

Parsons involved a challenge to the constitutionality of an early piece of consumer protection legislation in Ontario which standardized the terms of insurance policies. The statute regulated the terms of insurance policies; it was challenged on the grounds that legislation of this sort affected trade and commerce, a matter which falls under the exclusive jurisdiction of the federal government.[31]

The decision rendered by Sir Montague Smith, speaking for the Judicial Committee, is interesting in the first instance for the light it sheds on the JCPC's methodology. *Parsons* forced the Judicial Committee to address itself to the structure of sections 91 and 92 of the

BNA Act, the core sections of the act which divided legislative power between the national Parliament and the provincial legislatures respectively. The obvious difficulty in interpreting these two sections, Smith admitted frankly, was that subjects assigned to each level of government did not appear to be "altogether distinct and different"[32] from each other. Indeed, it seemed at first blush that "some of the classes of subjects assigned to the provincial legislatures unavoidably ran into and were embraced by some of the enumerated classes of subjects in sect. 91."[33] If that were the case, Smith understood that conflicts were bound to arise such that it would be impossible to allow both federal and provincial legislation to stand, and he drew the conclusion that in "cases of a conflict of power" the BNA Act itself gave "pre-eminence to the dominion parliament."[34]

The ready acknowledgment of jurisdictional overlap and conflict was, however, something of a false methodological start. While Smith could imagine any number of ways in which an "*apparent* conflict"[35] between federal and provincial governments might arise, he simply could not believe that those who drafted the BNA Act could possibly have intended "that a conflict should exist"[36] between provincial and federal governments in the ordinary course of things. For one thing, the federal government's allotment of power was so general and open-ended that the rule of routine conflict and federal paramountcy would inevitably eviscerate provincial power. If the federal government were allowed to act freely on every aspect of "marriage and divorce," with the additional guarantee that in the case of conflict their law would prevail, provincial initiatives would be utterly vulnerable to competing federal legislation, even though section 92 clearly granted them exclusive authority over the "solemnization of marriage in the province."[37] And that, Smith argued, simply made nonsense of the division of powers. "The legislature" that promulgated the BNA Act, he concluded, "could not have intended that the powers exclusively assigned to the provincial legislature should be absorbed in those given to the dominion parliament."[38]

The alternative to reading sections 91 and 92 as a set of overlapping and potentially conflicting jurisdictional claims was to define conflict away, as much as possible, by limiting the meaning of the key provisions. Smith put the point clearly as follows:

> It could not have been the intention that a conflict should exist; and in order to prevent such a result, the two sections must be read together, and the language of one interpreted, and, where necessary, modified, by that of the other. In this way it may, in most cases, be found possible to arrive at a reasonable and practical construction

of the language of the sections, so as to reconcile the respective powers they contain, and give effect to all of them.[39]

This is arguably the critical methodological statement of the Judicial Committee's early Canadian decisions. Jurisdictional conflict had to be avoided if the exclusive areas of provincial power were to be saved; it could be avoided if the courts defined sections 91 and 92 as spheres of legislative entitlement that were contiguous rather than overlapping, and limited rather than open-ended.

This premise led Smith to view the constitution as a set of mutually exclusive spheres of legislative powers, and it led him, further, to argue that the essential function of the Judicial Committee was to illuminate and reinforce the jurisdictional boundaries created by the BNA Act. When confronted with a jurisdictional controversy such as the one at issue in *Parsons*, the task of the Judicial Committee, therefore, was to ascertain the nature, the "pith and substance," of the legislation and match it against one of the classes or subject headings contained in sections 91 and 92. True to his methodological word, Smith proceeded in *Parsons* to consider first whether the Ontario legislation fit under the rubric of "property and civil rights," then to consider whether it was also a matter involving "trade and commerce." Having explained why the Ontario regulations directly affected civil rights and why the fire insurance business was not really a trade, he concluded neatly that the federal government's "legislative authority does not in the present case conflict or compete with the power over property and civil rights assigned to the legislature of Ontario...."[40] Ontario's legislation therefore stood, its sovereignty over the regulation of trade contracts within the province firmly staked.

Parsons provides the clearest exposition of the Judicial Committee's method, but it is not an isolated example. In a decision rendered a year later, Sir Montague Smith reiterated the basic "principle of construction"[41] that stressed the mutually exclusive nature of federal and provincial power under the BNA Act. The task of the Judicial Committee, Smith asserted, was to determine "the true nature and character of the legislation in the particular instance under discussion...in order to ascertain the *class* of subject to which it *really* belongs"[42]— not the *classes* to which it might *arguably* belong. Legislation was ordinarily either federal or provincial, but not both, because this was the only way to preserve the exclusive authority, the sovereignty, of each legislature over the subjects granted to it by the constitution. This remained the prevailing assumption throughout the 1880s and 1890s, and, judging by the continued appeal to legislative autonomy, it remains a part of the legal mind to this day.[43]

Patrick Monahan has suggested that *Parsons* illustrates a "categorical" model of legal reasoning. The term is useful because it hints at two crucial assumptions behind the JCPC's approach. The Judicial Committee's method was categorical in the primary sense that jurisdictional spheres had to be understood (to use an image that would later become famous) as "watertight compartments" of mutually exclusive jurisdictional capacity. However terms like "commerce" or "property and civil rights" might be understood in other contexts, within the confines of the BNA Act they had to be read in light of each other so as to "reconcile" and "give effect to all of them." This form of judicial analysis therefore placed enormous emphasis—and this is the second sense of the term—on defining the categories themselves. The first question to be asked in a jurisdictional case was not whether each side had legitimate interests that ought to be balanced, or whether the policy implications made national legislation more desirable, much less whether the legislation was wise. Rather, the first task in cases like *Parsons* was to define the nature of the impugned legislation and match this to the categories of the BNA Act itself.

This methodological gloss on *Parsons* is useful in understanding Mills's own interpretation of the BNA Act, for Mills was relentless in his pursuit of the sort of definitional clarity that the JCPC's method required. Time after time Mills challenged the Macdonald government's assumption of federal jurisdiction over matters that he believed fell within provincial jurisdiction; and invariably his critique began with an inquiry into the essence or nature of the subject under consideration. Thus Mills was convinced that "there are numerous questions that in their nature are local"[44] and which therefore have been assigned to the local legislatures. "The subject of trade" was essentially different from and had "nothing to do with manufactures"[45]—an uncompromising conceptual distinction on which the U. S. Supreme Court later came to grief. The provincial control of property and civil rights was quite different from the federal power to regulate the criminal law. Indeed, as Mills suggested in his classical legal fashion, "the domain of civil rights ... lies contiguous to the criminal law."[46]

Nor did Mills lose sight of the purpose of the exercise. One had to pay strict attention to the categorical definitions of terms both in order to maintain the jurisdictional boundaries that were the crucial condition of federalism and to preserve the distinction between what was "law" and what "politics." As he put it on one occasion: "The House has, of course, before it two questions, which are entirely distinct in character. The first is whether it has jurisdiction to deal with this particular matter; and the second is, with regard to the merits of the measure.... Of course it is not necessary that we should go into the discussion of the merits of the Bill at all if in the opinion of the House it is *ultra vires.*"[47] The success of federalism depended on spotting constitutional landmarks and maintaining jurisdictional boundaries, and Mills the parliamentarian grew famous as a self-appointed constitutional border patrol.

The heart of Mills's approach thus involved defining the categories set out in sections 91 and 92 of the BNA Act and matching legislation to them. This exercise required considerable analytical nimbleness, and, following the JCPC's lead, Mills developed the necessary tools and refinements that allowed him, as a professional lawyer, to spot the crucial constitutional "landmarks." Thus, while the boundaries between federal and provincial jurisdiction were generally clear, Mills noted that sometimes a matter that was within one government's jurisdiction could still have an "incidental" effect on a matter exclusively within the power of another. In this case care had to be taken to distinguish "the principal matter" dealt with from the "subordinate" and "incidental."[48] To use the language that eventually triumphed with the JCPC, it all depended under which "aspect" legislation was viewed —which in turn made careful scrutiny of legislation and a clear understanding of the essential differences between, for instance, "criminal law" and the protection of "property and civil rights" all the more crucial.

Having made the basic distinctions between federal and provincial categories, Mills then proceeded to dissect each set ever more finely, and to carve certain exceptions (especially) from the broad list of federal powers. In the debate over factory labor legislation, for instance, he pointed out that the provincial legislatures had been granted power to impose fines, penalties or imprisonment in the course of enforcing laws made pursuant to provincial jurisdiction.[49] A provincial legislature, indeed, could effectively "make a disregard of certain of its mandates, a crime; but it does not by reason of this expediency, lose its jurisdiction over the principal subject, nor exceed its own authority in so legislating."[50] Federal and provincial governments enjoyed exclusive jurisdiction in the matters set out in the constitution; but that did not mean that the criminal law was "a kind of sacred enclosure into which a Provincial Legislature has no power to enter."[51]

Occasionally even Mills lost his constitutional bearings. Confronted with national legislation to regulate child labor, Mills had to admit that "it is not easy to draw the line where police regulation ends and where ordinary criminal regulation begins."[52] First he tried to reproduce the argument he had used in the factory labor debate by suggesting that there were "special subjects of criminal legislation which necessarily fall within the jurisdiction of the Province."[53] Then he maintained that this was really one of those cases which could plausibly be defined either as a federal or a provincial matter. In the end, and with just a hint of exasperation, he suggested that it might be prudent were both levels of government to look into it.[54]

Weaving all of this into a coherent whole proved to be enormously difficult, especially when the JCPC's jurisprudence itself was thin and fluid. The question that perhaps gave Mills (and many others) the greatest difficulty was liquor. During the 1880s, a series of constitutional cases had established that the regulation and licensing of alcohol consumption fit squarely in provincial jurisdiction. Prohibition was another matter. Oliver Mowat, the premier of Ontario, had fought hard to win exclusive control of licensing—in part, it appears, because licensing was a ready source of revenue and patronage. By the 1890s, he was under tremendous pressure from temperance forces to move beyond regulation and to enact compulsory anti-drink legislation in Ontario.[55] For various reasons he was little inclined to accede to their demands, but as Paul Romney has noted , he had to do something to show his "good faith."[56] Mowat responded, on the one hand, by freeing local communities within the province to prohibit the sale of liquor locally—that is, to adopt a scheme similar in spirit to the national program of prohibition with a local option. On the other hand, Mowat maintained that he would not feel entirely confident about the act until the people of Ontario had had an opportunity to declare themselves directly on the question of prohibition and before the act's legitimacy had been established by the courts. One of Mowat's reasons for hesitating was removed by a plebiscite that returned a clear majority in favor of prohibition. Mowat thereupon submitted seven questions to the court in the form of a reference case, all of which were concerned with one or another aspect of the basic jurisdictional question at issue: given the existence of a national prohibitory act, does Ontario have the right to enact its own prohibitory scheme?

The prohibitionists did not focus solely on the provincial legislature, however. Like Mowat, Mills found himself under tremendous pressure from a variety of temperance interests to support some form of prohibition legislation—only on a national rather than a provincial scale. And like his Liberal colleague Mowat in Ontario, Mills justified his unwillingness to act hastily on jurisdictional grounds. In Mills's view, the federal government's right to ban the sale of liquor was by no means clear. The JCPC, in the 1882 case *Russell v. the Queen*, had upheld the national Temperance Act. But that case had addressed only the question of national jurisdiction, and Mills was persuaded that it was not a precedent that would last anyway. Thus, until the courts had dealt with Mowat's reference case and cleared the constitutional air, Mills was unwilling to commit himself one way or the other.

Mills's position raised the ire of many prohibitionists, two of whom, the Rev. Dr. J. S. Ross and the Rev. W. A. Mackay, undertook to denounce him in a series of letters to the Toronto *Globe* in the summer and fall of 1895.[57] Their basic charge was that Mills refused to support the imposition of a national program of prohibition because he was beholden to certain "liquor interests." His reservations concerning the constitutionality of national prohibition, they argued, were simply a pretext to avoid having to take a position that would betray his alliance with brewers and liquor manufacturers. The JCPC, it was noted, had already concluded in *Russell v. the Queen* that the federal government had the power to pass prohibitory legislation. Moreover, the ministers argued that the reference case before the JCPC had to do with the provincial government's power, not the federal government's jurisdiction. The decision of their Lordships in London, Ross argued,[58] would have no bearing whatsoever on the federal government's right to legislate. At best it would determine if the provincial government might also legislate; that is, it would decide whether there is concurrent jurisdiction in the matter of prohibition.

Mills responded to these criticisms, first in the *Globe*, then in Parliament, by lecturing his interlocutors (as he was used to lecturing John A. Macdonald) on the meaning of the division of powers. The problem with the Rev. Ross's characterization of the constitutional question was that he assumed that federal and provincial governments could both be allowed to legislate because prohibition was a matter of concurrent jurisdiction. But this was wrong. "There are but two matters," Mills wrote, "that, by our constitution, are made concurrent—agriculture and immigration."[59] These two subjects were exceptions to the rule that power is divided into exclusive spheres; "there are no other matters upon which each may legislate upon the same express subject."[60] Mills of course admitted that the legislation of one level might "incidentally" affect or "overlap" with a subject matter belonging exclusively to the other. If, for example, the provincial government were to ban the manufacture of liquor, that would incidentally affect interprovincial trade and commerce inasmuch as it would remove goods from the national market. But that did not alter the basic constitutional fact that the provincial government alone has the right to regulate the manufacture, and the federal government the interprovincial trade, of liquor. As he put it to Parliament, sections 91 and 92 vest power "exclusively" in the respective legislatures, and "the word exclusively means exclusively."[61]

"Does not Mr. Ross know that exclusive does not mean concurrent?"[62] Mills's rejoinder to his critics degenerated into sarcasm because he believed they were obtuse in their refusal to understand a distinction that was self-evident; and having failed to recognize the elementary concepts of federal constitutionalism, they could not possibly understand why he was reticent to act before the JCPC had rendered its definitive judgment. If the JCPC granted exclusive jurisdiction over the question of prohibition to the provincial governments, Parliament's hands would be tied. For that reason it was only sensible to wait for the JCPC to speak.

Actually, Mills seems to have been confident that the JCPC would not view prohibition as an all-or-nothing proposition, in which one government, and only one government, had complete responsibility for all aspects of prohibition. His best guess, rather, was that the Judicial Committee would "divide the jurisdiction" over prohibition between the governments by assigning "importations and general traffic to the Dominion, and other matters relating to production or to local traffic, to the provinces."[63] But this in no way altered his strategy of patience. If their Lordships divided jurisdiction in the way he predicted they would, the federal government would still be prohibited from legislating on that part of the subject that fell within provincial jurisdiction—"matters relating to production or local traffic"—as, conversely, the provincial legislature would be barred from legislating on that aspect of prohibition that fell exclusively within federal jurisdiction. Thus, while the questions put to the JCPC addressed only the provincial legislature's right to act, the answers given would almost certainly affect the federal government's ability to act. That is why he believed the only "reasonable course" was "to have the debate adjourned"[64] until the Judicial Committee had rendered its decision.

When the Judicial Committee eventually ruled in May 1896, their Lordships confounded Mills's expectation and forced him to reconsider his intransigent opposition to the idea of concurrent jurisdiction. Instead of parceling out jurisdiction in the way Mills had predicted, the JCPC validated provincial jurisdiction, sustained its earlier broad view of national power in *Russell*, showed that the two prohibitory acts could both be left standing because they were different in detail, and touched briefly on the problem of jurisdictional collision and repugnancy. True, Lord Watson did not use the word "concurrent" explicitly and so did not vindicate Mills's opponents completely. All the same, the Judicial Committee did make it clear that under certain circumstances federal and provincial legislation could overlap, co-exist or directly conflict. These possibilities Mills had been at pains to deny since he had challenged John A. Macdonald's attempt in the 1870s to make federal and provincial governments jointly responsible for liquor control.

Mills knew how to take jurisprudential cues, and he responded to the interpretive innovations secured by the *Local Prohibition* case by adapting his own interpretive approach to the new jurisprudential terrain. Mills never renounced his belief that each level of government enjoys exclusive jurisdiction over the subjects listed in sections 91 and 92, and he never abandoned his attempt to define potential conflicts away. He continued to look to the JCPC's decisions to judge "where the line should be drawn which separates Dominion legislative authority from that legislative authority which is vested in the province."[65] Yet after 1896, he was forced by the weight of the Judicial Committee's own authority to find room for a whole set of jurisprudential terms and problems which simply had not entered his vocabulary before that time—*de facto* concurrency, the conflict of laws, and paramountcy chief among them.

Mills was quickest to probe the jurisprudential potential of federal paramountcy. As long as Mills held to the *Parsons* view that federal and provincial legislation could not conflict in the ordinary course of things, he had paid little attention to the possibility that legislation could collide directly. He allowed for the possibility of "incidental" overlap and conflict, but that was just about all. Once the *Local Prohibition* case and others established the possibility that frontal collisions might well occur, however, it was of cardinal importance to know which act would prevail in the case of conflict. The Judicial Committee, Mills argued before Parliament in 1899, had developed a clear doctrine on the matter:

> ... in every case of Dominion legislation which comes within the enumerated powers of the Dominion, it is in the power of Parliament to extend its legislation so far as may be necessary to make that legislation effective. It may overlap and encroach upon the enumerated powers of a province, but when it does so it is paramount, and the authority of the province, for the time being, is in abeyance, if the statutes cannot stand together.[66]

Paramountcy thus not only resolved inconsistencies; it also helped to maintain jurisdictional exclusivity.

Mills had a more difficult time adapting his thinking to the possibility of concurrency. His approach to the prohibition question before

1896, to recall, had been to say that jurisdiction could be "divided" but not shared, and that it was exclusive, not overlapping. In the wake of the *Local Prohibition* decision, he was forced to qualify his approach. Two years after the Judicial Committee's decision in the *Local Prohibition* case, Mills wrote to the MP John A. Macdonell to explain the limitations upon provincial jurisdiction in the matter of prohibition. A provincial government had the power "to prohibit the manufacture and sale (of intoxicating liquors) for provincial consumption or for consumption in any district of the Province."[67] What it could not do—as he had said all along—was to prohibit the manufacture of liquor bound for interprovincial or international export. But Mills could place no similar limitations upon the federal government's authority. He understood perfectly well that the JCPC had upheld the federal government's general right to suppress the sale of liquor; and he understood that this general right, if exercised, was bound to interfere with provincial legislation in a way that could not be defined away and which, therefore, could not be squared with the position he had defended against the Reverends Ross and Mackay. "The Judicial Committee," he wrote to Macdonell, "held that a Provincial Legislature has jurisdiction to restrict the sale within the Province of intoxicating liquors, but that if there was a general restriction by the Dominion, then the Dominion Law, would operate, and the local law would for the time being remain in abeyance."[68] In short, the Judicial Committee held in the *Local Prohibition* case what Mills had earlier said was impossible—namely, that federal and provincial governments could in such circumstances legislate on the same express subject.

One might well charge Mills with inconsistency here, but in a way that would miss the point of the episode. For the real point is that during the 1880s and 1890s there did not yet exist a standard, orthodox approach to interpreting the division of powers. Mills was typical of his generation of lawyers inasmuch as he was struggling, with the help of the Supreme Court of Canada and the JCPC, to develop a coherent method of constitutional construction during two decades when the "correct" method of interpretation was very much up for grabs. He was guilty of the occasional false start; he pursued some methodological dead ends; and, as in the prohibition question, he was compelled to adapt his approach, perhaps even to flip-flop, in light of the decisions rendered by the courts. But Mills is important and useful for understanding the period because he ultimately got it "right." That is, by the time he died in 1903, Mills had become conversant with, indeed had helped to develop, a paradigm of constitutional interpretation that would dominate Canadian legal scholarship for the next fifty years and which, even now, remains firmly ensconced in, even if it is no longer the sole occupant of, the Canadian legal mind.[69]

IV

Parsons was important for the clarity and authority of its methodological assumptions. It was no less important for the fact that it was one of the first decisions rendered by the JCPC to hint at the jurisdictional space available to the provinces. As Sir Montague Smith legitimated Mills's emphasis on the exclusivity of each sphere of legislative power, so he confirmed Mills's reading that the provincial power over "property and civil rights" was as capacious as the federal government's power over "trade and commerce" was limited.

Smith forcefully rejected a definition of "property and civil rights" that would have limited the reach of provincial power to "such rights as flowed from the law."[70] He quickly concluded, on the contrary, that these words were "sufficiently large to embrace, in their fair and ordinary meaning, rights arising from contract."[71]

The trickier question from Smith's perspective was whether the regulation of insurance contracts was not also, or more clearly, a matter of "trade and commerce." If so, it would fall within federal jurisdiction. As Smith pointed out, the bare words of section 91:2, which gave the federal government exclusive jurisdiction over the "regulation of trade and commerce" pure and simple, were potentially limitless. The precise words of this provision, he said, were "sufficiently wide, if uncontrolled by the context and other parts of the Act, to include every regulation of trade ranging from political arrangements in regard to trade with foreign governments, requiring the sanction of parliament, down to minute rules for regulating particular trades."[72] But Smith was not willing to define the words "trade and commerce" in this almost unlimited way. Such a reading, he argued, was inconsistent with the internal context of the BNA Act, with the evident intentions of those who had drafted it, and with the meaning of the term as it had been used historically in Britain. He allowed that the federal power over trade and commerce included the "regulation of trade in matters of interprovincial concern" and perhaps the "general regulation of trade affecting the whole dominion,"[73] although he defined neither category precisely. Either way it was clear enough that the federal government's power to regulate trade and commerce could not extend so far as to regulate the contracts of a business that operated "in a single province."[74] And even if there were an interprovincial aspect to the case, Smith wasn't sure that the fire insurance industry was really a "trade" anyway—at least in the sense in which the term was used in the BNA Act.

Such statements as these were highly significant to the provincialist enterprise. By allowing the Ontario legislation to stand, the Judicial Committee at the very least raised the possibility that the provincial governments could quite legitimately occupy the fields of business, consumer and industrial regulation—areas in which they are now firmly, and probably immovably, situated. What is still more significant is that the liberal reading of provincial power in *Parsons* is only one example of a string of provincial victories before the Judicial Committee. Broadly speaking, the JCPC continued throughout the final decades of the nineteenth century to treat provincial claims in the generous fashion established by *Parsons*. The conventional scholarly judgment is that the Judicial Committee's work as a whole can be understood as an attempt "to accord a greater degree of autonomy to the provinces and thereby to make the Canadian system of government a more authentic federal system"[75] than John A. Macdonald, for one, would have wanted. The point was not entirely lost on Macdonald himself. After Ontario's boundary claim was upheld in 1888, even he was forced to concede that the Mowat government had had considerable "luck"[76] before the Judicial Committee. The comment was directed specifically at the boundary decision, but it is surely a fair assessment of the larger trend of JCPC decisions as well.

Here again, however, the Judicial Committee's jurisprudence is considerably more textured, ambiguous and evasive than the preceding summary taken alone would suggest. For while it is true that the JCPC tended to uphold provincial claims, its support for the provincialist reading of the BNA Act was far from monolithic. Indeed, despite what has been termed its "provincialist bias," the Judicial Committee flirted seriously, especially in the early years of its Canadian jurisprudence, with a construction of the constitution that was much friendlier to federal claims than *Parsons* and its progeny were.

The most striking counterexample to the jurisprudential tendency represented by *Parsons* is the famous 1882 case of *Russell v. the Queen*.[77] The *Russell* case involved the constitutionality of the Canada Temperance Act, passed at the insistence of an increasingly powerful temperance lobby in 1878. Like the provincial legislation discussed above, the Canada Temperance Act was a form of prohibitory legislation that came into effect only when a local population voted by plebiscite to enforce its provisions. Charles Russell was a merchant convicted of selling liquor in Fredericton, one of the communities which had exercised its local option and to which, therefore, the act applied in all its force. Russell appealed his conviction on the grounds that "it was not competent for the Parliament of Canada to pass the Act in question."[78] He appealed, in other words, on the grounds that the Temperance Act was *ultra vires* the federal government and an invasion of provincial jurisdiction.

The Judicial Committee explicitly followed the method prescribed in *Parsons* in addressing the jurisdictional question. According to the "principle of construction"[79] developed in *Parsons*, the task of the JCPC was to determine "the true nature and character of the legislation in the particular instance under discussion,"[80] and to match the legislation against one of the sets of powers, federal or provincial, set out in sections 91 and 92 of the BNA Act respectively. The Judicial Committee admitted that legislation falling under one government's list might incidentally affect the other level's power, but it was also careful to say that such "incidental interference does not alter the character of the law"[81] or in any way weaken a government's claim to "exclusive" jurisdiction. This was the methodological argument developed in *Parsons;* in *Russell* it was applied without qualification.

The substance of the decision in *Russell*, however, was decidely less congenial to provincial claims than *Parsons* had been—especially as regards the scope of the provincial power over "property and civil rights." In *Parsons*, the Judicial Committee accepted a broad definition of the term "property and civil rights" in the course of validating provincial legislation that standardized the terms of insurance policies. In *Russell*, on the contrary, the JCPC explicitly rejected the argument that temperance legislation was a matter relating or belonging to the subjects "property and civil rights." Lord Smith admitted freely that a law that prohibited the retail sale of liquor might "incidentally" affect "the free use of things in which men have property,"[82] but he maintained that temperance legislation was "primarily" a matter "relating to public order and safety,"[83] not property, and "that incidental interference does not alter the character of the law."[84] Nor, for similar reasons, could temperance legislation be fit under the rubric of "civil rights." "Laws of this nature," he argued, were "designed for the promotion of public order, safety and morals" and "belong to the subject of public wrongs rather than to that of civil rights."[85] This was, in short, legislation designed to promote the "peace, order and good government" of the country as a whole. It was, consequently, quite within the jurisdiction of the federal government to act.

With the benefit of hindsight, it is easy enough to see that *Russell* represents "the high-water mark in the early tendency of judicial review to provide a broad interpretation of the Dominion's legislative capacities."[88] The Judicial Committee never went so far as to overturn the decision in *Russell,* but it ultimately drew back from its broad reading of the words "peace, order and good government" and, under the leadership of Lord Viscount Haldane, transformed it into a residual power that could be invoked by Parliament only in cases of national emergency. Similarly, the Judicial Committee subsequently demonstrated a willingness to interpret provincial claims more generously than it did in *Russell,* even, as in the case of temperance, at the price of clarity and consistency. Indeed, it is arguable that the *Local Prohibition* case of 1896 is so difficult to unpack because it captured the Judicial Committee in partial metamorphosis. Unwilling to extend the logic of *Russell* yet unable to repudiate it altogether, the JCPC chose to validate both federal and provincial powers over temperance; that is, it confirmed the broad federal power that *Russell* had discovered while it allowed the provincial partnership that *Russell* had denied. To this day, *Russell* and the *Local Prohibition* case, taken together, pose a challenge to any commentator who hopes to find a consistent set of jurisprudential principles underlying the division of powers in Canada. The fit between *Russell* and the later decisions of Lord Viscount Haldane is still less comfortable.

In the years immediately following *Russell,* however, none of this was clear. What was clear was, first, that the Judicial Committee had taken a position that pulled back from its original musings in *Parsons* on the subject of jurisdiction; and second, that if the principles of *Russell* were generalized, they would pose a grave threat to the provincialist position. It is hardly surprising, therefore, that committed provincialists like David Mills should have taken the judgment in *Russell* very seriously. Nor is it surprising that *Russell* forced them to develop a more vigorous and complete defense of their own position.

At one level Mills anticipated the modern reaction to *Russell* almost perfectly, for like many modern commentators he clearly believed that the case had been wrongly decided. Mills's criticism of the *Russell* decision was different from conventional modern criticisms, however, in that he was careful to deflect blame for the decision away from the JCPC itself and toward the lawyers who had presented the provincial case in London. The real difficulty with the *Russell* decision, Mills said, was that the lawyers arguing the provincial case had botched the job because they "did not seem to know that (the sale of liquor) would be a subject coming within provincial jurisdiction."[87] Mills was especially critical of Judah Benjamin, the former Confederate leader who argued the province's case before the Judicial Committee. Benjamin was "a most able and distinguished lawyer."[88] The difficulty was that he "had no knowledge whatever of the municipal institutions of the provinces of the Dominion,"[89] and he simply did not know that prohibitory legislation, especially in Ontario, had historically been undertaken at the local level as a form of municipal regulation. Being "wholly unacquainted with the local institutions of this country,"[90] Benjamin had missed the opportunity to defend prohibitory legislation as a form of municipal regulation properly under provincial control. He was, therefore, "not in that regard qualified to argue this question satisfactorily before the Judicial Committee of the Privy Council."[91]

From Mills's perspective, the recognition of Benjamin's negligence allowed provincialists to treat *Russell* as an anomalous case that possessed little authority. If the problem with the provincial case for control over prohibition was in the presentation, then it was only a matter of time before the case would be argued correctly and persuasively. By the mid-1890s, Mills was convinced that domestic courts more familiar with the historical context of prohibition in Canada had already removed much of the "foundation"[92] on which *Russell* rested. Indeed, it was precisely because he was certain that the Judicial Committee would reconsider *Russell's* broad grant of federal power that Mills acted throughout the 1890s as if jurisdiction over prohibition were still an open question. What his critics interpreted as a cynical attempt to avoid taking a stand on prohibition was, from Mills's perspective, a perfectly reasonable course of action in light of the fragility of the *Russell* precedent. If *Russell* really was about to be superseded, overturned or at least qualified, did it not make sense to wait for a new discussion of federal and provincial jurisdiction over prohibition before acting?

At a deeper level, however, Mills understood perfectly well that Judah Benjamin was not entirely to blame for *Russell*. The Judicial Committee, after all, had not merely overlooked the possibility that prohibition could be defended as a form of municipal regulation. The far more serious problem, from a provincialist perspective, was that the Judicial Committee had explicitly denied that prohibition fit under the rubric of "property and civil rights." *Russell* effectively posed a direct and potentially devastating threat to what Mills had assumed was the principal source of provincial power. He could not assume that the Judicial Committee would back away innocently from the subversive principle established in *Russell*, and he could not afford, therefore, to allow it to go unanswered.

Mills elaborated his alternative understanding of the meaning of the words "property and civil rights" in a remarkable series of speeches before Parliament in the mid-1880s, in which he declared his opposition to a number of regulatory initiatives undertaken by the Macdonald government. Of these, three stand out. The first involved legislation, brought to Parliament in 1884, that imposed penalties on manufacturers who had adulterated food and drugs by misrepresenting their contents. The government treated the food adulteration act as a routine piece of regulatory legislation. The minister who introduced the measure to the House, John Costigan, noted that the subject had "attracted very great attention in all countries," and he presumed that "no one in this House (would) deny the importance of a measure of this kind."[93] The Liberal opposition quibbled about the statute's wording and questioned minor details, but before Mills rose to speak no one had seriously questioned the federal government's right to pass the legislation. The participants, government and opposition alike, simply assumed that as the legislation affected the conditions under which goods were bought and sold, especially in the interprovincial and foreign market, it fell under the federal power to regulate trade and commerce.

What most members of Parliament assumed, Mills denied. The legislation before Parliament regulated the conditions under which goods might be bought and sold. That is, it forbade a manufacturer from producing goods that were impure and from labelling them in a way that was misleading. In this way it constrained the freedom of the seller just as it protected the rights of the consumer. Moreover, the legislation clearly and directly regulated the way in which property was transferred, and it directly affected the civil rights of the buyer and seller. In Mills's opinion the legislation could only be understood, therefore, as "a municipal regulation, not embraced by the definition, regulation of trade, but under the phrase civil rights."[94] He concluded: "You can no more regulate the manufacture of drugs or any other class of articles than you can deal with the growth of a particular article. In all these cases you are dealing with property and the rights of property, as incident to property, and not making any regulation respecting trade."[95] Mills's rather extraordinary claim, in other words, was that the exclusive provincial power to regulate "property and civil rights" embraced "every relation in the state of society relating to private life."[96] It extended to virtually every imaginable transaction involving the relation between individuals (as in the case of manufacturers and consumers) or between the individual and the state (as in the cases of "religious liberty, civil liberty and political liberty").[97]

Mills sought support for his interpretation of the scope and meaning of the term "property and civil rights" in English and American law. What the Canadian constitution called the power to regulate "property and civil rights," English and American law called the "police power," but the object and effect of the law, Mills argued, were the same. The English courts had held that "the subject of trade and commerce has nothing to do with manufactures,"[98] and Mills maintained that according to English law "matters of this sort—adulteration of food, the selling of bread of light weight, everything of that sort... (had) been regarded as a matter of police regulation."[99] Of even greater authority was the American interpretation of English practice provided by Mills's former teacher at the University of Michigan, Thomas Cooley. "I have here," said Mills, "a small work by Justice Cooley, in which he deals with the question of civil rights, as they have been recognized by a series of decisions extending over centuries, rendered by the English common law courts.... With respect to these powers, Justice Cooley says:

> The authority to establish for the intercourse of the several members of the body politic with each other those rules of good conduct and good neighborhood which are calculated to prevent a conflict of rights and to ensure to each the uninterrupted enjoyment of his own, so far as is reasonably consistent with a corresponding enjoyment by others, is usually spoken of as the authority or power of police.'[100]

This was "precisely"[101] what the measure before Parliament concerned. The adulteration of food legislation was, Mills concluded, "beyond our power. It looks very much like a Police Bill, and should properly come under the jurisdiction of the Local Legislatures. It is an interference with their rights."[102]

Mills elaborated on his understanding of the meaning and scope of the "police power" the next year, 1885, in the course of objecting to a federal initiative to regulate the conditions under which women and children were employed in factories. From Mills's perspective, the regulation of factory owners, like the control of food manufacturing, clearly fell under provincial jurisdiction inasmuch as it went to the heart of the meaning of the term civil rights—the attempt to define and regulate "the relations between the employer and the employed" by interfering with "the freedom of contract."[103] Mills protested that he did not "complain of this interference"[104] in principle; indeed he throught that factory legslation was "very important" and its principle "thoroughly sound."[105] Like many other moderate liberal reformers— among them the Mowat government which had already enacted factory legislation for Ontario—he understood perfectly well that the liberty of contract had to be interfered with precisely "in order to prevent one man from interfering with the comfort and well-being of another."[106] But Mills maintained that "we," that is the federal Parliament, "are not the parties who are authorised to interfere"[107] in such matters. If Parliament were permitted to regulate factory conditions, then it could "claim jurisdiction, not only over the relations of employer and employed, but over the whole subject of property, except its transfer, and over all our civil relations," including "laws relating to public health and morals, and the protection of one individual against possible injury by another."[108]

In short, in giving the provincial governments the exclusive power to deal with "property and civil rights," the BNA Act conferred upon them the responsibility "to preserve peace and good order, and to see that one man, in doing as he pleases, does not please to interfere with the property, health, comfort or freedom of another."[109] The scope of the power over property and civil rights, in other words, included both the community's right to limit individual liberty "for the purpose of promoting morality, decency and good health"[110] and the community's obligation to enhance liberty by protecting "one individual against possible injury by another."[111] Grounded in respect both for community power and individual liberty, the provinces' exclusive jurisdiction over "property and civil rights" became for Mills the pivotal provision of sections 91 and 92.

Mills's broad definition of "property and civil rights" was presumably intended to offset the JCPC's hint in *Russell* that the "peace, order and good government" clause in effect granted an expansive police power to the federal government. But in the parliamentary context of the mid-1880s, his more direct purpose was to limit the interpretation of the enumerated federal powers, among them the federal government's apparently broad power to regulate trade and commerce. Mills's clearest statement of the relation between provincial and federal power in commercial matters was made in the debate, again in 1885, on a federal bill which stipulated the type of labelling that must appear on canned goods manufactured in the country. Mills admitted that the federal government had the sole responsibility for foreign trade. It could quarantine foreign goods on their way to the Canadian market, and it could of course impose tariffs upon foreign goods entering the country. But the routine regulation of the conditions under which canned goods could be sold, he maintained, was "not a regulation of trade at all in any sense":

> You are undertaking to say what shall be done in order that property may be preserved from destruction, or that the purchaser may be protected from fraud on the part of the vendor. All that has to do with the ownership of property and its transfer. Now the transfer of property, its purchase or sale, is a matter relating to property and civil rights, not a matter relating to commerce.[112]

A definition such as this, which treats buying and selling as actions that are in no sense commercial, is obviously destructive of federal power. Indeed, once the contractual transfer of property is defined as a matter of exclusive provincial jurisdiction, all that would seem to remain for Ottawa, beyond the control of international trade, is the regulation of the actual physical transfer, that is the interprovincial transportation, of goods:

> Take a farmer engaged extensively in raising cattle, he might go into manufacturing canned beef upon his estate. What right would this Parliament have to interfere with the manner in which he puts up his goods for market, any more than with the manner in which he may carry his grain or fruit to market? Anything of that kind relating to the products of the farm or factory are matters relating to his property and civil rights, and are determined and regulated by the Province to which he belongs. It is a regulation made as in incident to property, and it applies just as much to a case of property that might be transferred from father to son and disposed of by gift as to property disposed of by contract. We have no right to interfere with one more than the other. The law of contract is regulated by the laws of the Province where the contract was made and where the goods were manufactured and sold; and when the goods are transported into another portion of the Dominion or to a foreign country we make regulations in regard to them; but in regard to the production and sale by one party to another, that is a civil right under the control of the Legislatures.[113]

The federal initiative to regulate the labelling and sale of canned goods was thus deficient not merely because it was too broadly conceived or because it failed to exempt from its coverage those canned goods that were to be consumed locally, although this was part of what troubled Mills about the proposed legislation. Rather, the Canned Goods Act was "altogether"[114] beyond the jurisdiction of the federal government because it dealt with a matter—the production and transfer of property—that was essentially within provincial jurisdiction. In Mills's view neither more careful drafting nor a narrower scope could remedy that basic flaw.

Why did Mills insist on interpreting provincial power over "property and civil rights" so broadly? And what lay behind his defense of provincialism more generally? In one way, of course, Mills the constitutional lawyer would not have recognized these as legitimate questions. Even in a political forum such as Parliament, Mills distinguished sharply between law and politics, and his dissertations on the division of powers were usually narrowly focused and rather formal. In arguing that Parliament had no business legislating on a given matter, he would quote from past cases, ransack British common law precedents, or cite leading authorities—like Cooley on the meaning of the police power—as a way of illuminating the meaning of crucial terms; he would typically not explain why it was a good thing to interpret provincial jurisdiction broadly. As a legal liberal, he believed that his task was to interpret the plain meaning of the constitution, not offer an explicit political or ideological defense of provincial power.

Yet Mills's rhetoric was not always so confined. While he produced no systematic treatise defending provincial power, he did drop enough hints that one can piece together two distinct, but related, lines of argument. On the one hand, Mills argued that the success of representative government turned on the creation of something like provincial legislatures to deal with the "numerous questions that in their nature are local and which can only be adequately considered by the community immediately interested":[115]

> I am of the opinion that the system of representative Government is one which never can be satisfactorily carried out over a very great extent of territory except we divest the national assembly of those local and minor questions which may properly be dealt with by local representatives of the people, who are to be immediately affected by them. I think it may be laid down as a general proposition to which there can be no exception, that no Parliament can be successful in undertaking to legislate for the people except the people themselves sympathise with the Government in the work in which they are engaged.[116]

As usual, Mills supported his general assertions with specific historical examples. The imperial authorities created problems for themselves in the 1830s because they were indifferent to the very things that were most important to their British North American colonists; their indifference, indeed, led them to support an oligarchy that was completely unrepresentative, out of tune with the views of the population and finally fell. The history of the legislative union which existed from 1841–1866 taught the same lesson, for there "people were legislated for by others than those representing them, and thus with regard to a matter which peculiarly concerned the people of Lower Canada we find the representatives of Upper Canada to whose constituencies the law did not extend and upon whose people the law did not in any way operate, assisting in legislation of that character."[117] The result, predictably, was a system in which jointly administered powers "became elements of repulsion by which the ties, which naturally bound the two Provinces together, were well nigh severed."[118] The only way to combine truly representative government with diversity, therefore, was to give local populations the freedom to deal with the "numerous questions" that were "in their nature local":

> The only way to secure the effective operation of a representative government is by calling into existence local representative bodies to deal with such (local) questions, and so we find that the theory of a legislative union is only applicable to a very limited extent of territory and that with a wide area and diversified interests, a Federal system is a necessity if the government and legislature are to be really representative.[119]

Indeed, Mills's description of the virtues of local, representative government at times sounded like the Anti-Federalist criticism of the U. S. Constitution: "A government under the representative system is a government founded upon assent and sympathy; but a centralized representative government is compelled to rely on force in but a little less degree than a military despotism."[120]

If distant representatives lacked sympathy for and interest in local problems, so they lacked the local knowledge to address such problems in a way that was consistent with the distinctive traditions, approaches and solutions that distinguish one community from another. Mills, like so many other Canadian politicians both before and since, made much of diversity and of the difficulties created by strong social and cultural identities. But unlike some others, Mills considered diversity more than an uncomfortable and inevitable part of Canadian politics; it was, rather, a positive good that had to be protected. In that sense, broad provincial authority to deal with matters of "police" was important not only to realize representative government, but to preserve diversity as well. It was necessary not only to offset centralized indifference, but to protect the various and diverse regional communities that were otherwise vulnerable (as minorities are typically vulnerable) to enforced uniformity.

Here again, Mills's public defense of provincial power is disappointing largely in that it was unsystematic. Perhaps the best place to begin reconstructing his views on the connection between diversity and provincial power is with his contribution to the factory labor debate of 1885, where he struggled to explain to Parliament why it had no business regulating an area that was clearly a matter concerning property and civil rights and therefore within exclusive provincial jurisdiction. The argument took two forms. On the one hand, he wanted to show that regulatory policies such as these were matters of "police," and that the "police power" could be exercised only by provincial legislatures. On the other, he went out of his way to demonstrate that the federal government could not bring the question under the criminal law power simply by creating stiff penalties for those who did not comply with the act. The term criminal law, Mills argued, applied to those "wrongs committed against society which are *in themselves bad;*"[121] it did not embrace such "police" regulations as these.

Mills did not flesh out the distinction between crimes that are "in themselves bad" and mere police regulations, but even in this bare form it is suggestive. For what Mills clearly was attempting to claim was that crimes and police regulations are qualitatively different types of acts that draw on different forms of practical judgment. In some cases of criminal behavior judgment is scarcely required because certain actions are "in themselves bad" and have a clear, almost self-evident moral status. Though he did not furnish an example, murder would presumably qualify under this test. Moreover, in cases that do require moral choice, the judgment, according to Mills, would typically come down to an irreducible alternative between right and wrong. As he once put the point, "(i)n most cases crimes do not mean more or less, but yes or no."[122]

By contrast, Mills believed that police regulations involve a whole range of choices that defy the hard alternatives that he associated with clear, even unqualified, moral judgments. Where Mills would have said that murder is "bad in itself," his language when describing "police" regulations was far more conditional and his list of the activities that fell under it much longer. Provincial legislatures "may" regulate the construction and working conditions of factories. They "may" regulate the hours of labor. They "may" act to protect public health by controlling industrial sewage. They "may" punish prize fighting and cruelty to animals.[123] But they are not compelled to act in any of these areas, much less act in a single way, because there is nothing inherently right or wrong, wicked or innocent, about such measures as these. And where Mills would have said that most moral questions could be satisfied by a "yes or no" answer, he believed that the rightness of police regulations depended on finding the most "advantageous" solution, that is, one which gave individuals "the largest amount of freedom without interfering with the freedom of others."[124] Since "police"-style regulatory measures in some way affected the balance between individual liberty and community power, each would have to be weighed and assessed in light of the perceived needs and desires of the community affected by them.

Here, of course, lies the connection to federalism. For if there is no inherently correct balance between public authority and private liberty, then for Mills it followed that such decisions ought to be made at the provincial level, where those who belong to the community and are most familiar with it would be able to strike the balance that is best for their own situation. This notion that sound legislation depended on local knowledge was one theme of Mills's defense of home rule and provincial autonomy. The imperial authorities had created resentment in the North American colonies in the 1830s, not only because they had been indifferent to Canadian affairs but because they had been "ignorant" of them.[125] Similarly, the problem with disallowance, according to Mills, was that it permitted "strangers of other Provinces" to second-guess what ought to be properly a decision for Ontarians alone. That was wrong because these strangers "know much less of our local wants than the men who are on the ground—the men whom the people have trusted. They are much more likely to blunder."[126]

Mills used the same logic to rebuke those who, in 1889, urged him to support the disallowance of the financial settlement, negotiated by the Quebec government, to compensate the Jesuits for the appropriation of their land. "You must bear in mind," he told them, "that what is exclusively within the authority of a province is wholly outside Dominion authority. With regard to these matters, the province is the best judge. Authority over them is entrusted to it because it is assumed to be most competent."[127] Disagreement about religious "truth" was a notorious cause of political discord in the "old" Canada, as in the Old World. Since Protestant Ontario and Catholic Quebec "entertained widely different views of public policy," one of the chief aims of Confederation had been "to allow each province to pursue that course, on these old questions, most satisfactory to the majority of its own people."[128] Some Ontarians might think "that Quebec is going all wrong and that they could set it right."[129] To his credit, and it should be noted that he delivered the speech in his own constituency and at the risk of editorial censure, Mills distanced himself from that attitude of moral self-righteousness:

Permit me to say, gentlemen, that (it) is a duty under our constitution, that the electors of this province are not at liberty to perform for their neighbors. We have as much on hand...as we can well undertake. We have fallen far short of a standard of ideal perfectability and I am sure we could do infinitely greater service to the country, were we to devote ourselves to those abuses which the constitution of the country places directly within our reach.[130]

Again, Mills did not develop the argument completely systematically, and for that reason it is difficult to generalize with complete assurance. Still, it seems clear that his case for provincial power was grounded ultimately in a respect for diversity, and his (perhaps surprising) insight that most questions facing modern governments simply are not morally monolithic.

V

Murray Greenwood, one of a handful of modern commentators to take Mills's constitutional thought seriously, has concluded from this and like evidence that Mills was "a persuasive theorist of decentralization"[131] whose great virtue was his "coherent thinking."[132] There is no doubt that Mills demonstrated a sophistication of analysis that was extremely impressive; indeed, he anticipated a number of crucial methodological and substantive developments in constitutional interpretation. But in his own historical context, it is not immediately clear that Mills was either as persuasive or as coherent as Greenwood suggests. It is significant, for example, that while provincial jurisdiction over property and civil rights eventually did expand in roughly the way Mills suggested, his own interventions typically did not persuade the federal government to back away from the initiatives he opposed. With a few notable exceptions,[133] the federal government proceeded to build a regulatory apparatus on matters that Mills considered to be within provincial jurisdiction; in several instances, indeed, it appears that Mills was unable even to persuade his own Liberal colleagues to oppose the government's measures.[134] And if a test of coherence is consistency, then it is surely telling that once Mills became a federal minister he came to act in a way that, at first blush, cannot easily be squared with the uncompromising provincialism for which he was, and remains, best known.

Mills was given the opportunity to serve as a member of the government in 1897 when he was invited by Wilfrid Laurier to become minister of justice and government leader in the Senate. The justice portfolio was among the most important in the cabinet, and Mills, predictably, "plunged into his duties in the Department of Justice with gusto."[135] He took personal responsibility for the day-to-day administration of penitentiaries, reformed the parole system, toured the entire prison system, and made patronage appointments at virtually every level of the federal justice system. All of this left less time for, but did not supplant, his abiding interest in federal-provincial affairs. As minister of justice, Mills was responsible for advising the prime minister on the constitutionality of provincial statutes and for exercising the veto of disallowance—a duty which, as we have seen with regard to British Columbia's anti-Asian legislation, he did not hesitate to perform. In addition, Mills introduced several bills relating to the administration of justice which raised jurisdictional questions. And as the government leader in the Senate he took it upon himself to defend vigorously his government's national policies, especially its aggressive efforts to attract both capital and immigrants to the West.

The irony, therefore, is that as Mills became increasingly committed to his department's and to his government's program, he came increasingly to view the division of powers in a way that was uncharacteristically generous to the federal government. Where in the 1880s he strongly opposed federal efforts to regulate the manufacture and sale of adulterated foods as an invasion of provincial jurisdiction, as minister of justice he defended federal legislation that prohibited the manufacture and sale of oleomargarine within the Dominion.[138] While he defined the protection of morals as a police regulation rather than as a matter of the criminal law, and thus within provincial rather than federal jurisdiction, he hoped that as minister of justice he could amend the Criminal Code to regulate the playing of lotteries,[137] a classic form of late nineteenth-century morality legislation.

Most surprising of all, Mills introduced legislation as minister of justice to allow mortgage companies to incorporate themselves with the federal government even though the mortgage business clearly involves the loaning and transferring of property—that is, with a general subject that Mills had claimed only a few years before was a matter of exclusive provincial jurisdiction. When the premier of Ontario, A. S. Hardy, complained that the loan societies bill violated provincial jurisdiction, Mills replied by making the claim, extraordinary in light of his provincialist principles, that the incorporation of loan societies "is a regulation of commerce" because "the loaning of money upon any security is primarily not a question of property, but a question of commerce."[138] His argument before Parliament was still more eccentric. To the extent that loan companies have "the power to receive moneys on deposit, and to deal with them for the purpose of profits," he said, they are "to a limited extent, banking institutions"[139] and therefore fall within federal jurisdiction. Mills could find no comparable power under the enumerated heads of provincial power "to authorize any company to receive money on deposit, and to deal with it in the way that this is usually done."[140] And even if the federal power in this instance did "overlap and encroach upon the enumerated powers of a province," federal authority under the banking power was "paramount, and the authority of the province for the time being, is in abeyance, if the statutes cannot stand together."[141]

Even the tone of his discourse changed. Mills's official response to Premier Hardy's complaint was curt, formal and adversarial. His un-official response, captured in a letter to his old comrade-in-arms Oliver Mowat, betrayed the exasperation of a federal minister who, as if for the first time, had tumbled to the awareness that ambitious pro-vincial governments may not be a completely unmixed blessing. "There are a good many things that I would like to talk over," he wrote in the course of accepting an invitation to visit his old friend Mowat, now lieutenant-governor of Ontario. One of these was the combativeness of the Hardy government in pressing its jurisdictional claims. "I have always been in favor of maintaining Provincial rights," he wrote, "but I have never favored the notion of handing over the absolute control of Dominion affairs to the local authorities which some of our Local friends seem to think it a part of the duties that now devolve upon us."[142]

Nor was this an isolated example that reflected momentary frus-tration. In the course of replying to a letter which had posed the ques-tion whether it was possible to maintain "free institutions under a single Chamber," Mills was moved to wax expansive on one of his favorite subjects—the genius of the English constitutional system for preserving the "principles of personal liberty" through parliamentary government.[143] What the English understood, Mills argued, was that liberty could really only be protected if there was some other body, like the Lords (or the Senate in Canada) to check the popular legislature, for "there is nothing more wholesome than that a body should feel that it is not entrusted with absolute power, and that there is always some other body whose consent is necessary to the adoption of its opinions and theories." The express targets of this criticism were "the French, who are disposed to be governed by logic rather than by experience" and those American states which, inspired by Tom Paine and Thomas Jefferson, had established constitutions on the French model of "pure democracy."

Yet Mills seems to have realized that if "personal liberty" was at risk in the states because there were inadequate institutional checks to control a tyrannical majority, then the same criticism could be applied quite as easily to the Canadian provinces. If it were "utterly impossible to maintain the English Parliamentary system with a single Chamber," and if "no country (had) ever yet succeeded in maintaining its free institutions under a single Chamber," then did it not follow that the provincial legislatures, being uni-cameral, could not really be trusted to protect individual liberty? Mills did not deny the implication:

> If you had a single Chamber, in a period of great excitement, the majority would without hesitation trample under foot the rights of a minority. I have already see (sic) a single Chamber in some of our Provinces disregarding, in time of excitement, compacts by which they agreed to be bound without a moment's hesitation, and measures have been carried at the instance of powerful organizations, who could use their influence at elections, which measures were essentially unjust, and were expected to disregard the settled principles of our constitutional system and to destroy measures which were, beyond all question, within the authority of the Province, in which the Dominion has no concern, for the sole purpose of saving the Province from the disagreeable consequences of its own Act, which a representative Chamber had not the courage to face.

Considering that Mills had spent the better part of his career defending the provincial legislatures both as fully clothed parliamentary governments and as the true guardians of "personal liberty," this direct attack upon the provinces seems bizarre indeed.

Donald McMurchy, the author of the only full-scale study of Mills, has concluded from the sort of evidence presented above that as minister of justice Mills underwent a "rather amazing reversal of form"[144] on the question of provincial rights. It raises this obvious question: what accounts for the evident discrepancy between the hard-line provincialism of his early career and the more accommodating view of central power that informed his view while minister of justice?

McMurchy himself argues that one can explain Mills's flip-flop on the question of provincial rights "by the responsibilities of high federal office," and he concludes that as minister of justice Mills simply saw "more clearly the legitimate powers of the federal government."[145] McMurchy does not develop this argument at any great length, but one of its virtues is that it fits nicely with, indeed implicitly extends, J. C. Morrison's larger and extremely influential interpretation of the rise of the provincial rights movement in Ontario. For Morrison, whose study of the rise of the provincial rights movement focuses on the pivotal role played by Premier Oliver Mowat, the doctrine of provincial rights is best understood as a "political strategem"[146] inspired by "the necessities of Ontario politics"[147] and governed by calculations of partisan competition. As it had been "politically expedient, between 1864 and 1867" for the Reformers to portray Confederation as a deal in which Upper Canada got "everything it desired,"[148] so after Confederation it was in the party's interest to defend provincial rights against a Tory regime in Ottawa, hoping thereby "to make the greatest amount of capital out of a popular policy."[149] In this sense, McMurchy's interpretation of Mills can best be understood as an extrapolation of Morrison's argument. On the premise that the provincial rights movement was inspired above all by political expedience, Mills's "reversal" is neither surprising nor particularly difficult to explain. As the ruling party in Ontario, it was in the Reformers' interest to expand provincial rights. Once they were themselves in power in Ottawa, however, they changed their tune and became much more sensitive to national needs and federal possibilities. Mills's behavior, by this interpretation, is simply part of a larger piece in which the calculations of political self-interest played a dominant part.

The difficulty with this explanation when applied to Mills is that it cannot account for the numerous instances in which the minister of justice did not act to enhance federal jurisdiction even when it would seem to have been expedient to do so. He was urged by petitioners both private and public to claim federal jurisdiction over Sunday closing laws, horse racing, sanatoria, labor relations and other "police" regulations, usually on the argument—used by subsequent federal administrations—that these could be brought under federal control with little difficulty. But in each instance Mills refused to take up the suggestion, even though in so doing he passed up the opportunity both to extend federal regulatory control and to create a host of federal sinecures and patronage positions.[150] As he put it in a letter recommending that the federal government discontinue the practice of making queen's counsel appointments:

> I am aware that the conferring of this distinction bring (sic) a certain amount of influence and prestige to whoever may exercise the authority, but I think under our Federal constitution, it is most important not to minimize the rights which pertain to the different Provinces.[151]

In short, while Mills surely came to adopt a more charitable interpretation of federal power in these last years, he did not completely abandon the provincialism on which he had staked his career any more than the Judicial Committee completely abandoned the centralism it had espoused in *Russell v. the Queen.*

If Mills's mature position on the question of provincial rights cannot be reduced to calculations of political expedience, Morrison and others are still surely right to emphasize the importance of party. As numerous commentators have pointed out, the struggle over provincial rights in the generation after Confederation was closely connected to the partisan rivalry between Reform-Liberals and Conservatives that dominated late nineteenth-century Canadian politics. Questions of federalism, it is argued, were inevitably bound up with and served partisan ends. That the Reform or Liberal party typically aligned itself with the provincial rights position can best be understood, therefore, in terms of the necessities of partisan competition— the need to mobilize electoral support and to accommodate socioeconomic elites chief among them.

Yet as Brian Beaven has argued in detail,[152] the leaders of the Reform-Liberal party throughout this era interpreted the party's role more broadly and, in a word, more ideologically than the foregoing summary might suggest. Liberalism in late nineteenth-century Canada was only partly an electoral machine and a collection of sellable planks. It was, beyond this, an ideology in the basic sense that it furnished a set of principles that were meant to order and organize political life. The Liberalism that was expounded and defended up and down the hustings and through the popular press was a set of cultural symbols that connected a heroic past to an even more promising future—and which therefore provided a keen insight into the threat to both posed by the present rule of John A. Macdonald's Tories.

In the conventional Liberal view, Toryism was associated with arbitrary government, tyranny, privilege and corruption. In their earlier incarnation, Tories had fought hard to preserve the Family Compact, religious establishment, French "domination" and legislative union. Those iniquities had been defeated, but the Tory party had not. It remained, transmogrified, under the leadership of John A. Macdonald, so that while times had changed "the animating principle"[153] of Toryism remained the same. "The tory party in Canada to-day," the editorialist for the Toronto *Globe* opined in a typical outburst:

> is a compound of the relics of the Family Compact, the uneducated and unenlightened of the people—the selfish and mercenary—and of the drift wood of society that seeks a temporary resting place under the protection of Sir John Macdonald. It is the party of contractors, speculators, office holders, rings and monopolists. It is the hope of those having evil designs on the community—it is reinforced and kept afloat by constant contributions and assistance from those having interests at variance with the welfare of the people.... It is a party of disorganization and anarchy—it has substituted the tyranny of the vicious and selfish for the tyranny of a favoured few.[154]

Liberalism, by contrast, built on a tradition of respect for the rule of law, popular and individual rights, equality and honesty. These were the central symbols of the Liberal tradition, and they became the essential rhetorical weapons with which Canadian Liberals both defined their own identity and attacked the Macdonald administration. Just before the federal election of 1882, the leading Reform paper in Edward Blake's constituency presented the choice this way:

> Electors! The issues to be decided in the present contest are of vital importance to every one of you. They are issues that should appeal to the conscience of every man who loves his country—who wants a government of the people, by the people, and for the people—who values the blood-bought privileges of representative and responsible government as his dearest birth-right—who resents the usurpation of his inalienable rights by bare-faced monopolies, by reckless extravagance, by cowardly legislation and by treacherous acts, and this, too, by a corrupt autocracy which seeks to drive its fangs far and deep into the most vital axioms of government, and to sap the foundations of the strength and prosperity of our great Province of Ontario.[155]

The choice, therefore, was between the local Conservative candidate "who prefers the rule of a cabal at Ottawa" and the Liberal leader, Mr. Blake, who stood for "the people's rule."[156]

As this quotation suggests, the contrast between Tory and Liberal principles was drawn out with special clarity and emphasis at election time. But such outbursts were by no means confined to electoral campaigns. The beauty of Liberal ideology, indeed, consisted precisely in its versatility. For if the Liberal party presented a clear electoral alternative to the "lineal descendants of the family compact,"[157] the Tory party's very corruptness also helped to explain how the Conservatives continued to win national office and how they acted while in office. As undesirable as the old Tory party may have been, it at least had principles. "The Conservative party of to-day," by contrast, "is literally devoid of any guiding principle of action, save the retention of office."[158] The Conservatives under Macdonald were "wholly guided by expediency," and if they were successful in holding onto office it was apparently only because they practiced "bribery on an extensive scale."[159] The choice between Liberal and Conservative, therefore, was not simply campaign rhetoric trotted out before every election in a desperate effort to win votes. Indeed, Liberal editorialists frequently warned their readers against reducing the electoral choice to a "mere question of parties." The struggle, rather, was greater; it was for "popular freedom insidiously assailed under a new and most dangerous form," for the people's rights against "this new species of despotism."[160] So understood, this basic construction anchored the Liberal self-understanding, suffused their partisan rhetoric, and guided national political debate in the last quarter of the nineteenth century.

By and large, the defense of provincial rights squared nicely with Liberal principles. Macdonald's allegedly arbitrary use of the disallowance power became one of the chief exhibits in the Reformers' indictment of Toryism—which is precisely why Blake, Mills and others were so preoccupied with it. Sir John A.'s use of the reservation power provided the Reformers with some of the strongest evidence for their claim that Toryism was incompatible with the principles of responsible self-government. The provincial governments were struggling for their "independence," their "autonomy," their "rights"—all of them solid Liberal virtues to which the centralism and paternalism of Toryism were openly opposed. Even the Rivers and Streams case, which set McLaren's Tory-sponsored monopoly against the larger public interest in the use of navigable streams, was grist for the Liberals' mill.

Yet the fit between Liberal ideology and provincial autonomy was by no means perfect, and although the Liberals did not go out of their way to advertise the fact, it is at least arguable that the very Liberal principles that reinforced the claim for provincial autonomy also rendered the division of powers unstable. For interpreted ideologically, the threat posed to freedom in Canada came not from the central government as such but from Macdonald's extravagant, unprincipled and expedient use of national power. The Reformers did not reject the goal of westward expansion, increased immigration or commercial growth. They did not hesitate to say that theirs was the true "National Policy"[161] from which would spring a genuine "national sentiment".[162] And they did not deny that, to accomplish their program, the federal government would have to use its constitutional powers to the utmost. What the Reformers did reject was Macdonald's management of national affairs, and that, more than anything, supplied a powerful incentive to interpret federal jurisdiction narrowly. Stated baldly, as long as Macdonald's Tories were in office nationally, the cherished values of liberty and equal rights were in jeopardy; as long as Reformers ruled in Ontario, they were safe.

Given the highly ideological nature of partisan dispute, it was only prudent for someone like Mills to interpret provincial "police powers" broadly and federal power to regulate commerce and criminal law narrowly. But once the Liberals finally gained power in 1896, it was no longer necessary to interpret federal jurisdiction as exiguously as their leading constitutionalists had come to interpret it in the depths of the mid-1880s—that is, when Macdonald's hold on national power seemed unshakable. That Mills came to interpret national power more generously when in government than when in the opposition is therefore perfectly understandable and quite consistent with his underlying ideological principles. With a Liberal government in charge, the federal government could be entrusted with greater power needed to build the nation, without, at the same time, threatening liberty.

There were, of course, limits to this jurisdictional redirection. Provincial autonomy remained a firm Liberal slogan; Mills and others were too deeply imbued with legalist ideas to think that jurisdiction was infinitely plastic or "flippable"; and since most provincial governments remained firmly in Liberal hands it was unnecessary to push the jurisdictional point very far anyway. All Mills wanted to say was that a somewhat broader national power could be entrusted to Liberals where it would not be safe with Tories. To that extent he was willing to argue late in his life that the boundaries separating provincial from federal jurisdiction were perhaps more manipulable than he had earlier suggested; that, indeed, definitions were not static, but that at least some subjects could be actively "*brought* within our jurisdiction."[163]

Still, to say that Mills's jurisdictional shift is understandable in light of his underlying ideology is not to say that his position is altogether coherent. For here, as in the case of disallowance, Mills's late awakening to the possibilities of national power raises as many questions as it answers. According to Mills, the first object of government was to "legislate so that people will mind their own business and leave other people alone,"[164] and he believed deeply that provincial governments were by and large better suited to legislate in this liberal spirit. The difficulty is that, ultimately, Mills could find no logically necessary and empirically rigorous connection between liberalism and provincialism. Such bare-bones liberal principles could, and usually did, support the constitutional authority of provincial communities; in different circumstances, however, Mills the federal officeholder found that similar liberal arguments could be used in ways that worked against provincial power.

Mills's defense of provincial autonomy, in other words, relied for its strength on the deep association—analogy is too weak a word— between liberty and community, individual rights and provincial rights. Yet, in the end, Mills had to acknowledge, indeed he exploited, the contingency and instability of that association as he explored the possibilities of national power. In that sense, Mills's defense of provincial power under section 92 serves as a microcosm of the larger conception of provincial autonomy. It captures both the power and the powerful ambiguity of the provincialist idea.

Conclusion

I began this study by noting the extent to which constitutional discourse in Canada has come to center on various competing visions of what the country is and should be. Naturally enough, these "visions" are described somewhat differently by different observers. In one version the essence of the conflict is characterized by the contrasting terms provincialism and pan-Canadianism;[1] in others the essential tension is between the traditional discourse of federalism and the new language of judicially protected rights;[2] in still another we are left with two packages, the one emphasizing community, the other parasitic upon an atomistic liberalism.[3] Moreover, these visions produce quite different political attitudes. For some, these models are "binary opposites" which resist reconciliation because "one ideal is the negation of the other."[4] For others, it seems possible in principle—and maybe even in practice—to find a compromise position that will accommodate elements of both views.[5] Still and all, there seems to be considerable agreement among students of Canadian federalism about the basic tension between liberty and community that has produced so much constitutional conflict over the past twenty-five years.

If the dichotomy between liberty and community were simply the product of the academic mind, one might be able to dismiss it as an excursion in "theory" which bears little relation to the real world of Canadian federalism. In fact, however, this is not the case. One of the hallmarks of the intense academic debate that has occurred in recent years is the extent to which it has built upon, and taken its bearings from, the rhetorical signals sent by politicians, judges, social groups and others. Academics probably have attempted to describe the various "competing visions" somewhat more tidily than they may appear in political debate, on the hustings and before parliamentary committees, but the conceptions themselves remain deeply rooted in political practice.

Perhaps the most vivid, as well as important, example of the way in which the dichotomy between liberty and community has infected the terms of recent ground level political debate concerns the Quebec sign law controversy. In December 1988, the Supreme Court of Canada struck down those sections of Quebec's Bill 101, the Charter of the French Language, which required the exclusive use of French on commercial signs and posters, and in firm names.[6] The court held that these French-only provisions of Bill 101 violated the right to freedom of expression guaranteed both by the Canadian Charter of Rights and the Quebec Charter of Human Rights and Freedoms. Under the court's ruling, commercial expression can be considered to be a "fundamental freedom" for the purpose of constitutional analysis, in part, as the court put it, because "commercial expression...plays a significant role in enabling individuals to make informed economic choices, an important aspect of individual self-fulfillment and personal autonomy."[7]

Two days after the ruling was handed down, Robert Bourassa, the premier of Quebec, announced that he intended to introduce legislation into the Quebec National Assembly that would require the use of unilingual, French-only signs outside stores but permit the use of bilingual signs indoors. Premier Bourassa argued at the time that such a solution was consistent with the spirit of the Supreme Court's decision, but in order to foreclose future legal challenges to the new law, better known as Bill 178, the National Assembly invoked the "notwithstanding" or override provision of section 33 of the Charter of Rights.

The "notwithstanding" provision is arguably Canada's most distinctive contribution to contemporary constitutionalism.[8] It permits a provincial legislature or the national Parliament in effect to override certain sections of the Charter of Rights for a renewable period of five years,[9] and while most legislatures have not rushed to use it,[10] the override has elicited considerable interest from commentators and active politicians alike—especially in light of the Quebec case. The override has been defended as a uniquely Canadian way of reconciling judicial review with democratic accountability and decried as an unprincipled and tawdry political compromise that undermines the protection of rights. But most importantly, the controversy over the status and use of the override has reinforced the legitimacy of viewing the constitution as if it posed a stark, zero-sum choice between the values of liberty and community.

Thus, when Premier Bourassa was asked immediately following the court's ruling whether he would invoke the override clause, he explained that his task was to "reconcile two fundamental values: my unique duty to protect the French language and culture, and my duty to enforce the Quebec Charter of Rights and Freedoms, which is quite clear about freedom of expression."[11] Once the government had chosen its course of action, Premier Bourassa defended Bill 178 in similar terms, calling it "the best possible compromise between two apparently irreconcilable imperatives: the protection of the French language and the protection of individual freedom of expression."[12] Once Bill 178 had passed and the override was in place, Mr. Bourassa's tone hardened, but the analysis remained firmly anchored to the tension between these two fundamental values. When pressed by certain Quebec nationalists who believed that Bill 178 did not go far enough, the premier defended his actions by noting that "for the first time in the history of Quebec a premier went so far as to suspend civic liberties, to protect and defend the French language."[13]

By this point, the most visible critics of the override had adopted an equally uncompromising position. In an extraordinary parliamentary outburst, Prime Minister Mulroney called the override clause "that major fatal flaw of (the constitutional settlement of) 1981, which reduces your individual rights and mine":

> The Government of Canada surrendered a notwithstanding clause in 1981–82, which said, in effect, 'we hereby guarantee Canadians their fundamental right to language, to religion and to association, but, by the way, we forgot to tell you, these fundamental rights can be overridden if the Premier of Prince Edward Island or Saskatchewan or Québec decides that it is in his interest to take them away.[14]

A provision like the override "holds (individual rights) hostage." Worse, "(a) constitution that does not protect the inalienable and imprescriptible individual rights of individual Canadians is not worth the paper it is written on."[15]

One of the purposes of this book has been to show, by way of a historical case study, just how deeply rooted this tension between liberty and community is in the Canadian public mind. And, indeed, having reconstructed the ideology of provincial rights in detail, it is tempting to strike a blow against the relentless "presentism" of much current political coverage by cataloguing the numerous ways in which recent constitutional debate, both about Quebec and the country as a whole, resonates powerfully with the constitutional tradition. The view, espoused by Premier Bourassa, that someone in his position "cannot abdicate his responsibility to protect the French culture to another government which is responsible to a majority of another culture"[16] is completely familiar—thanks in part to the provincial rights movement. Prime Minister Mulroney's attempt to portray the provincial

governments as the real threat to individual rights echoes the senti-
ments of several past prime ministers. And the habit among some
English Canadians to be quick in denouncing Quebec's treatment of its
anglophone population while doing little to protect minority francophone rights in their own provinces also has deep roots in Canadian
constitutional politics.

Yet it is important to approach neat historical comparisons
between the provincial rights movement then and the problems of
liberty and community now with extreme caution. For one thing, all
governments are much more active than they were in the late nineteenth century, with the result that the patterns of intergovernmental
competition and cooperation are much more complex; indeed, some
would argue that the central constitutional desideratum of the
provincial rights movement—jurisdictional autonomy—is hopelessly
anachronistic. Modern Quebec provincialism/nationalism has responded to social and economic change in ways that render it in
crucial respects different from what preceded it, and which therefore
make the attempt to draw clear historical parallels highly dubious.
And the Charter of Rights has shifted the center of gravity in
Canadian political discourse in significant ways that may also skew
any simple comparison between past and present.

More crucially, I have tried to argue that even considered on its
own terms—that is, understood in the language of liberty and community—past and present are difficult to match because the forms of
constitutional debate have changed in subtle, but important, ways.
For while the provincial autonomists were indeed forced to address
the problems of liberty and community, and while the tension between
the two was often deep, the provincialist vision did not manifest itself
in quite the neat, self-contained, dichotomous way that has so come to
dominate recent constitutional discourse. In essence, I have wanted
to argue that the autonomists would not share the view that liberty
and community are "binary opposites," or that one is forced to choose
between these two "apparently irreconcilable values," because their
claim for community was based on, and was intimately tied to, their
liberalism.

The insight that liberty and community are in some sense code-
pendent complicated the autonomists' worldview immensely, and in
the course of this study we have encountered numerous examples of
the peculiarities to which it gave rise. Thus the autonomists struggled
to secure the "rights" of the provinces understood as political communities, but their defense of provincial independence was explicitly
based on a deep commitment to liberal individualism and a character-
istically liberal mode of expression. The autonomists were strongly

committed to the view that collective identity or "race" is constitutive of individual identity, but when it came to applying their analysis of "race" politically, they retreated to the comfortable liberal foundation of individual rights. The autonomists went to considerable lengths to shore up the sovereignty of the provincial legislatures, but they also insisted on viewing "the people" as the source of, and the ultimate check on, governmental authority. The provincial autonomists struggled to defend provincial jurisdiction against the nationalizing pretensions of the Macdonald government; yet after more careful examination, it appears that their reservations had as much to do with Macdonald as with the legitimacy of a robust central government. Indeed, while the provincial autonomists offered what is arguably the most systematic and far-reaching account of "provincialism" English Canada has ever produced, we have seen that their own principles could be used, and sometimes were used, to support a position far more congenial to the competing, nationalist vision of community. And while the provincial autonomists developed a discourse of federalism that suffuses Canadian politics to this day, they also developed a rights-based political vocabulary that one normally associates with the ostensibly rival discourse of nationalism.

The ideology of provincial autonomy, in short, was both considerably more ambiguous and considerably more subtle than is usually thought. Both qualities seem painfully absent from the current debate; which is why, despite their many imperfections, the autonomists' thought may help to illuminate the current situation. On the surface, for example, the Bourassa government's use of the notwithstanding clause would seem to be an open and shut case of provincial supremacy. The novelty of the institutional mechanisms aside, here were the representatives of the majority acting in full knowledge to protect their culture, especially when, as the editorialist from the 1880s said in another context, "the minority have called to their aid an outside power."[17] What gives pause is that the editorialist who argued against external interference also maintained that the moral claim for provincial autonomy rests on the same basis as the moral claim for individual autonomy. Is it not in some sense self-contradictory to "suspend" an individual's linguistic autonomy when it is precisely on its right to linguistic autonomy that Quebec, as a collectivity, would say that other societies and governments ought not to interfere in Quebec's affairs? Or to put a similar thought in language more congenial to the late twentieth century, Quebec as a society bases its moral claim for recognition from others on its status as an equal. Is that claim not to some degree undercut when it denies to individuals the same equality and respect that it would demand for itself?

Yet the Mulroney position, that the override clause is the "fatal flaw" of the Constitution Act, 1982, seems equally open to question. The argument that "inalienable and imprescriptible individual rights" can only be secure if the Supreme Court is granted the last say is persuasive only if one assumes that judges are uniquely able to find "right answers" to hard cases involving the relation of individual and state, and that legislatures cannot be trusted to question those decisions. Yet even the provincial autonomists—who had enormous faith in law and the ability to discern "right" answers—would not have gone that far. What the autonomists understood, and what is surely open to discussion, is that different communities may strike the balance between individual and state somewhat differently, yet remain firmly within the liberal universe. That is one reason that provincial control of matters concerning property and civil rights was so important to the leading autonomists like Mills; it is an observation worth noting in the context of the sign law decision as well. The court's crucial argument in that case was that commercial expression must be accorded constitutional protection because the ability to make informed economic choices "is an important aspect of individual self-fulfillment and personal autonomy." Yet it hardly seems illiberal or tyrannical to suggest that some communities might have good reason to resist that claim because they might not agree that consumerism is such a fundamental good. Indeed, it is quite possible that some communities would consider that consumerism is actually at tension with the requirements of liberal citizenship. In such a case, is it really so clear that to place restrictions on commercial speech is to deny "an inalienable and imprescriptible individual right"? Even the current U. S. Supreme Court has backed away from that position.[18]

What is so deeply troubling about the current, highly polarized situation is the apparent inability to see beyond, or see through, the "competing visions" that animate, but also divide, most constitutional discussions. It is in that sense that we are witness to a failure of constitutional vision. I would not deny that much of the bitterness and rancor that has characterized federal-provincial relations over the past two decades has been caused by real and serious differences of purpose. I would only insist that beneath the constitutional polarization there exists another federal-provincial dynamic, deeply embedded in the Canadian political tradition, that has been obscured in the rush to find a "model" that would clarify our options by treating liberty and community as simple antinomies. At their best, the provincial autonomists in Ontario "saw" the constitution slightly differently than we do. They saw that the tensions and conflicts in Canadian constitutional politics arise, paradoxically, both because the alternative visions are so different and because they are so much alike; that the source of the deep tension between the defense of self-governing communities and the protection of individual and minority rights, between community and liberty, is a common commitment to liberalism. The autonomists themselves did not face up squarely to the tension because they stopped short of drawing out the full implications of their insight. That is a luxury we can no longer afford.

The challenge posed by the contemporary debate, therefore, is to find principles that will allow the different strands of the Canadian constitutional tradition to grow and intertwine from their common source. There is no instant recipe for success; nor is there any guarantee that the future will be any less fractious than the recent past. But it remains crucial, all the same, to insist that the tension between liberty and community ought to begin, rather than end, serious constitutional discussion in Canada. The Supreme Court of Canada has taken a few tentative steps in this direction, especially in its attempts to develop flexible standards under the "reasonable limits" test of section 1 of the Charter of Rights.[19] The challenge, however, needs to be taken up beyond the courts as well, for it must be realized that the interaction of community and liberty affects everyone in sundry ways. One of the reasons that the notwithstanding clause of section 33 is attractive to some observers, indeed, is that it has the potential to democratize constitutional politics by forcing governments to explain to their citizens precisely why it is necessary to exercise the override power in a given case, to enter into a conversation with their citizens —and to be accountable for the decision taken.[20] Either way, it is time to begin thinking afresh about the relation between liberalism and federalism in Canada. If law is a way by which we all "imagine the real," one can scarcely imagine a challenge for Canadian constitutional politics more real than this.

Notes

Chapter 1.

1. Cited in Alan Cairns, "The Other Crisis of Canadian Federalism," in Douglas E. Williams, ed., *Constitution, Government, and Society in Canada* (Toronto: McClelland and Stewart, 1988), 183.

2. The response to the 1982 settlement is nicely captured in the title of a collection of essays, edited by Keith Banting and Richard Simeon, which explored the struggle over constitutional reform in Canada. *And No One Cheered: Federalism, Democracy and the Constitution Act* (Toronto: Methuen, 1983).

3. The Meech Lake Accord is the name given to a series of proposed amendments to the Constitution Act, 1982, negotiated among the First Ministers in May–June 1987. The proposed amendments limited the federal government's spending power; provided provincial input into the selection of senators and Supreme Court justices; and altered the constitutional amending formula in certain cases. Most importantly, the accord proposed an amendment that would acknowledge the existence of Quebec as a "distinct society" within Canada, while recognizing the existence of English-speaking Canadians in Quebec and French-speaking Canadians outside of Quebec as a "fundamental characteristic" of the country.

To take effect, the Meech Lake amendments had to be ratified by the House of Commons, the Senate, and all ten provincial legislatures by June 23, 1990. In the end, the legislatures in two provinces—Newfoundland and Manitoba—did not pass the amendments before the deadline and the Accord died.

4. The phrase is taken from a paper written by Professor G. P. Browne of Carleton University and distributed by the Manitoba Government at the First Ministers' Conference on the Constitution in September 1980.

5. Sterling Lyon, "Notes for a Statement on the Entrenchment of a Charter of Rights," First Ministers' Conference on the Constitution, 9 September 1980, 6.

6. The quotations in this paragraph are taken from Richard Simeon, "Meech Lake and Shifting Conceptions of Canadian Federalism," 14 *Canadian Public Policy* (1988), S14, S23. Obviously, the precise understanding of these competing visions varies somewhat from author to author. Still, the dualistic analysis I have sketched is, in one form or another, pervasive. See Richard Simeon, "Constitutional Development and Reform," in Michael S. Whittington and Glen Williams, eds., *Canadian Politics in the 1980's*, 1st ed. (Toronto: Methuen, 1981), 243–259; Keith Banting and Richard Simeon, "Federalism, Democracy and the Constitution," in *And No One Cheered*, 2–26; Richard Simeon, "Meech Lake and Visions of Canada," in K. E. Swinton and C. J. Rogerson, eds., *Competing Constitutional Visions: The Meech Lake Accord* (Toronto: Carswell, 1988), 295–306; Alan Cairns, "The Canadian Constitutional Experiment," *Dalhousie Law Journal* 9 (1984), 87–114; Alan Cairns, "The Politics of Constitutional Conservatism," in Banting and Simeon, *And No One Cheered*, 28–58; Patrick Monahan, "At Doctrine's Twilight: The Structure of Canadian Federalism," *University of Toronto Law Journal* 34 (1984), 47–99; Patrick Monahan, *Politics and the Constitution: The Charter, Federalism and the Supreme Court of Canada* (Toronto: Carswell/Methuen, 1987), esp. ch. 5; Charles Taylor, "Alternative Futures: Legitimacy, Identity and Alienation in Late Twentieth Century Canada," in Alan Cairns and Cynthia Williams, eds., *Constitutionalism, Citizenship and Society in Canada* (Toronto: University of Toronto Press, 1985), 183–229; Patrick Macklem, "Constitutional Ideologies," *Ottawa Law Journal* 20 (1988), 117–156; Roy Romanow, John Whyte and Howard Leeson, *Canada...Notwithstanding: The Making of the Constitution 1976–1982* (Toronto: Carswell/Methuen, 1984), Introduction, especially xvii; Pierre Trudeau, "Prime Minister's Remarks at Close of Discussion on the Charter of Rights," First Ministers' Conference on the Constitution, 10 September 1980, 5–7.

For the relation between Trudeau's pan-Canadianism and the Charter of Rights, see Peter H. Russell, "The Political Purposes of the Canadian Charter of Rights and Freedoms," *Canadian Bar Review* 61 (1983), 36–42; and Rainer Knopff and F. L. Morton, "Nation-Building and the Canadian Charter of Rights and Freedoms," in Cairns and Williams, *Constitutionalism, Citizenship and Society in Canada*, 133–182.

7. I concentrate on reconstructing the English-Canadian constitutional mind for two reasons. First, the ideology of provincial rights in English Canada has received less attention than it deserves. While many of the episodes studied in this book are well-known, relatively few scholars have interested themselves principally in the ideological dimension of the provincial rights dispute. In Quebec, on the other hand, the connection between nationalism, provincial autonomy and ideology during this period has been more widely discussed. Works in English include: Denis Monière, *Ideologies in Quebec: The Historical Development* (Toronto: University of Toronto Press, 1981); A. I. Silver, *The French-Canadian Idea of Confederation, 1867–1900* (Toronto: University of Toronto Press, 1982); and Susan Mann Trofimenkoff, *The Dream of Nation: A Social and Intellectual History of Quebec* (Toronto: Gage, 1983), ch. 10.

Second, I concentrate on English Canada because the contemporary debate about liberty and community in Quebec, while sharing some of the characteristics of the English-Canadian debate, has an added dimension that makes it distinctive. As I note in the text, the terms of the recent political/constitutional debate in Quebec, filtered as they are through intergovernmental negotiations and court challenges, are at least recognizable in English Canada. The socio/psychological debate about the bases of individual and community identity is quite different, however. There are important differences, both in tone and substance, between English-Canadian claims of community and Quebec nationalism. Recognizing that, I limit myself to discussing English-Canadian social thought, while attempting to point out areas of confluence in political and constitutional discourse.

8. The term is taken from Monahan, "The Structure of Canadian Federalism," 84.

9. Canada, Legislative Assembly, *Parliamentary Debates on the Subject of the Confederation of the British North American Provinces* (Quebec: Hunter, Rose and Company, 1865), 29. (Hereafter cited as *Confederation Debates.*)

10. Ibid.

11. Ibid.

12. Ibid.

13. Ibid., 32.

14. Ibid.

15. Ibid., 29.

16. Ibid., 33.

17. Cited in Ramsay Cook, *Provincial Autonomy, Minority Rights and the Compact Theory 1867–1921* (Queen's Printer, 1969), 10.

18. The *Constitution Act, 1867* was formerly known as the *British North America Act.* For reasons of historical accuracy, I will refer to the constitution throughout this book as the Confederationists referred to it, that is as the BNA Act. In the notes, however, I will refer to it by its present and correct name.

19. See *Constitution Act, 1867*, section 91 (Preamble) and section 92 (Preamble).

20. *Constitution Act, 1867*, Preamble.

21. Cook, *Provincial Autonomy*, 1.

22. *Constitution Act, 1982*, section 92A.

23. *Attorney General of Manitoba et al. v. Attorney General of Canada et al.* (Patriation Reference case), (1981) 1 S.C.R. 753.

24. As one of its conditions for entering into constitutional negotiations with the Mulroney government, Quebec insisted that limitations be placed on the federal spending power. A perceptive analysis of the proposal as it appears in the Meech Lake Accord is provided by J. Stefan Dupré, "Section 106A and Federal-Provincial Fiscal Relations," in Swinton and Rogerson, *Competing Constitutional Visions*, 203-211.

25. On the Supreme Court as umpire, see Peter Russell, Rainer Knopff, and Ted Morton, eds., *Federalism and the Charter: Leading Constitutional Decisions* (Ottawa: Carleton University Press, 1989), 9-10 and the cases presented in Part One, 162-288. The Supreme Court's continued willingness to hear jurisdictional cases stands in contrast to the current situation in the U.S. See *Garcia v. San Antonio Metropolitan Transit Authority* 105 S. Ct. 1005 (1985).

26. See Cook, *Provincial Autonomy* 20; Peter B. Waite, *Canada 1874–1896, Arduous Destiny* (Toronto: McClelland and Stewart, 1971), 175; Donald G. Creighton, *Canada's First Century* (Toronto: Macmillan, 1970), 48; John T. Saywell, *The Office of Lieutenant-Governor* (Toronto: University of Toronto Press, 1957), 260; J. C. Morrison, "Oliver Mowat and the Development of Provincial Rights in Ontario: A Study in Dominion-Provincial Relations, 1867–1896," in *Three History Theses* (Toronto: Ontario Department of Public Records and Archives, 1961), 79, 215-219, 228-231; and Alan Cairns, "The Judicial Committee and Its Critics," *Canadian Journal of Political Science* 4 (1971), 321-322.

27. Richard Simeon, *Federal-Provincial Diplomacy* (Toronto: University of Toronto Press, 1972), ch. 1.

28. Christopher Armstrong, *The Politics of Federalism* (Toronto: University of Toronto Press, 1981), 8, 31; Norman McL. Rogers "The Genesis of Provincial Rights," *Canadian Historical Review*, 14:1 (March 1933), 9-23; Paul Romney, *Mr. Attorney* (Toronto: Osgoode Society, 1986), 240-281; and Robert Bothwell, *A Short History of Ontario*, (Edmonton: Hurtig, 1986), 82.

29. Alan Cairns, "The Judicial Committee," 323. See also Edwin Black and Alan Cairns, "A Different Perspective on Canadian Federalism," *Canadian Public Administration* 9 (1966), 29. This account is echoed by many others. Waite, *Arduous Destiny*, emphasizes the importance of "strong regional identities," at 176. This is also a constant theme of Edwin Black, *Divided Loyalties* (Montreal: McGill-Queen's University Press, 1975).

30. Garth Stevenson, *Unfulfilled Union*, 1st ed (Toronto: Macmillan, 1979), 66. See also Armstrong, *The Politics of Federalism, passim;* and Monière, *Ideologies in Quebec*, ch. 5.

31. For examples, see F. R. Scott, "The Consequences of the Privy Council Decisions," *Canadian Bar Review* 15 (1937), 485; W. P. M. Kennedy, "Interpretation of the British North America Act," *Cambridge Law Review* 8 (1943), 156; V. C. MacDonald, "The Constitution in a Changing World," *Canadian Bar*

Review 26 (1948), 29; and Bora Laskin, "Peace, Order and Good Government, Re-examined" *Canadian Bar Review* 25 (1947), 1054.

32. Cairns, "Judicial Committee," 319. A particularly graphic illustration of the legalistic interpretation of Canadian federalism is provided by R. Mac-Gregor Dawson, who noted that "the true nature of Canadian federalism is disclosed only through the long series of judgments which have been rendered by the Courts, and particularly by the Judicial Committee of the Privy Council." See R. MacGregor Dawson, *Constitutional Issues in Canada 1900–1931* (London: Oxford University Press, 1933), 431.

33. See Clifford Geertz, *Local Knowledge: Further Essays in Interpretive Anthropology* (New York: Basic Books, 1983), 167–234. See also Clifford Geertz, *The Interpretation of Cultures* (New York: Basic Books, 1973), ch. 8, 193–233.

34. Geertz, *Local Knowledge*, 218.

35. For an application of this approach to a comparative study of abortion law, see Mary Ann Glendon, *Abortion and Divorce in Western Law* (Cambridge: Harvard University Press, 1987), 8. For another extremely useful application, again in the American case, see H. N. Hirsch, "Law, Facts, and Persons: Police Powers, Neutral Principles, and Constitutional Change," *Constitutional Commentary* 4 (1987), 93–113.

36. Geertz, *Local Knowledge*, 184.

37. Ibid., 234.

38. Cairns, "The Canadian Constitutional Experiment," 98.

39. An excellent study of constitutionalism executed in this spirit is Michael Kammen, *A Machine That Would Go Of Itself: The American Constitution in American Culture* (New York: Vintage, 1986). On federalism in particular, see Michael Kammen, *Sovereignty and Liberty: Constitutional Discourse in American Culture* (Madison: University of Wisconsin Press, 1989), especially chapter 6, "The Revival of States' Rights in American Political Culture, ca. 1918–1938: Reflections on the Ambiguities of Ideological Constitutionalism," 157–188.

40. Armstrong, *The Politics of Federalism*, 3.

Chapter 2.

1. I adopt this conventional nomenclature in part to remind readers of the exclusive and elitist nature of mid-nineteenth-century Canadian politics. Unlike the resolutions adopted at Philadelphia in 1787, the Confederation proposal, known as the Quebec Resolutions, did not require ratification by specially designed constitutional assemblies. The resolutions themselves called only for approval by the various local parliaments, and even here there was some reluctance in some of the affected colonies to enter into a full-scale

legislative debate. Moreover, even if there had been some form of official referendum on the proposals, the restrictions on the franchise would have severely limited participation. In Upper Canada (Ontario), the franchise at the time of Confederation excluded both women and those who did not hold a sizeable amount of real property. Indeed, in 1866 the Canadian Legislative Assembly actually raised the property qualification, in part as a reaction against what was perceived as the dangerously democratic tendencies at work in the U. S. This limitation on the franchise may help to explain why, with the exception of cultural questions, the theme of minority rights does not loom as large in the Canadian Confederation debates as it did in the American constitutional debates. One way of ensuring that the property-less many do not cancel debts or redistribute the property that belongs to the few is to disenfranchise those who do not possess the requisite amount of property. On the franchise in mid-nineteenth-century Ontario, see D. G. G. Kerr, "The 1867 Elections in Ontario: The Rules of the Game," *Canadian Historical Review* 51 (1970), 369–377.

2. Peter B. Waite, *The Life and Times of Confederation, 1864–1867* (Toronto: University of Toronto Press, 1962), 33.

3. The Constitution Act, 1867 was formerly known as the British North America Act. For reasons of historical accuracy, I will refer to it in the text itself as the Fathers of Confederation referred to it, that is as the BNA Act. In the notes, however, I will refer to it by its present and correct name.

4. Bruce Hodgins, "The Canadian Political Elite's Attitudes Toward the Nature of the Plan of Union," in Bruce W. Hodgins, Don Wright and W. H. Heick, eds., *Federalism in Canada and Australia: The Early Years* (Waterloo: Wilfrid Laurier University Press, 1978), 43. Of course, the view that the Confederation settlement was at best "quasi-federal" is no more monolithic than the views of the Confederationists themselves. Moreover, the emphasis on the Confederationists' hostility to the federal principle varies somewhat from author to author. Still, the view that, as a body, the Fathers of Confederation did not embrace the federal principle is widespread. See André Bernard, *La Politique au Canada et au Québec* (Montréal: Les Presses de L'Université du Québec, 1977), ch. 11; Ramsay Cook, *Provincial Autonomy, Minority Rights and the Compact Theory, 1867–1921* (Ottawa: Queen's Printer, 1969), ch. 2; Donald Creighton *Dominion of the North* (Toronto: Macmillan, 1957), ch. 6; Donald Creighton, *The Road to Confederation* (Boston: Houghton Mifflin, 1965), ch. 6; Kenneth McNaught, *The Pelican History of Canada* (Middlesex: Penguin, 1969), ch. 9; W. L. Morton, "Confederation, 1870–1896," in A. B. McKillop, ed., *Contexts of Canada's Past* (Toronto: Macmillan, 1980), 208–228; J. C. Morrison, "Oliver Mowat and the Development of Provincial Rights in Ontario: A Study in Dominion-Provincial Relations, 1867–1896," in *Three History Theses* (Toronto: Ontario Department of Public Records and Archives, 1961), ch. 1; J. R. Mallory, "The Five Faces of Federalism," in P.-A. Crépeau and C. B. Macpherson, eds., *The Future of Canadian Federalism* (Toronto: University of Toronto Press, 1965), 3–15; John T. Saywell, *The Office of Lieutenant-Governor* (Toronto: University of Toronto Press, 1957), ch. 1; Norman Ward,

Dawson's The Government of Canada, 6th ed. (Toronto: University of Toronto Press, 1987), ch. 14. See also Gil Rémillard, *Le Fedéralisme Canadien* (Montréal: Québec/Amérique, 1983). Mr. Rémillard notes the view, propounded by Wheare, that the BNA Act was "quasi federal" (149). His own view seems to be closer to the one developed here, however. Thus, he says, "d'une facon générale, il semble bien que les Canadiens de l'époque aient tout simplement confondu fédéralisme, comme il était alors courant de le faire. Cependant, le Canada est bien une fédération et non une confédération" (64). Mr. Rémillard's views are of special interest because he was the Quebec minister of intergovernmental affairs at the time the Meech Lake Accord was negotiated.

5. K. C. Wheare, *Federal Government*, 4th ed. (London: Oxford University Press, 1963), 18.

6. See W. L. Morton, *The Critical Years, 1857–1873* (Toronto: McClelland and Stewart, 1964). I am dealing here only with the pre-Confederation politics in the Province of Canada, what is now Ontario and Quebec. On the politics of Confederation in the other colonies, see, for instance, Kenneth G. Pryke, *Nova Scotia and Confederation, 1864–74* (Toronto: University of Toronto Press, 1979), ch. 1; G. A. Rawlyk and Doug Brown, "The Historical Framework of the Maritimes and Confederation," in G. A. Rawlyk, ed., *The Atlantic Provinces and the Problems of Confederation* (Breakwater, 1979), 1–47. Frederick Vaughan provides useful insights into the Atlantic debates over Confederation in "Critics of the Judicial Committee of the Privy Council: The New Orthodoxy and an Alternative Explanation," *Canadian Journal of Political Science* 19 (1986), 495–519, especially 511–512. See also Jennifer Smith, "Canadian Confederation and the Influence of American Federalism," *Canadian Journal of Political Science* 21 (1988), 443–463.

7. Canada, Legislative Assembly, *Parliamentary Debates on the Confederation of the British North American Provinces* (Quebec: Hunter, Rose and Company, 1865), 107 (Brown); 143, 130 (McGee).

8. A. I. Silver, *The French-Canadian Idea of Confederation, 1867–1900* (Toronto: University of Toronto Press, 1982), 33.

9. Ibid, ch. 3,4.

10. Ibid., ch. 2.

11. For a survey of French-Canadian arguments for Confederation, see Silver, *French-Canadian Idea*, ch. 2; see also Cartier's speech in the *Confederation Debates*, 60, where he argues that the central government would have jurisdiction over the "large questions of general interest in which the differences of race and religion had no place."

12. J. M. S. Careless, *Brown of the Globe*, 2 vols. (Toronto: Macmillan, 1959), volume I, ch. 4.

13. Toronto *Globe*, 11 November 1859, speeches of Wilkes and Brown at the Reform Convention. Also see *Confederation Debates*, 92 (Brown).

14. Toronto *Globe*, 24 May 1859, "Federation."

15. Cited in Charles R. W. Biggar, *Sir Oliver Mowat*, 2 vols. (Toronto: War-wick Bro's and Rutter, 1905), volume I, 93.

16. *Confederation Debates*, 92 (Brown).

17. Ibid.

18. Ibid.

19. Ibid.

20. Ibid., 87 (Brown)

21. On the *Federalist Papers* and the myth of founding, see Judith N. Shklar, "*The Federalist* as Myth," *Yale Law Journal* 90 (1981), 942–53.

22. *Confederation Debates*, 45.

23. Ibid.

24. *Constitution Act, 1867*, Preamble.

25. See, for instance, the comments of M. C. Cameron and Christopher Dunkin, *Confederation Debates*, 459, 482.

26. *Confederation Debates*, 947–950.

27. Ibid., 33.

28. Quebec Resolutions, section 29:37, reprinted in G. P. Browne, ed., *Documents on the Confederation of British North America* (Toronto: McClel-land and Stewart, 1969), 154–165. See *Confederation Debates*, 30, 33. More importantly, the *Constitution Act, 1867* itself enshrines the exclusivity of pro-vincial jurisdiction. See section 92 (Preamble) and section 93, where the pro-vincial legislatures are granted the power "exclusively" to make laws in the matters listed therein.

29. *Constitution Act, 1867*, section 91 (Preamble). It should be noted that this grant of power to legislate for the "peace, order and good government" of the country was meant, as Macdonald said, to avoid the errors of the American Constitution. See *Confederation Debates*, 33.

30. See J. A. Maxwell, *Federal Subsidies to Provincial Governments in Canada* (Cambridge, Mass., 1937).

31. *Constitution Act, 1867* section 92:10:c.

32. Ibid., section 56, 90.

33. Ibid., section 55, 58, 90.

34. Ibid., section 93:4.

35. *Confederation Debates*, 859, 858 (J. B. E. Dorion).

36. Ibid., 858 (J. B. E. Dorion); 690 (A. A. Dorion).

37. William Blackstone, *Commentaries on the Laws of England* I:ii:7.

38. Gordon S. Wood, *The Creation of the American Republic, 1776–1787* (New York: Norton, 1969), 529.

39. See Blaine Baker, "The Reconstitution of Upper Canadian Legal Thought in the Late-Victorian Empire," *Law and History Review* 3 (1985), 255. Peter Waite suggests that a similar understanding of sovereignty informed Joseph Howe's opposition to Confederation. For Howe, the most prominent anti-Confederationist from Nova Scotia, "(o)ne government or another had to be supreme. Apparently both could not be." See Peter B. Waite, "Halifax Newspapers and the Federal Principle, 1864–1865," in J. M. Bumsted, ed., *Canadian History Before Confederation*, 2nd ed. (Georgetown: Irwin-Dorsey, 1979), 505.

40. *Confederation Debates*, 250 (A. A. Dorion).

41. Ibid., 689 (A. A. Dorion).

42. Ibid., 858 (J. B. E. Dorion).

43. Ibid., 623–24 (Perrault).

44. Ibid., 33 (Macdonald).

45. Ibid., 33, 41.

46. Ibid., 42, 33.

47. The Reform party was not monolithic in its support of the Confederation settlement. Not all Reformers supported Confederation, and a few prominent members of the party, among them John Sandfield Macdonald, were openly critical of it. Most, however, did support it, and most of the Reform press rallied behind it. On the participation of the Reform press, see Waite, *Life and Times of Confederation*, 126–33. On John Sandfield Macdonald and other Reform critics, see Bruce W. Hodgins, *John Sandfield Macdonald* (Toronto: University of Toronto Press, 1971), ch. 5.

48. On George Brown's centralism, see Careless, *Brown of the Globe*, vol. II, 164–169, 232.

49. Toronto *Globe*, 1 August 1864. See also *Confederation Debates*, 674 (Hope Mackenzie), and 807 (Walsh), for a similar line of argument based on a similar reading of the U. S. Constitution.

50. Toronto *Globe*, 1 August 1864. See also Ottawa *Union*, 1 November 1864.

51. Toronto *Globe*, 1 August 1864, 29 August 1864, 15 October 1864; St. Catharine's *Journal*, 27 September 1864; Ottawa *Union*, 12 September 1864; *Confederation Debates*, 433 (Alexander Mackenzie).

52. Toronto *Globe*, 4 October 1864.

53. Ibid.

54. Toronto *Globe*, 8 October 1864.

55. J. C. Morrison, "Oliver Mowat and the Development of Provincial Rights in Ontario," 11, 1. Also see Peter Waite, *Life and Times of Confederation*, 133, who argues that the Reformers "did not in fact concern themselves much about local government." W. L. Morton goes further when he argues that "(t)he provinces were not, in fact, expected to be self-supporting as they were not thought sovereign even in their spheres of exclusive jurisdiction. They were subordinate governments both in appearance and in fact. They had no great tasks to perform and were given no great powers." W. L. Morton, "Confederation, 1870-1896," in A. B. McKillop, ed., *Contexts of Canada's Past*, 209. See also Frederick Vaughan, "Critics of the Judicial Committee of the Privy Council: The New Orthodoxy and an Alternative Explanation," *Canadian Journal of Political Science* 19 (1986), 505.

56. For a challenging interpretation of the political and constitutional roots of localism in Ontario, see Paul Romney, "From Constitutionalism to Legalism: Trial by Jury, Responsible Government, and the Rule of Law in the Canadian Political Culture," *Law and History Review* 7 (1989), 121-174; and Paul Romney, "From the Rule of Law to Responsible Government: Ontario Political Culture and the Origins of Canadian Statism," Canadian Historical Association, *Historical Papers 1988 Communications Historiques*, 86-119.

57. See Elwood H. Jones, "Localism and Federalism in Upper Canada to 1865," in Hodgins, Wright, and Heick, eds., *Federalism in Canada and Australia*, 19-41.

58. Toronto *Globe*, 17 September 1864.

59. Toronto *Globe*, 29 August 1864, 3 September 1864, 4 October 1864, 15 October 1864. See also *Confederation Debates*, 108 (Brown).

60. Alexander Hamilton, James Madison and John Jay, *The Federalist Papers* (New York: Bantam, 1982), 195.

61. Wheare, *Federal Government*, ch. 1.

62. For a useful analysis of various issues of concern to Americans arising from the gradual acceptance of Blackstone's doctrine of parliamentary sovereignty, see Thomas Grey, "Origins of the Unwritten Constitution: Fundamental Law in American Revolutionary Thought," *Stanford Law Review* 30 (1978), 865-93.

63. *Federalist Papers*, #78, 397.

64. These images are taken from *The Federalist Papers*, #49 (255) and #46 (237) respectively. My debt to Gordon Wood's presentation of the question should be obvious. See Wood, *Creation*, 372-383.

65. Shklar, *"The Federalist* as Myth," 950.

66. See Wood, *Creation*, 529 and Hamilton, Madison and Jay, *The Federalist Papers*, No. 39 (194). Madison did not rest the protection of state interests solely on a judicially patroled division of powers. Jennifer Smith is quite right to point out that Madison's theory of federalism "extends beyond that to encompass" representation in national institutions. See Jennifer Smith, "Canadian Confederation and the Influence of American Federalism," *Canadian Journal of Political Science* 21 (1988), 446. See also Samuel H. Beer, "Federalism, Nationalism and Democracy in America," *American Political Science Review* 72 (1978), 9–21.

67. Toronto *Globe*, 1 August 1864; see also the edition of 30 August 1864.

68. Ibid., 30 August 1864.

69. For references to a constitution in this "American" sense of a written, fundamental law, see Toronto *Globe*, 15 October 1864 ("Surely we can safely put into our constitution . . ."); 20 June 1867 ("The constitution excludes local and sectional questions from the federal Parliament. . . . The people of Ontario have got the absolute control of their local affairs, and they have a just representation in the Parliament which deals with the affairs of the Dominion. So far as these cardinal points in the *Constitution* are concerned, we have all that we asked or could ask").

70. Toronto *Globe*, 4 October 1864; see also London *Free Press*, 26 September 1864; Hamilton *Times*, 12 August 1864, 7 October 1864; Toronto *Leader*, 27 September 1864.

71. Hamilton *Weekly Times*, 30 September 1864.

72. Toronto *Leader*, 27 September 1864. The *Leader* was in fact a Conservative newspaper, but as Peter Waite notes, it had a "liberal Conservative" slant on the Confederation proposal that brought it closer to Reform doctrine (*Life and Times of Confederation*, 126).

73. Toronto *Globe*, 30 August 1864.

74. Toronto *Globe*, 28 June 1867.

75. Ibid.

76. Ibid. See also *Confederation Debates*, 446–47 (Burwell).

77. Cited and reproduced in the Toronto *Globe*, 22 June 1867.

78. Toronto *Globe*, 20 June 1867. One of the great advantages of emphasizing the constitutional protection of local control from external interference is that the Reformers did not have to face the important intra-party differences that existed about the precise definition of "local." Bruce Hodgins has argued, for instance, that the highly centralist rhetoric that George Brown preferred between 1864 and 1866 was in many ways inconsistent with Reform

traditions. Yet as he goes on to point out, there was little discussion, much less recognition of disagreement, about the scope of federal and provincial responsibilities at the time. That evidence fits with the interpretation I have advanced that the central issue for the Reformers was to find a way to insulate local governments—however powerful—from national interference. See Bruce Hodgins, "Disagreement at the Commencement: Divergent Ontario Views of Federalism, 1867-1871," in Donald Swainson, ed., *Oliver Mowat's Ontario* (Toronto: Macmillan, 1972), 52-59.

79. Silver, *French-Canadian Idea*, 43.

80. *Confederation Debates*, 547.

81. Ibid., 690.

82. Ibid., 876.

83. Ibid., 697 (Cauchon).

84. Ibid.

85. *Confederation Debates*, 575-576 (Cauchon); see also Joseph Cauchon, *L'Union des Provinces de L'Amérique Britannique du Nord* (Quebec: A. Cote, 1865), 40; and *Confederation Debates*, 690 (Cartier).

86. See 28 above. Macdonald also adopted the Reform image that emphasized the novelty of the Confederation proposal, calling it a "happy medium" between a legislative and a federal union. See *Confederation Debates*, 33, and Toronto *Globe*, 15 October 1864. Compare that with Madison's characterization of the American Constitution as a "composition" of national and confederal elements.

87. 32 Vict. ch. 3.

88. W. E. Hodgins, comp., *Correspondence, Reports of the Ministers of Justice, and Orders in Council upon the Subject of Dominion and Provincial Legislation, 1867-1895* (Ottawa: 1896), 83. (Hereinafter cited as *Dominion and Provincial Legislation.*)

89. See Hodgins, *John Sandfield Macdonald*, ch. 5.

90. Hodgins, *Dominion and Provincial Legislation*, 88.

91. Ibid., 87.

92. 33 Vict., ch. 5.

93. Hodgins, *Dominion and Provincial Legislation*, 256.

94. W. L. Morton, "Confederation: 1870-1896," in McKillop, ed., *Contexts of Canada's Past*, 227.

95. Canada, Parliament, *House of Commons Debates*, 28 November 1867, 149.

96. On Cooley, see Alan R. Jones, *The Constitutional Conservatism of Thomas McIntyre Cooley* (New York: Garland Publishing Inc., 1987).

97. (Boston: Little Brown, 1874).

98. Mills Papers, Box 4285, Notes on Prof. Cooley's "State Constitutional Law and Legislative Limitations," 1.

99. Ibid., 8.

100. Ibid.

101. Ibid., 2.

102. Canada, Parliament, *House of Commons Debates*, 28 April 1869, 96.

103. Ibid., 28 February 1871, 200.

104. Ibid., 28 November 1867, 149.

105. Ibid., 28 February 1871, 200.

106. Ibid., 28 April 1869, 96.

107. Ibid., 28 November 1867, 154.

108. Ibid., 149.

109. W. L. Morton, "Confederation, 1870–1896," in McKillop, ed., *Contexts of Canada's Past*, 227.

110. My discussion of the Nova Scotia question in the next paragraphs draws heavily upon the accounts of the "better terms" episode found in Kenneth G. Pryke, *Nova Scotia and Confederation 1864-1874* (Toronto: University of Toronto Press, 1979), 46-97; and Colin D. Howell, "Nova Scotia's Protest Tradition and the Search for a Meaningful Federalism," in David Jay Bercuson, ed., *Canada and the Burden of Unity* (Toronto: Macmillan, 1977), 169-191.

111. Howell, "Nova Scotia's Protest Tradition," 172.

112. The financial terms of the Confederation settlement were spelled out in section 118 of the *Constitution Act, 1867*. The section was first rendered obsolete and then repealed in 1950.

113. See Canada, Parliament, *House of Commons Debates*, 11 June 1869, 728 (motion by Blake); and 16 June 1869, 828 (motion by Mills).

114. Ibid., 16 June 1869, 806.

115. Ibid., 11 June 1869, 726.

116. Ibid.

117. Ibid., 11 June 1869, 727.

118. Ibid., 12 June 1869, 766 (Burpee).

119. Ibid., 11 June 1869, 728 (Blake).

120. Ibid., 727 (Blake).

121. Ibid., 737.

122. Ibid.

123. Ibid., 741–742.

124. Ibid., 723.

125. See the speeches of Harrison, 12 June 1869, 766–767; Killam, 12 June 1869, 768; and McLelan, 16 June 1869, 822–825.

126. The final vote on second reading of the "better terms" resolution passed by a vote of 97–50. See *House of Commons Debates*, 16 June 1869, 828.

Chapter 3.

1. London *Advertiser*, 25 January 1883.

2. Canada, Legislative Assembly, *Parliamentary Debates on the Subject of the Confederation of the British North American Provinces*, (Quebec: Hunter, Rose and Company, 1865), 33 (Macdonald).

3. Canada, Parliament, *House of Commons Debates*, 14 April 1882, 920.

4. Ibid.

5. Gerald M. Craig, ed., *Lord Durham's Report* (Toronto: McClelland and Stewart, 1963), 141–142.

6. See W. P. M. Kennedy, *Documents of the Canadian Constitution, 1759–1915* (Toronto: Oxford University Press, 1918), 696–698.

7. These figures are calculated from tables furnished in Great Britain, Parliament, *Parliamentary Papers* (House of Commons), 1864, vol. XL, 665.

8. Kennedy reports that between 1867 and 1878, 21 Canadian bills were reserved under the Instructions, or about 2 per year. See Kennedy, *Documents*, 696, footnote 1.

9. Canada, Parliament, *House of Commons Sessional Papers*, 1877, no. 13, 4.

10. Ibid., 8.

11. *Confederation Debates*, 33 (Macdonald). See also Carl Berger, *The Sense of Power* (Toronto: University of Toronto Press, 1970), 153–159.

12. *Constitution Act, 1867* sections 55, 90.

13. John Saywell, *The Office of Lieutenant-Governor* (Toronto: University of Toronto Press, 1957), 195–196.

14. W. E. Hodgins, comp., *Correspondence, Reports of the Ministers of Justice, and Orders in Council upon the Subject of Dominion and Provincial Legislation, 1867–1895* (Ottawa, 1896), 443, 447.

15. Ibid., 336.

16. Ibid., 770.

17. Totals tabulated from Hodgins, *Dominion and Provincial Legislation.*

18. For example, see Hodgins, ibid, 661 and 1011.

19. The bills are described and Macdonald's comments are recorded in Hodgins, *Dominion and Provincial Legislation*, 773.

20. Ibid., 772.

21. Public Archives of Manitoba, Macdonald to Morris, 9 December 1872. Cited in M. S. Donnelly, *The Government of Manitoba* (Toronto: University of Toronto Press, 1963), 19.

22. One apparent exception to the rule is the reservation of a Quebec bill incorporating the St. Louis Hydraulic Co. in 1869. The Lieutenant-Governor reserved the bill on jurisdictional grounds. When Macdonald, the minister of justice, came to consider the matter he noted the jurisdictional problem, but added that it would not be "in the public interests" to allow the bill to stand when it "might be the means of injuring private property." Since there were also jurisdictional objections, however, it cannot be taken as a clear exception to the rule I have suggested. See Hodgins, *Dominion and Provincial Legislation*, 150.

23. The words are C.F. Fraser's, the only Catholic in Mowat's cabinet. Margaret Evans, "Oliver Mowat and Ontario, 1872-1896: A Study in Political Success," Unpublished Ph.D. thesis, University of Toronto (1969), 140.

24. Canada, Parliament, *House of Commons Debates*, 14 April 1882, 920.

25. Ibid.

26. Hodgins, *Dominion and Provincial Legislation*, 104-105.

27. Ibid., 104.

28. Ibid., 105.

29. Cited and reproduced in Saywell, *Lieutenant-Governor*, 198-199.

30. Ibid.

31. Canada, Parliament, *House of Commons Debates*, 14 April 1882, 911.

32. Ibid., 910.

33. Canada, Parliament, *House of Commons Sessional Papers*, 1877, no. 13, 9.

34. Canada, Parliament, *House of Commons Debates*, 14 April 1882, 910.

35. Ibid., 913.

36. Ibid.

37. Ibid.

38. Hodgins, *Dominion and Provincial Legislation*, 78.

39. Ibid.

40. Ibid.; emphasis added.

41. Neither Gérard La Forest, (whose *Disallowance and Reservation of Provincial Legislation* [Ottawa: Queen's Printer, 1955] is an otherwise excellent account of the subject), nor John Saywell, *Lieutenant-Governor*, notes the significance of the change. La Forest glosses over the 1882 report completely (ch. 5), while Saywell says merely that the "Prime Minister's report was little more than a repetition of his comments in 1873" (203).

42. The bill in question had been passed by the New Brunswick legislature over the protests of some residents in Maine. Their protest was registered in Ottawa, and the lieutenant-governor was apparently instructed to look closely at it. See Hodgins, *Dominion and Provincial Legislation*, 706-708. Two other bills, both from B. C., were reserved in the early years of this century (1919-1920) on instructions from Ottawa. See Saywell, *Lieutenant-Governor*, 207 and Appendix B. Saywell's thorough account of the use of reservation during the period is excellent. See especially chapter 8, 206-213.

43. According to Saywell, reservation was used sporadically in the 1890s and 1900s, usually on jurisdictional grounds. By the time of the Great War, its use had become very infrequent and it has been used only six times since. See Saywell, *Lieutenant-Governor*, Appendix B.

44. Mills Papers, Brief to the Ontario Court of Appeals in the Matter of Queen's Counsel, 1896, 136.

45. J. C. Morrison, "Oliver Mowat and the Development of Provincial Rights in Ontario: A Study in Dominion-Provincial Relations, 1867-1896," in *Three History Theses* (Toronto: Ontario Department of Public Records and Archives, 1961), 63.

46. *Constitution Act, 1867*, section 10.

47. Ibid., section 58.

48. Cited in Morrison, "Oliver Mowat and Provincial Rights," 51.

49. Ontario, Legislative Assembly, *Sessional Papers*, 1888, no. 37, 7.

50. Cited in Morrison, "Oliver Mowat and Provincial Rights," 65.

51. Paul Romney, *Mr. Attorney* (Toronto: Osgoode Society, 1986), 243; emphasis in original.

52. 3 S.C.R. 575 (1879).

53. Ibid., 634.

54. Ibid.

55. Ibid., 631.

56. Ibid., 633.

57. Ibid., 635.

58. Ibid., 634.

59. *The Liquidators of the Maritime Bank of Canada v. The Receiver-General of New Brunswick* (1892) A. C. 437, at 441.

60. Ibid.

61. Ibid.

62. Ibid., 443.

63. Ibid.

64. *Lenoir v. Ritchie*, at 623.

65. Ibid., 622.

66. Ibid., 623.

67. *Constitution Act, 1867*, section 9, 10.

68. *Lenoir v. Ritchie*, at 623.

69. Ibid., 619.

70. For one typical expression of this view see Mills's editorial in the London *Advertiser*, 13 February 1883.

71. Albert Venn Dicey, *Introduction to the Study of the Law of the Constitution*, 10th ed. (London: Macmillan, 1959), 470.

72. Ibid., 470, note 2.

73. On the connection between Dicey's story of the decline of prerogative and his critique French *droit administratif*, see the introduction to *Law of the Constitution*, vi-vii.

74. Interestingly, Dicey did not believe that prerogative had disappeared. Rather, he argued that it had metamorphosed so that some of those discretionary powers once exercised by the sovereign were now exercised, in foreign policy for instance, by the cabinet. This concentration of executive power in the cabinet is also one strand of the story of the development of executive federalism in Canada. See *Law of the Constitution*, 464-470.

75. Ontario, Legislative Assembly, *Sessional Papers*, 1888, no. 37, 13; emphasis added.

76. Mills Papers, Brief to the Ontario Court of Appeals in the Matter of Queen's Counsel, 1896, 21-22.

77. Ibid., 9.

78. Ibid., 7-8; emphasis added.

79. Ibid., 7.

80. Ibid., 136.

81. For another expression of this view, this time from Mills the journalist, see London *Advertiser*, 29 October 1884.

82. Ontario, Legislative Assembly, *Sessional Papers*, 1888, no. 37, 21.

83. Ibid., 15.

84. Ibid., 16-18.

85. *(A. G. (Can) v. A. G. (Ont.)*, (1898) A. C. 254.

86. Donald V. Smiley, *The Federal Condition in Canada* (Toronto: McGraw-Hill Ryerson, 1987), ch. 4.

87. Richard Simeon, *Federal-Provincial Diplomacy* (Toronto: University of Toronto Press, 1972), ch. 1.

88. See note 21.

89. The metaphor of diplomacy is a venerable part of the Canadian political vocabulary. Edward Blake, upon being named premier of Ontario in 1871, outlined what the policy of his administration would be "with reference to what may be called the external relations of the Province." (Toronto *Globe*, 23 December 1871). Wilfrid Laurier reiterated the point in another context before the House of Commons a few years later. "In order to obtain a mere party triumph," he said, "they (the Conservative government of Quebec) ask the aid and co-operation of a foreign power—because I hold that the federal power, in purely Provincial matters, is a foreign power—." Canada, Parliament, *House of Commons Debates*, 12 March 1879, 325.

90. Reg Whitaker, "Democracy and the Canadian Constitution," in Keith Banting and Richard Simeon, eds., *And No One Cheered* (Toronto: Methuen, 1983), 240.

91. Whitaker quotes Macdonald's famous defense of an unelected Senate in this regard. The Senate was necessary, Macdonald urged, because "the rights of the minority ought to be protected, and the rich are always fewer in number than the poor." Ibid., 245.

92. Ibid., 244.

93. Ibid., 254.

94. The rights qualifications that have occasioned the most commentary are the "reasonable limits" provision and the so-called *non obstante* or override clause. See *Canadian Charter of Rights and Freedoms*, sections 1 and 33.

95. Whitaker, "Democracy and the Canadian Constitution," 256. For a recent account of the larger issues of democratic theory and practice involved in the amending process, see Alan Cairns, "Citizens (Outsiders) and Governments (Insiders) in Constitution-Making: The Case of Meech Lake," 14 [Supplement] (1988) *Canadian Public Policy*, 121-145.

96. See Robert C. Vipond, "Whatever Became of the Compact Theory? Meech Lake and the New Politics of Constitutional Amendment in Canada," *Queen's Quarterly* 96 (1989), 793-811.

97. Mills Papers, Mills to L. Goulet, 3 August 1898.

98. See, for example, an editorial comment, presumably written by Mills, on the proposed enfranchisement of native Canadians under the Franchise Act. "Mr. Laidlaw asks, when is an Indian going to be entitled to vote if not now. We answer, when he becomes a citizen. When he ceases to form one of a tribe standing apart from the rest of the community and exhibits the same qualifications as other voters. A white man must have property or income. An Indian may control neither." London *Advertiser*, 25 July 1885. Mills's view on this matter presumably had something to do with the fact that his parliamentary constituency contained a reservation at Walpole Island. The *Advertiser* argued that the franchise reforms had been proposed "for the purpose of swamping certain constituencies, making this one of the most scandalous propositions that have ever been submitted to Parliament. It is well known what the object is. There are several hundred Indians in the vicinity of Sarnia. These the Government proposes to enfranchise in order to defeat Mr. Lister. There are several hundred upon Walpole Island. These would be in Bothwell." London *Advertiser*, 25 April 1885.

99. The autonomists were not afraid to use and identify with the term "democracy." For example, the editorialist for the London *Advertiser* recounted approvingly a speech delivered by "Mr. Lowell, the United States Minister in England" on "English Democracy": "Not the least interesting part of the address, so far as an English audience is concerned, would be the thought which Mr. Lowell develops that democracy is essentially British.... Every colony that has gone out from the mother land has rapidly grown in the principles of self-government. Whether independent as in the United States, or nominally dependent as in Canada, the English colonist is a democrat; he believes in the rule of the people and tries to enforce it." London *Advertiser*, 29 October 1884. On the use and meaning of the term democracy in this era, see Brian Beaven, "A Last Hurrah: Studies in Liberal party development and ideology in Ontario, 1878-1893," Ph.D. thesis, University of Toronto, 1982, ch. 5.

As Beaven points out, the contrast between the Liberal support for democracy and the Tory defense of "privilege" became one of the central leitmotifs of partisan competition and self-definition in this period. The editorialist for the London *Advertiser* drew out the contrast with admirable succinctness: "There is no question of the relative fitness of Liberals and Tories to rule the Dominion. The first are for the people, and the latter are for pelf." London *Advertiser*, 19 May 1882.

The story of the evolution of franchise laws in Ontario suggests that this pride had at least some empirical foundation. In 1866, the franchise "had been narrowed to owners and occupants of real property, assessed at an actual value of $600." Property qualifications remained in effect at the federal level until reformed by the Laurier government in 1898. The Mowat government, by contrast, liberalized franchise laws in Ontario throughout its tenure, until by the mid- to late-1880s all adult, white males were eligible to vote regardless of property. As one might expect, the provincial autonomists made the most of the federal-provincial contrast to demonstrate their greater commitment to democratic principles. On the franchise, see Gregory S. Kealey, *Toronto Workers Respond to Industrial Capitalism, 1867–1892* (Toronto: University of Toronto Press, 1980), 367–368 (and his references). See also Roman Franko, "Social Movements, Politicians and the Extension of the Franchise in Post-Confederation Ontario," paper presented to the annual meeting of the Canadian Political Science Association, Windsor, Ontario, June 1988.

100. On occasion, the autonomists did slip into the more identifiably American language of popular sovereignty. For instance, in the course of denouncing the Macdonald government's use of disallowance in the Rivers and Streams case, the *Globe* observed: "It is obvious that this new policy of the Dominion Ministers indicates a crusade against the local supremacy of the Provinces, and an attempt to coerce and control their Local Government and Legislatures, which by the Constitution are as much the representatives of the supremacy and sovereignty of the people in the Provinces as the Dominion Parliament is of the people in the Dominion, and aims a death blow at the Federal system, and the responsibility of the Provincial Ministry to the Local Legislature and electorate." Toronto *Globe*, 6 June 1881. The use of the term supremacy to refer both to the federal and democratic arguments is especially revealing.

101. *Confederation Debates*, 407.

102. Ibid.

103. Ibid., 108.

104. 44 Vict. ch. 11.

105. Hodgins, *Dominion and Provincial Legislation*, 178.

106. For a more detailed account of the legal course followed, see Romney, *Mr. Attorney*, 255–256 and his references at note 37.

107. Blake Papers, "Federal and Provincial Rights," Series B, Box 114, 108, n.d.

108. Ibid.

109. As the editorials in the *Advertiser* were unsigned, it is difficult to verify Mills's authorship beyond the shadow of doubt. It seems clear, however, that most of the editorials written on the subject of federalism roughly between mid-1882 and 1885 were indeed written by Mills. I found the editorials written in 1883 to be an especially rich source, a fact which corresponds especially well with what we know of Mills's journalistic career. Mills spent 1883 without a seat in the House of Commons while he appealed his narrow defeat in the election of 1882. In the end, Mills won his appeal and was re-seated in the House of Commons. In the meantime, however, he held the position of editor-in-chief of the *Advertiser*. It is almost certainly not coincidental, therefore, that the *Advertiser's* editorials from 1883 are especially numerous and powerful on the question of provincial rights. Even if they were not actually written by Mills, they certainly bear the imprint of his thought as we know it from other sources.

110. London *Advertiser*, 7 February 1883.

111. Ibid., 25 January 1883.

112. Ibid., 7 February 1883.

113. Ibid.

114. Ibid., 28 April 1882.

115. Ibid., 23 March 1882.

116. Ibid., 14 October 1882.

117. Ibid., 18 December 1882.

118. Ibid., 25 January 1883.

119. Blake, "Federal and Provincial Rights," 110.

120. London *Advertiser*, 24 January 1883.

121. Ibid., 19 May 1882.

122. Blake, "Federal and Provincial Rights." 110.

123. Ibid.

124. London *Advertiser*, 19 May 1882.

125. Ibid., 14 October 1882.

126. Ibid.

127. Ibid., 18 October 1882.

128. Ibid.

129. Ibid.

130. Ibid., 19 May 1882.

131. Ibid., 18 January 1883.

132. Ibid., 12 February 1882.

133. Ibid., 9 February 1883. It is worth noting that Mills believed that, at the national level, the Senate could also act as a check against the House of Commons. Thus while "the people of the smaller Provinces, rightly or wrongly, look to the Senate for the protection of their provincial autonomy," the Senate was also meant to act as a second line of defense in the event that "the majority" went "wrong."

The difficulty, as Mills saw it, was that the Senate, being unelected, lacked the legitimacy to perform the functions it was meant to perform. He campaigned, therefore, for an elected Senate, one of the first in a long line of Canadian constitutional reformers to do so. See London *Advertiser*, 2 May 1882.

134. Ibid.

135. Ibid., 12 February 1883.

Chapter 4.

1. Carl Berger, *The Sense of Power: Studies in the Ideas of Canadian Imperialism 1867–1914* (Toronto: University of Toronto Press, 1970), 109.

2. Paul Rutherford, *A Victorian Authority: The Daily Press in Late Nineteenth-Century Canada* (Toronto: University of Toronto Press, 1982), 157.

3. Ibid., 156.

4. Ibid., 156 ff.

5. The intervention of the imperial authorities was particularly important in New Brunswick. Donald Creighton tells the story in *John A. Macdonald: The Young Politician* (Toronto: Macmillan, 1952), 422–430; see also Norman McL. Rogers, "The Compact Theory of Confederation," *Canadian Bar Review* IX (1931), 403.

6. David Mills, "The Evolution of Self-Government in the Colonies: Their Rights and Responsibilities in the Empire," *The Canadian Magazine* II (April 1894), 540.

7. Ibid.

8. David Mills, "The Unity of the British Empire: Its Helps and Hindrances," *The Empire Review* II:7 (August 1901), 4.

9. Mills, "Evolution of Self-Government," 540.

10. Ibid.

11. Mills, "Helps and Hindrances," 4.

12. Mills, "Evolution of Self-Government," 541.

13. Ibid., 538.

14. W. P. M. Kennedy, *Documents*, 696.

15. Mills Papers, Box 4278, Draft of a Speech on the Jesuit Estates Act, 1889, 8.

16. Ibid., 13. See also London *Advertiser*, 23 March 1883.

17. David Mills, *Reform Government in the Dominion: The Pic-Nic Speeches* (Toronto: Globe Printing and Publishing Company, 1878), 93.

18. London *Advertiser*, 5 April 1883.

19. Ibid., 15 January 1883.

20. Ibid., 7 September 1883.

21. Ibid., 5 April 1883.

22. Ibid., 30 August 1884.

23. Mills, "Jesuit Estates," 3.

24. London *Advertiser*, 14 October 1882.

25. Ibid.

26. Mills, "Jesuit Estates," 3.

27. Edward Blake, "The Irish Question," speech delivered to the Eighty Club, (London: 1892), 21.

28. London *Advertiser*, 19 August 1884.

29. Ibid., 13 September 1884.

30. Ibid., 26 September 1884; see also the issue of 15 January 1883.

31. Ibid., 30 June 1882.

32. See, for example, London *Advertiser*, 1 September 1883.

33. Mills Papers, "Lectures on the Federal Constitution of Canada," 1895(?), 216–219. The quotations in the next three paragraphs are all taken from this source. See also London *Advertiser*, 23 March 1882.

34. London *Advertiser*, 23 March 1882.

35. Ibid., 7 February 1883.

36. Mills, "Jesuit Estates," 28.

37. Mills, "Evolution of Self-Government," 540.

38. For examples of this usage, see London *Advertiser*, 12 February 1883 and 12 June 1882; Toronto *Globe*, 8 January 1883, 24 January 1883, and 24 February 1883; and see Edward Blake, "The Irish Question," 21.

39. See George Stocking, *Race, Culture, and Evolution* (New York: The Free Press, 1968), ch. 3-6.

40. There are numerous studies on the influence of Darwinism on social and political thought in Canada in the period covered by this study. See, for instance, Berger, *Sense of Power*, especially 116-119; Ramsay Cook, *The Regenerators* (Toronto: University of Toronto Press, 1985); and P. Roome, "The Darwin Debate in Canada: 1860-1880," in L. A. Knafla, M. S. Staum and T. H. E. Travers, eds., *Science, Technology and Culture in Historical Perspective* (Calgary: University of Calgary, 1976), 183-205.

41. David Mills, by way of example, took a keen interest in the Darwinism debate, so much so that he contributed his own refutation of Darwin to a popular magazine in 1894. See David Mills, "The Missing Link in the Hypothesis of Evolution, or Derivative Creation," *Canadian Magazine* III:4 (August 1894), 297-308. Such questions also surfaced in the House of Commons. In the course of the debate over language policy in the North-West, D'Alton McCarthy and David Mills took it upon themselves to discuss the question of "race" in light of recent anthropological analysis. See Canada, Parliament, *House of Commons Debates*, 22 January 1890, 39-46 and 13 February 1890, 625-630. On Mills's understanding and use of race, see David Mills, "Saxon or Slav: England or Russia?," *The Canadian Magazine* IV:6 (April 1895), 518-530.

42. Berger, *Sense of Power*, 117.

43. Canada, Parliament, *House of Commons Debates*, 13 February 1890, 623.

44. Ibid., 624.

45. On the use of the term "nation" to describe Ontario, see J. M. S. Careless, *Frontier and Metropolis: Regions, Cities, and Identities in Canada before 1914* (Toronto: University of Toronto Press, 1989), 85.

46. Canada, Parliament, *House of Commons Debates*, 13 February 1890, 623.

47. Ibid.

48. Ibid., 631.

49. Lewis Herbert Thomas, *The Struggle for Responsible Government in the North-West Territories, 1870–1897* (Toronto: University of Toronto Press, 1956), 185. The most incisive account of the affair is in Claude-Armand

Sheppard, *The Law of Languages in Canada*, Studies of the Royal Commission on Bilingualism and Biculturalism vol. 10, (Ottawa: Information Canada, 1971), 82–85.

50. See, for instance, *R. v. Mercure* (1988) D.L.R. 48 (4th) 1, which concerned the question whether Saskatchewan was still required to comply with the provision of the North-West Territories Act which permitted the use of English or French in legal proceedings.

51. Canada, Parliament, *House of Commons Debates*, 18 February 1890, 847.

52. Ibid., 22 January 1890, 51.

53. Ibid., 14 February 1890, 678.

54. Ibid., 13 February 1890, 629.

55. Ibid.

56. Ibid.

57. Ibid.

58. Ibid., 627.

59. Ibid.

60. Ibid., 622.

61. Ibid., 628.

62. Ibid., 621.

63. Ibid., 628.

64. Ibid., 623.

65. Ibid., 628.

66. Ibid., 634–635.

67. Ibid., 621.

68. Ibid., 632.

69. Ibid., 17 February 1890, 729.

70. Thomas, *Struggle for Responsible Government*, 185; Sheppard, *Law of Languages*, 84–85.

71. Cook, *Provincial Autonomy*, 55.

72. Ibid., 44. On the law and politics of the Manitoba schools question, see Gordon Bale, "Law, Politics and the Manitoba School Question," *Canadian Bar Review* 63 (1985), 461–518.

73. Donald McMurchy explains some of the political calculations in his biography of Mills. See Donald J. A. McMurchy, "David Mills: Nineteenth Century Canadian Liberal," Ph.D. thesis, University of Rochester (1969), 438-449. See also, Thomas, *Struggle for Responsible Government*, 185. In fact, Mills, who broke with his Liberal colleagues in his strong support in principle for remedial legislation, was defeated in the election of 1896. McMurchy draws out the electoral implications of his stand unambiguously: "The Liberals won the election of 1896 because they opposed remedial legislation, and Mills personally lost because he favoured it." See McMurchy, "David Mills," 448.

74. Blake, "The Irish Question," 20.

75. Ibid., 21.

76. Mills, "Jesuit Estates," 17-18.

77. Ibid., 18.

78. Ibid., 17; emphasis added.

79. Blake, "The Irish Question," 24.

80. Ibid., 26.

81. Mills, "Jesuit Estates," 27-28; cf. 16-17.

82. London *Advertiser*, 20 October 1883.

83. The way in which British politicians sought to use federalism as a model for solving "the Irish problem" has been admirably explained by John Kendle, *Ireland and the Federal Solution: The Debate Over The United Kingdom Constitution, 1870–1921* (Kingston and Montreal: McGill-Queen's University Press, 1989). On Edward Blake's activities as a British MP, see Margaret Banks, *Edward Blake, Irish Nationalist: A Canadian Statesman in Irish Politics, 1892–1907* (Toronto: University of Toronto Press, 1957), 60-62.

84. Blake, "The Irish Question," 29.

85. Canada, Parliament, *House of Commons Debates*, 13 February 1890, 742.

86. Ibid.

87. The *Advertiser* pronounced on Gladstone as follows: "Mr. Gladstone's ambition has long been to promote freedom; to elevate the masses of the population; to give security to life and property; by resting the authority of Government upon the broad basis of popular liberty." 20 September 1883. See also Brian Beaven, "A Last Hurrah: Studies in Liberal party development and ideology in Ontario, 1878-1893," Ph.D. thesis, University of Toronto, 1982, 400-404. For the broader connection to English Liberalism, see Beaven, 370-400.

Gladstone, for his part, was aware of the usefulness of the Canadian federal model in explaining the policy of home rule. Kendle reports, indeed, that "(o)ne of Gladstone's first requests preparatory to drafting his first home rule bill was for a copy of the BNA Act." See Kendle, *Ireland and the Federal Solution*, 6.

88. For an account of the Irish in Ontario that explodes a number of the common myths, see Donald H. Akenson, *Being Had: Historians, Evidence, and the Irish In North America* (Port Credit: P. D. Meany, 1985), ch. 4.

89. London *Advertiser*, 28 December 1885.

90. Ibid., 20 October 1883.

91. Blake, "The Irish Question," 20.

92. Ibid., 21.

93. London *Advertiser*, 21 August 1883.

94. Ibid., 17 February 1883.

95. Ibid., 9 August 1882.

96. Ibid., 15 February 1882.

97. Blake, "The Irish Question," 28-29.

98. London *Advertiser*, 27 February 1883.

99. Ibid., 21 August 1883.

100. Ibid., 27 February 1883.

101. Blake, "The Irish Question," 29.

102. See also London *Advertiser*, 15 February 1882 and Mills's speech on home rule, reproduced by the *Advertiser*, 10 November 1885.

103. Great Britain, Parliament, *House of Commons Debates*, 4th Series, XI, 11 April 1893, 72.

104. Ibid., 72-73.

105. Ibid., 73.

106. Ibid., 14 April 1893, 415.

107. Ibid., 419.

108. Ibid., 420.

109. Ibid., 415.

110. Ibid., 422.

111. Ibid., 11 April 1893, 66.

112. Blake, "The Irish Question," 23-24.

113. Ibid., 24.

114. Ibid.

115. Canada, Parliament, *House of Commons Debates*, 14 February 1890, 682.

116. Ibid., 680.

117. Ibid., 681.

118. Ibid., 688.

119. Ibid.

120. Canada, Parliament, *House of Commons Debates*, 3 March 1896, 2737.

121. On this point see the speech by Sir Charles Tupper, who was responsible for guiding the remedial legislation through Parliament. *House of Commons Debates*, 3 March 1896, 2719–2736.

122. Ibid., 2740–2741.

123. Ibid., 2741; emphasis added.

124. Ibid., 2742

125. Ibid.

126. Ibid., 2741; emphasis added.

127. Ibid., 2745.
128. Ibid., 2739.

129. Ibid., 2740.

130. Ibid., 2742.

131. Ibid., 2740.

132. In fact, Laurier did not rule out the use of remedial legislation altogether or in every situation, but he made the conditions for its use so demanding that this was, practically speaking, the effect. See the final part of his speech, ibid., 2753–2759, where he lays out the conditions for the use of remedial legislation.

133. On divisions within the Liberal party on the Manitoba schools question see McMurchy, "David Mills," 428–492. A lively, detailed account of Laurier's politics throughout the period is to be found in Joseph Schull, *Laurier: The First Canadian* (Toronto: Macmillan, 1965), ch. 13–15.

134. Canada, Parliament, *House of Commons Debates*, 18 March 1896, 3839.

135. Ibid., 3821.

136. Ibid., 3822.

137. Mills Papers, Box 4281,"Draft of a Speech on the Manitoba Schools Case," 1896, 11-12.

Chapter 5.

1. London *Advertiser*, 14 March 1883.

2. Ibid.

3. Ibid. Laurier made the same point in his speech on the Manitoba Schools question. See Canada, Parliament, *House of Commons Debates*, 3 March 1896, 2741.

4. London *Advertiser*, 14 March 1883.

5. *Constitution Act, 1867*, sections 56, 90.

6. See chapter 3.

7. Canada, Legislative Assembly, *Parliamentary Debates on the Subject of the Confederation of the British North American Provinces* (Quebec: Hunter Rose and Co.: 1865), 433.

8. Ibid., 108.

9. G. P. Browne, *Documents on the Confederation of British North America* (Toronto: McClelland and Stewart, 1969), 95.

10. Macdonald's report, dated 8 June 1868, is reproduced in W. E. Hodgins, comp., *Correspondence, Reports of the Ministers of Justice, and Orders in Council upon the Subject of Dominion and Provincial Legislation* (Ottawa: 1896), 61-62.

11. Ibid.

12. *Constitution Act, 1867*, section 91 (Preamble); section 92 (Preamble).

13. *Confederation Debates*, 32.

14. My interpretation of Macdonald's guidelines for the use of disallowance differs from the conventional interpretation championed by Eugene Forsey, "Disallowance of Provincial Acts, Reservation of Provincial Bills, and Refusal of Assent by Lieutenant-Governors Since 1867," *The Canadian Journal of Economics and Political Science* 4 (1938), 47-59; and J. R. Mallory, *Social Credit and the Federal Power in Canada* (Toronto: University of Toronto Press, 1954), ch. 2. Both want to argue that when Macdonald referred to "illegal" and "unconstitutional" acts in the report of 1868 he did so in order to distinguish them. They suggest that by "illegal" Macdonald was referring to acts that were *ultra vires* or beyond the jurisdiction of the provinces, whereas by "unconstitutional" he meant to bring within the pale of disallowance acts that were unsound, unreasonable or violations of property rights. My interpretation accords with that of Gérard La Forest, *Disallowance and Reservation of Provincial Legislation* (Ottawa: Queen's Printer, 1955), 37.

15. Hodgins, *Dominion and Provincial Legislation*, 83. Bruce Hodgins argues that, ironically, Edward Blake played an important part in this episode by actually persuading Macdonald to use the veto against the Ontario legislation. See Bruce W. Hodgins, "Divergent Ontario Views of Federalism, 1868-1871," in Donald Swainson, ed., *Oliver Mowat's Ontario* (Toronto: Macmillan, 1972), 63-64.

16. Hodgins, *Dominion and Provincial Legislation*, 83, 93.

17. Ibid., 472.

18. Ibid., 476.

19. Ibid., 97.

20. Ibid., 100-101. I have taken the small liberty of transposing the words used in the report of one bill (ch. 48, regarding the Grand Junction Railroad Co.) to the Goodhue case. This is unexceptionable because the Goodhue bill was allowed to stand, in the minister's words, "for the same reason as that given with respect to chapter 48."

21. For background to the New Brunswick schools question see Peter M. Toner, "New Brunswick Schools and the Rise of Provincial Rights," in Bruce Hodgins, Don Wright and W. H. Heick, eds., *Federalism in Canada and Australia: The Early Years* (Waterloo: Wilfrid Laurier University Press, 1978), 125-136. See also A. I. Silver, *The French-Canadian Idea of Confederation, 1864–1900* (Toronto: University of Toronto Press, 1982), ch. 5.

22. Canada, Parliament, *House of Commons Sessional Papers*, 1872, vol. 5, no. 7, no. 36.

23. Canada, Parliament, *House of Commons Debates*, 29 April 1872, 198-199.

24. Ibid., 198.

25. Ibid.

26. Ibid., 200.

27. Ibid., 199.

28. Ibid., 199.

29. Ibid., 199-200.

30. Ibid., 200.

31. Ibid.

32. Ibid.

33. Ibid., 201.

34. Canada, Parliament, *House of Commons Debates*, 14 May 1873, col. 177.

35. Ibid.

36. Ibid.

37. Ibid.

38. Ibid.

39. Ibid.

40. Ibid., 178

41. The prediction was made in 1864, following the Quebec Conference, and is cited in Bruce Hodgins, "Divergent Ontarian Views," 65–66.

42. The division is recorded at the end of the debate, column 179.

43. Brian Young, "The Defeat of George-Etienne Cartier in Montreal-East in 1872," *Canadian Historical Review* 51 (1970), 398–406.

44. I have tabulated these results from the tables in Hodgins, *Dominion and Provincial Legislation.*

45. Ibid., 274.

46. Ibid., 133.

47. For a more detailed treatment of this point, see La Forest, *Disallowance and Reservation*, 41–43.

48. Canada, Parliament, *House of Commons Debates*, 12 March 1879, 327.

49. Ibid.

50. Hodgins, *Dominion and Provincial Legislation*, 174.

51. Ibid., 178.

52. Ibid.

53. Ibid., 183

54. Ibid., 185. See also London *Advertiser*, 28 April 1882.

55. Canada, Parliament, *House of Commons Debates*, 14 April 1882, 908–909. In addition, see the speech by Guthrie on the same day, 896–897.

56. Toronto *Globe*, 24 January 1883.

57. Ibid., 26 January 1883.

58. Canada, Parliament, *House of Commons Debates*, 14 April 1882, 920.

59. Ibid., 921.

60. Ibid., 924.

61. London *Advertiser*, 9 February 1883.

62. La Forest notes that "nearly one-half of the thirty-eight Acts disallowed during this period (i.e. 1881-1896) were vetoed on the ground that they interfered with the railway policy of Canada" even though most were within provincial jurisdiction. See La Forest, *Disallowance and Reservation*, 58.

63. London *Advertiser*, 7 February 1883.

64. Toronto *Globe*, 24 January 1883.

65. London *Advertiser*, 14 March 1883.

66. Ibid., 10 December 1883.

67. Toronto *Globe*, 6 June 1881.

68. Robert Gordon, "Legal Thought and Legal Practice in the Age of American Enterprise," in Gerald L. Geison, ed., *Professions and Professional Ideologies in America* (Chapel Hill: University of North Carolina Press, 1983), 69.

69. My brief description of legal liberalism draws heavily on the work of Robert Gordon, especially his article "Legal Thought and Legal Practice in the Age of American Enterprise," cited in the previous note. I should note, however, that where Gordon (and others) refer to the phenomenon as "liberal legalism," I prefer to emphasize the political roots and call it "legal liberalism." For a critical analysis of this method and its relation to the Critical Legal Studies movement, see Rogers M. Smith, "After Criticism: An Analysis of the Critical Legal Studies Movement," in Michael W. McCann and Gerald L. Houseman, eds., *Judging the Constitution: Critical Essays on Judicial Lawmaking* (Glenview, Illinois: Scott, Foresman and Co., 1989), 92-124.

70. See David Sugarman, "The Legal Boundaries of Liberty: Dicey, Liberalism, and Legal Science," 46 *Modern Law Review* (1983), 102-111.

71. *Introduction to the Study of the Law of the Constitution*, 10th ed. (London: Macmillan, 1959).

72. On this point see Sugarman, "Legal Boundaries," 109-110; and H. A. Tulloch, "Changing British Attitudes Towards the United States in the 1880s," *The Historical Journal* vol. 20:4 (1977), 825-840. Indeed, in the final page of the *Law of the Constitution*, Dicey argues that "(t)he 'rule of law' is a conception which in the United States has received a development beyond that which it has reached in England." *Law of the Constitution*, 472.

73. Tulloch's description of the phenomenon of 'americomania' is especially suggestive in this regard. See Tulloch, "Changing Attitudes," 833-839.

74. The quotations in this paragraph are all taken from Duncan Kennedy, "Toward an Historical Understanding of Legal Consciousness: The Case of Classical Legal Thought in America, 1850-1940," *Research in Law and Sociology* 3 (1980), 3-24, at 7.

75. Writing in 1898, Mills noted: "I do not think that there is any (American) constitutional case reported before 1885, which I have not read more than once...." Mills Papers, Mills to Fitzpatrick, 3 September 1898.

76. See Blaine Baker, "The Reconstitution of Upper Canadian Legal Thought in the Late-Victorian Empire," *Law and History Review* 3 (1985), 219–263.

77. When Mills, who taught law at the University of Toronto from 1888 to 1896, was asked by a correspondent to furnish a set of readings on various legal subjects, he replied: "On Federal Constitutional law, my lectures have never been written out, and so I will not be able to place them at your disposal; but as a substitute therefor, I would recommend you to take the first volume of Kent's "Commentaries" and examine the students upon these lectures relating to United States jurisprudence, and the little volume by Cooley, and Mr. Clement's book on the "Constitution of Canada." Mills Papers, Mills to Perry, 6 January 1899.

78. Baker, "Upper Canadian Legal Thought," 263–292.

79. Mills seems to have considered Dicey an authority on parliamentary government. When he was asked about the constitutional propriety of prolonging the life of the legislature, Mills referred his correspondent to "Professor Dicey's book on the British Constitution," in which would be found "a very excellent discussion of this subject." Mills Papers, Mills to Cameron, 4 May 1901.

80. Next to Gladstone, Bryce was arguably the English Liberal with whom the provincial autonomists most clearly identified. Mills wrote glowingly of Bryce's eulogy of Gladstone, for example (Mills to Clarke, 25 May 1898); and Bryce appears to have encouraged Edward Blake to make the most of the Canada-Irish "home rule" analogy.

81. The idea that the provincial governments are supreme within the "sphere" alloted to them by the constitution; that this is the basis of their "autonomy," "independence" and "rights"; and that the federal government's exercise of disallowance therefore amounted to "usurpation" or "trespassing," suffused the autonomists' discussions of federalism. For representative samples, see London *Advertiser*, 28 April 1882; 13 October 1882; 18 October 1882; 2 December 1882; 10 January 1883; 24 January 1883; 7 February 1883; 9 February 1883; 12 February 1883; 14 March 1883. Also see Toronto *Globe*, 6 June 1881; 9 September 1881; 5 January 1883; 8 January 1883; 24 January 1883; 24 February 1883.

82. London *Advertiser*, 7 February 1883.

83. Ibid., 13 October 1882.

84. Ibid., 26 March 1883.

85. Ibid.

86. Ibid.

87. Ibid., 9 February 1883.

88. Ibid., 12 February 1883. For another example of the inter-state/individual-state analogy, see Mills's speech on Irish home rule, Canada, Parliament, *House of Commons Debates*, 26 April 1887, 115.

89. London *Advertiser*, 26 March 1883.

90. Ibid., 14 March 1883.

91. Toronto *Globe*, 24 February 1883.

92. London *Advertiser*, 10 December 1883.

93. Canada, Parliament, *House of Commons Debates*, 28 March 1889, 876.

94. London *Advertiser*, 10 December 1883.

95. Canada, Parliament, *House of Commons Debates*, 28 April 1869, at 97.

96. London *Advertiser*, 26 February 1883; 6 July 1883; 15 July 1883; 10 December 1883.

97. Toronto *Globe*, 6 June 1881.

98. For a thorough account of the Interprovincial Conference of 1887, see J. C. Morrison, "Oliver Mowat and the Development of Provincial Rights in Ontario: A Study in Dominion-Provincial Relations, 1867–1896," in *Three History Theses* (Toronto: Ontario Department of Public Records and Archives, 1961), ch. 5.

99. For a more detailed analysis of the compact theory see Ramsay Cook, *Provincial Autonomy, Minority Rights and the Compact Theory, 1867–1921* (Ottawa: Queen's Printer, 1969), ch. 4.

100. See Paul Gérin-Lajoie, *Constitutional Amendment in Canada* (Toronto: University of Toronto Press, 1950), 142–43.

101. Blake's successful amendment strengthened the reference case procedure. The reference case provided a judicial alternative to disallowance that combined the expeditiousness associated with disallowance with the appearance of neutrality associated with judicial proceedings. In fact, Blake presented the reference case procedure less as an alternative to disallowance than as a supplement to it. But most seem to have realized that with a more satisfactory reference procedure in place, there would be no need for disallowance. See the comments of the Conservative minister of justice, Sir John Thompson, who was responsible for administering the new procedure: "... if the court pronounced (an act) to be unconstitutional it would be most absurd, and practically impossible, for the Minister of Justice to advise that it should be disallowed, after the highest tribunal had decided that the Act was

within the powers of the Provincial Legislature." *House of Commons Debates*, 7 August 1891, 3587. Reference cases have since become an important feature of Canadian constitutional law whereas disallowance has passed into virtual disuse. Under the circumstances, it is not too much to connect the waxing of one with the waning of the other. Certainly there can be no question that, at a more general level, judicial review has replaced disallowance as a form of federal boundary management. On reference cases in this early context, see Gerald Rubin, "The Nature, Use and Effect of Reference Cases in Canadian Constitutional Law," in W. R. Lederman, ed., *The Courts and the Canadian Constitution* (Toronto: McClelland and Stewart, 1964), 220-248.

102. Canada, Parliament, *House of Commons Debates*, 29 April 1890, 4089.

103. Ibid.

104. Ibid., 4088.

105. Ibid., 4089.

106. Ibid.

107. London *Advertiser*, 14 March 1883; see also *House of Commons Debates*, 8 March 1875, 576: "The line which separated the powers of the Local Legislatures from those of the Parliament of Canada, was as distinct as if it was a geographical boundary marked out by the surveyor."

108. See La Forest, *Disallowance and Reservation*, ch. 8-10.

109. Canada, Parliament, *House of Commons Debates*, 1937, vol. 3, 2294.

110. That does not mean that the use of disallowance would never again be considered. Lapointe reserved the right to act in extraordinary cases, and on these grounds disallowed a series of acts passed by the Social Credit government in Alberta, all of which in one way or another conflicted with federal law or, in the federal government's opinion, supplanted federal institutions. The Social Credit episode is reviewed in La Forest, *Disallowance and Reservation*, 78-80, and is the subject of one of the classic studies of Canadian politics, James Mallory's *Social Credit and the Federal Power in Canada*.

A few years after the Social Credit incident, in 1945, the King government was asked, in one case by the Canadian Pacific Railway, to disallow two pieces of allegedly socialist legislation passed by the CCF government in Saskatchewan headed by T. C. (Tommy) Douglas. Douglas responded in good provincial rights fashion that this would be an entirely "arbitrary action." His attorney general argued in an official brief that any question of the constitutionality of provincial legislation ought to come before the courts, not the federal government. And the federal government rejected the petitions, arguing, according to Douglas's friend M. J. Coldwell, "that disallowance is conceivable only if provincial legislation interfered with the rights of the Dominion or placed the whole of Canada in a bad light." See Thomas H. McLeod and Ian McLeod, *Tommy Douglas: The Road to Jerusalem* (Edmonton: Hurtig, 1987), 138-39.

Disallowance has not been used since. According to La Forest's calculation, a total of 112 statutes have thus been disallowed since 1867. See La Forest, *Disallowance and Reservation*, 82.

111. Tabulated from the tables in Hodgins, *Dominion and Provincial Legislation*, vol. 1 (1867–1896) and 2 (1896–1920). Between 1887 and 1897, the federal government disallowed thirteen provincial acts, most of them from Manitoba.

112. Ibid., vol. 2, 594

113. Ibid., 595.

114. Ibid., 597.

115. Ibid., 556.

116. Mills Papers, Mills to Laurier, 18 May 1900.

117. Hodgins, *Dominion and Provincial Legislation*, vol. 2, 556; emphasis added.

118. Ibid., 557.

119. Ibid., 17–18.

120. Ibid., 26.

121. Ibid.

122. Ibid.

123. Ibid.

124. Ibid., 27.

125. Charles Taylor, "Alternative Futures: Legitimacy, Identity and Alienation in Late Twentieth Century Canada," in Alan Cairns and Cynthia Williams, eds., *Constitutionalism, Citizenship and Society in Canada* (Toronto: University of Toronto Press, 1985), 183–229; a study commissioned as part of the research program of the Royal Commission on the Economic Union and Development Prospects for Canada, vol. 33.

126. Ibid., 190.

127. Ibid., 193.

128. Ibid., 194.

129. Ibid., 206.

130. Ibid., 209.

131. Ibid., 211.

132. Ibid., 224.

133. Ibid., 211.

134. Ibid., 221-222.

135. Ibid., 225.

136. Ibid., 224.

137. Ibid., 225. Unfortunately, a typographical error in the sentence immediately prior to the one quoted here makes it sound as if Taylor ultimately supports the "centralist" solution. This is clearly not what he intended.

138. Ibid., 224.

139. Ibid., 211.

140. Ibid., 221.

141. London *Advertiser*, 26 March 1883. See also the issue for 23 March: "But it is not the question of the wisdom or justness of the measure which we have to consider in the case. The question is as to the constitutional rights of those to whom the people have entrusted with certain powers, to be the sole judges as to the legislation required in the public interest under these exclusive powers."

142. The Ontario government's various efforts to avoid dealing with the question of prohibition, to be discussed in the next chapter, are a good example.

143. London *Advertiser*, 19 July 1884.

144. I have elaborated on this point in "Constitutional Politics and the Legacy of the Provincial Rights Movement in Canada," *Canadian Journal of Political Science* 18 (1985), 267-294.

145. The constitutional conferences leading to the promulgation of the *Constitution Act, 1982* provided several good examples of the way in which the provincial governments exploited the analogy between liberalism and federalism. In arguing for greater constitutional control over the development of natural resources, both Alberta's Peter Lougheed and Saskatchewan's Allan Blakeney compared the provincial governments' position to that of (individual) property owners who simply wanted to vindicate "the rights of the owner," including the "right to receive value for the resource as a commodity." (Proceedings of the First Ministers' Conference on the Constitution, September 1980; Premier Lougheed, 119-120). As Premier Blakeney put it: "Ownership by a province becomes important, then, because it allows a province to do all those things that *any* owner can do...." (Saskatchewan position paper, 12; emphasis added).

Premier Lougheed drew out the analogy again in stating Alberta's position on changes to the amending formula. The priority of his government, he said, was for an amending formula "that protects us against the rights of the tyranny of the majority" (Proceedings, 124).

Chapter 6.

1. For a summary and critical analysis of this view, see Alan C. Cairns, "The Judicial Committee and Its Critics," *Canadian Journal of Political Science* 4 (1971), 301-345. The controversy has been rekindled recently by Frederick Vaughan, "Critics of the Judicial Committee of the Privy Council: The New Orthodoxy and an Alternative Explanation," *Canadian Journal of Political Science* 19 (1986), 495-519.

2. A good summary of Mowat's activities before the JCPC is to be found in Paul Romney, *Mr. Attorney* (Toronto: Osgoode Society, 1986), ch. 6.

3. Canada, Parliament, *House of Commons Debates*, 11 April 1877, 1371. Mills was speaking specifically of Parliament on this occasion, but the principle applied to both levels of government.

4. Ibid., 1368 (Robinson).

5. Ibid.

6. Ibid., 1368 (Blake)

7. Ibid.

8. Ibid., 1370.

9. Ibid.

10. Ibid.

11. Ibid., 1371.

12. Ibid., 1370.

13. Ibid., 1369.

14. Ibid.

15. See Alan Cairns, "The Other Crisis of Canadian Federalism," in Douglas E. Williams, ed., *Constitution, Government and Society in Canada* (Toronto: McClelland and Stewart, 1987), 171-191.

16. Canada, Parliament, *House of Commons Debates*, 11 April 1877, 1370.

17. See ch. 2 where I explain my use of this term.

18. Patrick Monahan, "At Doctrine's Twilight: The Structure of Canadian Federalism," *University of Toronto Law Journal* 34 (1984), 55.

19. Canada, Parliament, *House of Commons Debates*, 17 June 1869, 853.

20. Ibid., 19 May 1869, 392; 18 March and 15 April 1879, 507 and 1247.

21. Ibid., 21 March 1877, 890-891.

22. Ibid., 19 April 1872, 82.

23. *Confederation Debates*, 33.

24. Canada, Parliament, *House of Commons Debates*, 1 March 1875.

25. Canada, Parliament, *House of Commons Debates*, 17 June 1869, 853.

26. Jennifer Smith, "The Origins of Judicial Review in Canada," *Canadian Journal of Political Science* 16 (1983), 115-134.

27. Cairns, "The Judicial Committee and its Critics," 319.

28. Canada, Parliament, *House of Commons Debates*, 1 April 1884, 1250.

29. (1881) 7 A.C. 96.

30. Mills Papers, "Lectures on the Federal Constitution of Canada," Lecture 5, 24.

31. *Constitution Act, 1867*, section 91:2.

32. 7 A.C. 96, at 107.

33. Ibid.

34. Ibid., 108.

35. Ibid., emphasis added.

36. Ibid., 109.

37. This is Sir Montague Smith's own example, ibid., 108. See *Constitution Act, 1867*, section 91:26; section 92:12.

38. Ibid., 108.

39. Ibid., 109.

40. Ibid., 113.

41. *Russell v. the Queen*, (1882) 7 A.C. 829, at 836.

42. Ibid., 840; emphasis added.

43. On the larger challenge to the rule of law that was mounted by scholars in the 1930s, see R. C. B. Risk, "Volume I of the Journal: A Tribute and a Belated Review," *University of Toronto Law Journal* 37 (1987), 193-211.

44. Mills Papers, "Lectures on the Federal Constitution of Canada," Lecture 1, 10.

45. Canada, Parliament, *House of Commons Debates*, 1 April 1884, 1249.

46. Canada, Parliament, *House of Commons Debates*, 1 April 1885, 882.

47. Canada, Parliament, *House of Commons Debates*, 27 February 1885, 288.

48. See, for instance, Canada, Parliament, *House of Commons Debates*, 1 April 1884, 1249; 27 February 1885, 288; 1 April 1885, 884.

49. *Constitution Act, 1867*, section 92:15.

50. Canada, Parliament, *House of Commons Debates*, 1 April 1885, 883.

51. Ibid.

52. Ibid., 21 May 1888, 1660.

53. Ibid.

54. Ibid., 1661.

55. For a discussion of the politics of prohibition, see Margaret Evans, "Oliver Mowat and Ontario, 1872-1896: A Study in Political Success," Ph.D. thesis, University of Toronto (1969), 321-339. For an extremely valuable analysis of the legal cases concerning liquor, see R. C. B. Risk, "Under the Influence: The Courts, Federalism and Liquor, 1867-1900," paper presented to the Toronto Area Legal History Group, March 1990.

56. Romney, *Mr. Attorney*, 264.

57. See Toronto *Globe*, 17 August 1895, 2 September 1895, 14 September 1895, 19 October 1895.

58. Ibid., 17 August 1895.

59. Ibid., 7 September 1895. See Garth Stevenson, "The Origins of Co-operative Federalism," David Shugarman and Reg Whitaker, eds., *Federalism and Political Community* (Peterborough: Broadview Press, 1989), 7-31.

60. Ibid.

61. Canada, Parliament, *House of Commons Debates*, 24 February 1896, 2227.

62. Toronto *Globe*, 7 September 1895.

63. Canada, Parliament, *House of Commons Debates*, 24 February 1896, 2227.

64. Ibid.

65. Ibid., 15 June 1899, 375.

66. Ibid., 377.

67. Mills Papers, Mills to Macdonell, 2 June 1898.

68. Ibid.

69. To understand more clearly where Mills fits in the larger context of legal thought in Canada, see Risk, "Volume I Of The Journal," especially 207-211; and Monahan, "The Structure of Canadian Federalism," 64-69. R. C.

B. Risk has analyzed in detail one of Mills's legal soulmates in "A. H. F. Lefroy: Common Law Thought in Late-Nineteenth-Century Canada: On Burying One's Grandfather," *University of Toronto Law Journal* (forthcoming).

70. (1881) 7 A.C. 96, at 110.

71. Ibid.

72. Ibid., 112.

73. Ibid., 113.

74. Ibid.

75. Vaughan, "Critics of the Judicial Committee," 519.

76. Campbell Papers, Macdonald to Campbell, 18 December 1888.

77. (1882) 7 A.C. 829.

78. Ibid., 833.

79. Ibid., 836.

80. Ibid., 840.

81. Ibid., 839.

82. Ibid.

83. Ibid., 838–839.

84. Ibid., 839.

85. Ibid.

86. Peter H. Russell, ed., *Leading Constitutional Decisions*, rev. ed. (Toronto: McClelland and Stewart, 1973), 1.

87. Canada, Parliament, *House of Commons Debates*, 11 June 1885, 2473.

88. Ibid., 24 February 1896, 2226.

89. Ibid.

90. Toronto *Globe*, 23 August 1895.

91. Canada, Parliament, *House of Commons Debates*, 24 February 1896, 2226.

92. Toronto *Globe*, 23 August 1895.

93. Canada, Parliament, *House of Commons Debates*, 27 March 1884, 1137.

94. Ibid., 1 April 1884, 1249.

95. Ibid.

96. Ibid., 1247.

97. Ibid., 1249.

98. Ibid.

99. Ibid., 1247.

100. Ibid., 1249. On Cooley's understanding of the police power, see Alan R. Jones, *The Constitutional Conservatism of Thomas McIntyre Cooley* (New York: Garland, 1987), ch. 5.

101. Canada, Parliament, *House of Commons Debates*, 1 April 1884, 1249.

102. Ibid., 1137. The bill passed despite Mills's objections. The vote was unrecorded.

103. Ibid., 1 April 1885, 883.

104. Ibid.

105. Ibid., 886.

106. Ibid., 882.

107. Ibid., 883.

108. Ibid., 882.

109. Ibid., 883.

110. Ibid.

111. Ibid., 882.

112. Ibid., 15 June 1885, 2535.

113. Ibid., 2536.

114. Ibid., 2537. Here again Mills was unable to persuade the government, and the bill passed.

115. Mills Papers, "Lectures on the Federal Constitution of Canada," I:10.

116. Canada, Parliament, *House of Commons Debates*, 1 March 1875, 400.

117. Ibid., 401.

118. Ibid.

119. Mills, "Lectures," I:11.

120. Ibid., I:12. Compare Mills's understanding of the connection between local control and representative government with, for instance, the Federal Farmer—one of the most reflective Anti-Federalist critics of the U. S. Constitution. See Herbert J. Storing, ed., *The Anti-Federalist*, 1 volume abridgement (Chicago: University of Chicago Press, 1981), 39–54. The Address

of the Pennsylvania Minority also provides room for comparison (201–223), as do the letters of Brutus (especially #4, 127–132).

121. Canada, Parliament, *House of Commons Debates*, 1 April 1885, 883.

122. Mills Papers, Mills to Hardy, 4 December 1897.

123. Canada, Parliament, *House of Commons Debates*, 1 April 1885, 886.

124. Ibid., 886, 882.

125. Mills Papers, Box 4278, "Draft Speech on the Jesuit Estates Question," (1889) 12.

126. London *Advertiser*, 18 January 1883.

127. "Jesuit Estates," 12.

128. Ibid., 17.

129. Ibid., 18.

130. Ibid.

131. Murray Greenwood, "David Mills and Co-ordinate Federalism, 1867–1903," *University of Western Ontario Law Review* 16 (1977), 112.

132. Ibid., 111.

133. Greenwood notes, for instance, that Mills's opposition to factory legislation (discussed above) "helped convince the government that this was a provincial matter, an important decision as it prepared the way for the assumption of jurisdiction by the provinces over most of the field of labour relations." Ibid., 105.

134. In addition to the examples noted above, several other bills passed over Mills's objections—among them a bill to regulate carriers by land (1885), a bill regulating the quarantining of animals brought into the country (1885), and a bill concerning 'offences against the person' (1885).

135. Donald J. A. McMurchy, "David Mills: Nineteenth Century Canadian Liberal," Ph.D. thesis, University of Rochester (1969), 527.

136. Mills Papers, Mills to John Boiser, 21 November 1899.

137. Ibid., Mills to E. L. Bond, 9 March 1900.

138. Ibid., Mills to A. S. Hardy, 9 May 1899.

139. Canada, Parliament, *Senate Debates*, 15 June 1899, 378.

140. Ibid.

141. Ibid., 377.

142. Mills Papers, Mills to Mowat, 19 April 1899.

143. Ibid., Mills to L. Goulet, 3 August 1898. The quotations in the next two paragraphs are all from this source.

144. McMurchy, "David Mills," 538.

145. Ibid.

146. J. C. Morrison, "Oliver Mowat and the Development of Provincial Rights in Ontario: A Study in Dominion-Provincial Relations, 1867–1896," in *Three History Theses* (Toronto: Ontario Department of Public Records and Archives, 1961), 300.

147. Ibid., 295.

148. Ibid., 294.

149. Ibid., 295.

150. See Greenwood, "David Mills and Co-ordinate Federalism," 97.

151. Mills Papers, Mills to Fitzpatrick, 22 February 1898.

152. Brian Beaven, "A Last Hurrah: Studies in Liberal party development and ideology in Ontario, 1878–1893," Ph.D. thesis, University of Toronto (1982), ch. 1.

153. Ottawa *Free Press*, 16 February 1882.

154. Toronto *Globe*, 2 June 1883.

155. Bowmanville *Canadian Statesman*, 2 June 1882.

156. Ibid.

157. Ottawa *Free Press*, 16 February 1882.

158. Toronto *Globe*, 2 June 1883.

159. Ibid.

160. Ottawa *Free Press*, 16 February 1882.

161. See Beaven, "A Last Hurrah," 444, quoting David Mills.

162. Ibid., 445, again quoting Mills.

163. Mills Papers, Mills to Campbell, 10 January 1900; emphasis added.

164. Canada, Parliament, *House of Commons Debates*, 11 June 1894, 4095.

Conclusion.

1. Perhaps the clearest and most subtle statement of this view is Richard Simeon, "Meech Lake and Shifting Conceptions of Canadian Federalism," *Canadian Public Policy* 14 (1988), S7–S24. For a more complete list of works

in this and the other categories suggested in this paragraph, see chapter 1, note 6.

2. An extremely insightful analysis along these lines is provided by Alan Cairns, "Citizen (Outsiders) and Governments (Insiders) in Constitution-Making: The Case of Meech Lake," *Canadian Public Policy* 14 (1988), S121–S145.

3. The outstanding example is Charles Taylor, "Alternative Futures: Legitimacy, Identity and Alienation in Late Twentieth Century Canada," in Alan Cairns and Cynthia Williams, eds., *Constitutionalism, Citizenship and Society in Canada* (Toronto: University of Toronto Press, 1985), 183–229.

4. Patrick Monahan, "At Doctrine's Twilight: The Structure of Canadian Federalism," *University of Toronto Law Journal* 34 (1984), 84.

5. See Richard Simeon, "Meech Lake and Visions of Canada," in K. E. Swinton and S. J. Rogerson, eds., *Competing Constitutional Visions: The Meech Lake Accord* (Toronto: Carswell, 1988), 295–306.

6. *Ford v. Quebec (Attorney General)* (1989) 54 D.L.R. (4th), 577.

7. Ibid., 618.

8. See Paul C. Weiler, "Rights and Judges in a Democracy: A New Canadian Version," *University of Michigan Journal of Law Reform* 18 (1984), 51.

9. The override provision applies to the fundamental freedoms of section 2, the legal rights of sections 7–14, and the equality provisions of section 15.

10. For a description of its use to date, see Peter H. Russell, Rainer Knopff, and Ted Morton, eds., *Freedom and the Charter: Leading Constitutional Decisions* (Ottawa: Carleton University Press, 1989), 5 (note 5).

11. Toronto *Globe and Mail*, 16 December 1988, A1.

12. Ibid., 19 December 1988, A4.

13. Ibid., 15 March 1989.

14. Canada, Parliament, *House of Commons Debates*, 6 April 1989, 153.

15. Ibid.

16. Toronto *Globe and Mail*, 7 April 1989, A1.

17. London *Advertiser*, 18 October 1882.

18. See *Posadas De Puerto Rico Assoc. v. Tourism Co.* 106 S. Ct. 2968 (1986). The opinion for the 5 members who formed the majority was written by Justice Rehnquist (as he then was).

19. See, for instance, the concurring opinion of Justice LaForest in the recent Sunday closing case. *Edwards Books and Art Ltd. v. the Queen* (1986), 35 D.L.R. (4th) 1, at 44. See Lorraine E. Weinrib, "The Supreme Court Of

Canada And Section One Of The Charter," *The Supreme Court Law Review* 10 (1988), 469–513; and Katherine Swinton, "Competing Visions of Federalism and Rights," in K. E. Swinton and C. J. Rogerson, eds., *Competing Constitutional Visions: The Meech Lake Accord* (Toronto: Carswell, 1988), 279–294.

20. See for instance Peter H. Russell and Paul C. Weiler, "Don't scrap the override clause—it's a very Canadian solution," Toronto *Star*, 4 June 1989, B3. The supporters of the override have been more active in suggesting how section 33 might be used than in explaining how to prevent its abuse. Some dismiss the problem of abuse by arguing that a government would not use the override to "violate clearly defined and widely accepted rights" because governments "must fact the ultimate check in a democracy—the judgment of the voters." That "check" seems insufficient in itself when one considers that some of the most serious, often systemic, forms of discrimination and rights abuse make extremely popular electoral politics. Which is why the legal and political rules for the use of the override need to be developed with considerably greater clarity than they are at the moment. See F. L. Morton, "The Political Impact of the Canadian Charter of Rights and Freedoms," *Canadian Journal of Political Science* 20 (1987), 55.

Index

Adulterated foods, 183
Agriculture, 117, 165
Alberta, 233n.110, 235n.145
Amending formula, 42, 235n.145
Anglin, Timothy, 120
Anti-Federalists, 179, 240n.120
Archibald, Adams, 55
Armstrong, Christopher, 12
Articles of Confederation, 28
Asian immigration, 140, 142, 183
Aspect doctrine, 163

Beavan, Brian, 187
Benjamin, Judah, 172-173
Berger, Carl, 92
Blackstone, William, 23, 26, 28, 30
Blake, Edward, 13, 38, 42-44, 51, 56,
    59-60, 63, 67, 75, 85, 86, 88, 94, 97-98,
    101, 125, 127, 137, 152, 154, 157,
    188-189, 216n.89, 232n.101
Blakeney, Allan, 235n.45
Blanchet, Joseph, 34
Bleu party (Conservative), 16, 17-18,
    33-35
Bourassa, Robert, 192-197
British Columbia, 183, 214n.42; disallow-
    ance of provincial acts, 140-142
British constitution, 47-48, 52, 56, 64,
    70-72, 132, 184, 231n.79
British Empire, 24, ch.4 *passim*, 181;
    India, 87-89; Egypt, 88
British North America Act, 5, 15, 31, 33,
    36, 40, 43, 57, 65, 69, 72, 108, 113, 116,
    117. *See also* Constitution Act (1867)
Brown, George, 16-17, 18-20, 25, 26, 33,
    76, 97, 99, 115, 209n.78

Bryce, James, 132, 134, 231n.80

Cairns, Alan, 7-8, 11, 158
Calhoun, John, 25, 30
Canada Temperance Act, 164, 170-171
Canned Goods Act, 176-177
Cardwell, Edward, 65-66
Cartier, George-Etienne, 16-17, 20, 44, 76
Categorical legal reasoning, 162-164
Cauchon, Joseph-Edouard, 34
C.C.F., 233n.110
Centralism, 19, 31, 34-36, 47, 75, 85,
    115-118, 124, 126, 128-129, 130,
    145-149, 155, 157, 179, 182, 183, 186,
    187, 189, 191, 195, 209n.78
Chamberlin, Brown, 38, 40
Charter of Rights and Freedoms, 74, 82,
    143, 145, 148, 192, 194, 197; notwith-
    standing clause, 192, 195-197,
    244n.20. *See also* Constitution Act
    (1982)
Child labor legislation, 163
Citizen alienation, 146
Citizen participation, 144
Citizens Insurance of Canada v.
    Parsons, 159-162, 167
Civil War (U.S.), 15-16, 24-25, 157
Coldwell, M.J., 233n.110
Common Schools Act (N.B.), 121
Communitarianism, 92-93
Community, 2-3, 143, 148, 152, 176, 179,
    180, 181, 190, conclusion, *passim*
Compact theory, 6, 43, 137
Compulsory vaccination, 157
Concurrent jurisdiction, 117, 161,
    165-168

245

Confederation Debates (1865), 3, 21, 34, 49, 123
Confederation settlement, chap. 2, *passim*, 116, 121-122, 124, 157, 181
Conservative party, 63, 80, 93, 118, 124-126, 139, 143, 187-190, 217n.99
Constitution Act (1867); criminal law, 118, 163, 180, 183; declaratory power, 24; immigration, 141, 165; peace, order and good government, 4, 24, 37, 44, 91, 142, 171, 172, 176; property and civil rights, 127, 128, 157, 161, 163, 169, 171, 173-182, 196, 224n.87, 235n.145; trade and commerce, 4, 142, 159, 161, 169, 174, 176, 186
Constitution Act (1982), 1-2, 74, 196, 199n.3. *See also* Charter of Rights and Freedoms
Constitutional amendment, 42
Constitutional federalism, 30, 36
Control of contagious diseases, 157
Cook, Ramsay, 97
Cooley, Thomas, 39-40, 134, 175, 178
Costigan, John, 174
Courts: umpires of federal system, 158
Crooks, Adam, 127
Cultural identity, 17-19, 92, 179, 192, 193, 195; and state role in formation of, 93-95

Darwinian science, 92, 222n.41
Declaration of Independence, 28
Decentralism, 182
Declaratory power, 22, 24. *See also* Constitution Act (1867)
Delegation doctrine, 155
Denis, Paul, 34
Dicey, A.V., 70-71, 132-134, 215n.74, 231n.79
Disallowance, 15, 22, 24-25, 108-110, 156, 181, 231n.81, 232n.101; and changing use of, 126-127, 129-130, 138, 233n.110, and Confederation settlement, 75-76; imperial use of, 50-51, 80, 116; and individual rights, 118-119, 125, 127, 139-143, 148; as jurisdictional veto, 119-125, 129, 143; and privileges and immunities act, 36; and Rivers and Streams case, 76-82, 126-131, 218n.100

Dorion, Antoine-Aimé, 22, 31, 34, 75, 123-124
Dorion, Jean Baptiste Eric, 22-24, 31, 75
Douglas, T.C., 233n.110
Dual mandate (dual representation), 36, 37-41
Durham, Lord, 30, 49-50, 98

Edwards Books and Art Limited v. the Queen, 243n.19
Executive federalism, 73

Factory labor legislation, 157, 163, 175-76, 179, 180, 241n.133
Family Compact, 78, 88, 187-188
Fathers of Confederation, 7, 15, 20, 26, 74, 103, 114-115
Federal principle, 113, 118, 121-122, 127, 129-130, 131
Federal spending power, 42-43
The Federalist Papers, 20
Federalists (U.S.), 16, 20, 28-30
Food and drug adulteration, 174-175
Foreign trade, 176-177
Forsey, Eugene, 227n.14
Fournier, Télesphore, 124
Franchise, 203-204n.1, 217n.98, 218n.99
French domination: fears of, 17-19, 56-57, 76, 79, 97-98, 102, 187

Geertz, Clifford, 9-11
Gordon, Robert, 230n.69
Gladstone, William, 101, 104, 224n.87, 231n.80
Goodhue will case, 127
Great coalition (1864), 115
Greenwood, Murray, 182, 241n.133
Gwynne, (Justice) John Wellington, 67-69

Haldane, Lord Viscount, 172
Hamilton, Alexander, 20
Hamilton Weekly Times, 32
Hardy, A.S., 183-184
Health, 176, 186
Holton, Luther, 43, 123
Home rule, 84-91, 113, 181, 224n.87; and Ireland, 100-107; and Quebec, 104
Howe, Joseph, 41-42

Howland, Lieutenant-Governor William, 57-59

Immigration, 117, 165
Imperial Parliament, 24, 30-33, 35, 85, 89, 113, 184
Individual rights, 143, 144, 148, 188, 190, 192-197; as model for provincial rights, 135-136, 139-140, 195-196, 235n.145; as threat to community, 144
Industrial regulation, 170
Insurance, 159
Interprovincial Conference (1887), 137
Ireland: home rule, 84, 100-107
Irving, Aemilius, 33

Japan: and anti-Asian legislation in B.C., 141
Jefferson, Thomas, 20, 74, 184
Jesuit Estates Act, 98, 110, 181
Le Journal (Quebec), 34
Judicial Committee of the Privy Council (JCPC), 8, 68, 77, ch. 6 *passim*

Kendle, John, 224n.83, 224n.87
Kennedy, Duncan, 133
Earl of Kimberley, 66
King, William Lyon Mackenzie, 138, 233n.110

Laflamme, Rodolphe, 125
La Forest, Gérard, 227n.14, 230n.62, 243n.19
Lapointe, Ernest, 138, 233n.110
Laskin, Bora, 8
Laurier, Wilfrid, 7, 38, 94, 96, 101, 108-11, 125, 140, 182, 216n.89, 218n.99, 226n.132, 227n.3
Law of the Constitution, 133. *See also* A.V. Dicey
Legal liberalism, 132-139, 153, 156, 158-159, 178-182, 230n.69; Oxford school, 132; Harvard school, 132
Legislative Assembly, Canada, 21, 203-204n.1
Legislative privileges and immunities, 36
Lenoir v. Ritchie, 66-72
Lekvesque, Renek, 1
Liberal party, 7, 63, 77, 97, 111, 118, 124-125, 126, 128, 139, 143, 174, 182,

187-190, 217n.99. *See also* Reform party
Liberalism, 2-3, 47-48, 92-96, 131-143, 148, 152, 176, 180, 184-185, 187-190, conclusion, *passim*, 231n.80. *See also* individual rights
Licensing Act (Ontario), 142
Lieutenant-Governor, ch. 3, *passim;* and colonial government, 48; and colonial governor; 48-50, 54; creation of, 24; prerogative powers, exercise of, 63-70; as representative of Queen, 63-69; and reservation power, 52-63
Linguistic and cultural homogeneity, 95
Loan societies bill, 183
Local Prohibition case, 166-168, 172
Locke, John, 144
London *Advertiser*, 78-81, 88, 98, 102, 130-131, 135, 137, 218n.99, 219n.109, 224n.87
Lougheed, Peter, 235n.145

Macdonell, John A., 168
Macdonald, John A., 3-6, 9-10, 11-12, 44, 48-49, 55, 60, 63, 74, 84-85, 114, 170, 187, 189, 195; and Confederation settlement, 15, 16, 19, 20, 21, 24, 35, 36; and disallowance, 36, 114-124, 136, 218n.100, 227n.14; and minority rights, 216n.91; and Nova Scotia, 42; and prerogative powers, 66; and prohibition, 154-156, 167; and provincial lieutenant-governorship, 47-49; and reservation of provincial legislation, 52-63, 213n.22; and Rivers and Streams case, 77-80
Macdonald, John Sandfield, 37, 207n.47
MacDonald, V.C., 8
Mackay, Rev. W.A., 165, 168
Mackenzie, Alexander, 60, 114, 124-125
Madison, James, 16, 20, 28, 30, 31, 114, 209n.66
Mallory, J.R., 227n.14
Manitoba, 17; and reservation of legislation, 55-56; schools question, 96, 108-112, 227n.3
Marriage and divorce, 160
McCarthy, D'Alton, 93-96, 101, 106
McMurchy, Donald, 185-186
Meech Lake Accord, 1-2, 148, 199n.3
Mercier, Honorek, 12

Mill, John Stuart, 132
Mills, David, 13, 38, 43, 67, 74, 75, 97, 98, 101, 123, 134, 137, 138, 196, 219n.109, 222n.41, 224n.73, 231n.77, 231n.79, 240n.120, 241n.133, 241n.134; and British empire, ch.4 *passim;* and disallowance, 78-82, 140; and division of powers, ch.6 *passim;* and dual representation, 38-41; and language rights, 94-96; and Manitoba schools question, 111-112; and prerogative powers, 71-72; and prohibition, 153, 164; race, definition and use of term, 92
Ministerial responsibility, 58-59
Minority-majority relations, 99
Minority rights, 76, 84, 97-100, 115, 117, 141, 142, 197, 216n.91, 235n.145; Anglo-Quebeckers, 75-76, 99, 105, 114, 192, 194, 199n.3; educational, 96-97, 108-112, 119-123; federal protection of, 108-111; linguistic, 94-95, 96, 148, 192-193
Modernity, 149; defined, 144
Monahan, Patrick, 156, 162
Morris, Alexander, 55
Morrison, J.C., 26, 185-186
Morton, W.L., 38, 41
Mowat, Oliver, 7, 13, 19, 56-57, 66, 67, 71, 75, 76, 77, 128, 137, 152, 164, 170, 175, 184, 185, 218n.99
Mulroney, Brian, 193, 196

Nation, 133
National interest, 117, 130, 156, 189
Native Canadians, 74, 217n.98
New Brunswick, 17, 214n.42; schools question, 100, 110, 119-124, 129
de Niverville, C.B., 21
North-West Territories Act: use of French language, 93-96, 97, 101, 106-107
Nova Scotia: better terms, 36, 41; disallowance of acts, 118-119

Ontario: boundary dispute, 170; as leader of provincial rights movement, 12-13
Orange Association (Orange Lodge), 18, 56-59, 61-62, 106

Paine, Tom, 184
Paramountcy doctrine, 167
Parish Schools Act (1858), 119. *See also* New Brunswick
Parliament, 154, 155, 219n.109, 220n.133
Parliamentary privileges and immunities, 118
Parti Québécois, 1
Participatory model, 145, 146
Police powers, 174-176, 179-180, 183, 186, 189. *See also* Constitution Act, 1867, property and civil rights
Political culture, 9, 73, 146, 152
Political federalism, 25, 156
Prerogative powers, 28, 60, 63-70; democratization of, 71-72
Prison reform, 182
Progress: Victorian idea of, 83, 91
Prohibition, 153-156, 164-169
Property rights, 78, 125, 126-131, 142, 183
Provincial autonomy, 6, 27, 34, 36, 38-41, 44-45, 53, 67, 73, 153, ch.5 *passim*, 181
Provincial rights movement: definition of federalism, 5
Public-Private distinction, 133-134

Quarantine, 176, 241n.134
Quebec, 6, 12, 17-18, 105, 149, 191-197, 199n.3, 200-201n.7, 202n.24, 213n.22, 216n.89; and Bill 101 (Charter of the French language), 192; and Bill 178 (sign law), 192, 196; Charter of Rights and Freedoms, 192-193; and Confederation settlement, 4, 122; National Assembly, 192; nationalism, 1-2
Quebec Conference, 31
Quebec Resolutions, 21, 41, 203n.1
Queen's counsel, 64-72

Race: definition of, 91-93, 195; and Irish question, 103; and language, 95-96; political recognition, 98
Reform Convention (1859), 19, 33
Reform party, 4, 12, 16, 17, 25-33, 38, 76, 102, 185-186, 207n.47, 209n.78, 224n.73. *See also* Liberal party

Regionalism, 4, 6, 145-149; and individuality of provinces, 24
Remedial legislation, 22, 108-112, 120, 226n.132
Representation by population, 27, 33, 98
Representative government, 179, 184-185, 240n.120
Reservation power: decline in use of, 61-63; as federal veto of provincial legislation, 52-63, 213n.22, 214n.42; as imperial veto, 50, 86; and Manitoba, 55-56. *See also* Lieutenant-Governor
Responsible government, 48-53, 55, 58, 59, 78-82, 189, 195. *See also* Self-government
Riel, Louis, 97, 100
Ripon, Lord, 88-89
Rivers and Streams Act, 77, 126-131, 189. *See also* Disallowance
Robinson, J.B., 153-155
Romney, Paul, 66, 164
Rose, John, 76, 114
Ross, George, 142
Ross, Rev. J.S., 165-166, 168
Rouge party, 22
Rule of law, 111-112, ch.5 *passim*, 152, 156, 188
Russell v. the Queen, 164, 166, 170-173, 176, 186
Russell, T.W., 104-106
Rutherford, Paul, 83

St. Thomas Journal, 33
Saskatchewan, 233n.110, 235n.145
Scotland, 103
Scott, F.R., 8
Self-government, 30-31, 48, 51-53, 56, 60, 113, 131, 144, 146, 148; colonial, 68, 84-89
Senate, 26, 184, 199n.3, 216n.91, 220n.133

Shklar, Judith, 29
Silver, A.I., 17, 33
Simeon, Richard, 7, 73, 145
Smiley, Donald, 23
Smith, Sir Montague, 159-161, 169, 171
Social Credit, 233n.110
Sovereignty, 23-36, 153, 156, 218n.100, 231n.81; of the people, 73-75, 235n.141
Stevenson, Garth, 7
Stocking, George, 91
Sugarman, David, 132
Supreme Court Act, 138
Supreme Court of Canada, 6, 66-69, 74, 159, 168, 192, 197, 199n.3

Tariffs, 176
Taschereau, (Justice) Henri-Elzéar, 69-72
Taylor, Charles, 143-149, 152
Thomas, Lewis Herbert, 93
Thompson, Sir John, 232n.101
Toronto Globe, 18, 25, 26, 27, 30-33, 78, 128, 137, 165, 187, 218n.100
Transcontinental railroad, 90
Trudeau, Pierre, 1-2

Union Act, 18
United States, 145, 157; Constitution, 5, 23, 25, 28, 73, 117, 133-134, 179; federalism, 38; Supreme Court, 134, 162, 196

Waite, Peter, 15
Watson, Lord, 68-69, 72, 106
Wheare, K.C., 15
Whitaker, Reg, 73
Wilson, James, 16
Wood, Gordon, 23
Women, 203-204n.1